Graph-Theoretic Techniques
for Web Content Mining

SERIES IN MACHINE PERCEPTION AND ARTIFICIAL INTELLIGENCE*

Editors: **H. Bunke** (Univ. Bern, Switzerland)
P. S. P. Wang (Northeastern Univ., USA)

---

*For the complete list of titles in this series, please write to the Publisher.

Series in Machine Perception and Artificial Intelligence – Vol. 62

Graph-Theoretic Techniques for Web Content Mining

Adam Schenker

University of South Florida, USA

Horst Bunke

University of Bern, Switzerland

Mark Last

Ben-Gurion University of the Negev, Israel

Abraham Kandel

University of South Florida, USA

World Scientific

NEW JERSEY • LONDON • SINGAPORE • BEIJING • SHANGHAI • HONG KONG • TAIPEI • CHENNAI

Published by

World Scientific Publishing Co. Pte. Ltd.

5 Toh Tuck Link, Singapore 596224

USA office: 27 Warren Street, Suite 401-402, Hackensack, NJ 07601

UK office: 57 Shelton Street, Covent Garden, London WC2H 9HE

British Library Cataloguing-in-Publication Data
A catalogue record for this book is available from the British Library.

GRAPH-THEORETIC TECHNIQUES   **FOR WEB CONTENT MINING**
Series in Machine Perception and Artificial Intelligence — Vol. 62

ISBN-13 978-981-256-339-2
ISBN-10 981-256-339-3

Printed in Singapore

Dedication

Dedicated to The Honorable Congressman C. W. Bill Young, House of Representatives, for his vision and continuous support in creating the National Institute for Systems Test and Productivity at the Computer Science and Engineering Department, University of South Florida.

Preface

Graphs are mathematical constructs for representing objects or systems which contain structural (*i.e.* relationship) information. Graphs have been used in many domains, from software engineering to artificial intelligence. However, the use of graphs in machine learning has been limited, compared to the more prevalent vector model which does not capture structural information. This can be attributed to the fact that until recently we have not had suitable graph-theoretic tools for dealing with graphs, and that comparing graphs for the purpose of evaluating structural matching is often of high time complexity. For these reasons, most machine learning approaches that deal with graph-based data introduce either restrictions on the type or related attributes of the graphs used, or they require a totally new mathematical foundation for handling graphs (such as probability theory). An unfortunate drawback of these types of methods is that existing machine learning algorithms either cannot be applied or require extensive modifications.

In this book, we present methods for utilizing graphs with well-known machine learning algorithms, such as k-means clustering and k-nearest neighbors classification, with virtually no significant modifications; the extensions for allowing these algorithms to use graphs is direct and intuitive. Further, we show how we can achieve polynomial time complexity with the restriction that the graphs contain unique node labels. This is the only restriction we place on the graphs, and we can even discard this limitation if we use a sub-optimal approximation approach for determining graph distance or if the graphs are relatively small.

To demonstrate the effectiveness of these approaches for performing clustering and classification with graphs, we apply them to the domain of web content mining. We show how web document content can be modeled with different graph representations, and how these graphs contain additional information not found in traditional vector representations of document content. We perform experiments comparing the clustering and classification performance of the graph-based approach to that of the vector approach. Other interesting results show how we can visualize the graph space through multidimensional scaling, and how we can create a multiple classifier system that contains both statistical (vector) and structural (graph) classifiers. We also present the details of a web search clustering system that we developed and show how the system was easily modified to use graph-based representations instead of vector representations; the graph representations have a noticeable benefit in that they allow the terms in the cluster labels to have the correct ordering, and also provide differentiation between isolated terms and multi-term phrases.

Acknowledgements

This work was supported in part by the National Institute for Systems Test and Productivity at the University of South Florida under the U.S. Space and Naval Warfare Systems Command Contract No. N00039–02–C–3244.

A. Schenker

H. Bunke

M. Last

A. Kandel

Contents

Chapter 1

Introduction to Web Mining

With the recent explosive growth of the amount of content on the Internet, it has become increasingly difficult for users to find and utilize information and for content providers to classify and catalog documents. Traditional web search engines often return hundreds or thousands of results for a search, which is time consuming for users to browse. On-line libraries, search engines, and other large document repositories (*e.g.* customer support databases, product specification databases, press release archives, news story archives, *etc.*) are growing so rapidly that it is difficult and costly to categorize every document manually. In order to deal with these problems, researchers look toward automated methods of working with web documents so that they can be more easily browsed, organized, and cataloged with minimal human intervention.

In contrast to the highly structured tabular data upon which most machine learning methods are expected to operate, web and text documents are semi-structured. Web documents have well-defined structures such as letters, words, sentences, paragraphs, sections, punctuation marks, HTML tags, and so forth. We know that words make up sentences, sentences make up paragraphs, and so on, but many of the rules governing the order in which the various elements are allowed to appear are vague or ill-defined and can vary dramatically between documents. It is estimated that as much as 85% of all digital business information, most of it web-related, is stored in non-structured formats (*i.e.* non-tabular formats, such as those that are used in databases and spreadsheets) [Pet]. Developing improved methods of performing machine learning techniques on this vast amount of non-tabular, semi-structured web data is therefore highly desirable.

Clustering and classification have been useful and active areas of machine learning research that promise to help us cope with the problem of information overload on the Internet. With clustering the goal is to separate a given group of data items (the data set) into groups called clusters such that items in the same cluster are similar to each other and dissimilar to the items in other clusters. In clustering methods no labeled examples are provided in advance for training (this is called *unsupervised learning*). Under classification we attempt to assign a data item to a predefined category based on a model that is created from pre-classified training data (*supervised learning*). In more general terms, both clustering and classification come under the area of knowledge discovery in databases or data mining. Applying data mining techniques to web page content is referred to as web content mining which is a new sub-area of web mining, partially built upon the established field of information retrieval.

When representing text and web document content for clustering and classification, a vector-space model is typically used. In this model, each possible term that can appear in a document becomes a feature dimension [Sal89]. The value assigned to each dimension of a document may indicate the number of times the corresponding term appears on it or it may be a weight that takes into account other frequency information, such as the number of documents upon which the terms appear. This model is simple and allows the use of traditional machine learning methods that deal with numerical feature vectors in a Euclidean feature space. However, it discards information such as the order in which the terms appear, where in the document the terms appear, how close the terms are to each other, and so forth. By keeping this kind of structural information we could possibly improve the performance of various machine learning algorithms. The problem is that traditional data mining methods are often restricted to working on purely numeric feature vectors due to the need to compute distances between data items or to calculate some representative of a cluster of items (*i.e.* a centroid or center of a cluster), both of which are easily accomplished in a Euclidean space. Thus either the original data needs to be converted to a vector of numeric values by discarding possibly useful structural information (which is what we are doing when using the vector model to represent documents) or we need to develop new, customized methodologies for the specific representation.

Graphs are important and effective mathematical constructs for modeling relationships and structural information. Graphs (and their more restrictive form, trees) are used in many different problems, including sorting, compression, traffic/flow analysis, resource allocation, *etc.* [CLR97] In addition to problems where the graph itself is processed by some algorithm (*e.g.* sorting by the depth first method or finding the minimum spanning tree) it would be extremely desirable in many applications, including those related to machine learning, to model data as graphs since these graphs can retain more information than sets or vectors of simple atomic features. Thus much research has been performed in the area of graph similarity in order to exploit the additional information allowed by graph representations by introducing mathematical frameworks for dealing with graphs. Some application domains where graph similarity techniques have been applied include face [WFKvdM97] and fingerprint [WJH01] recognition as well as anomaly detection in communication networks [DBD⁺01]. In the literature, the work comes under several different topic names including graph distance, (exact) graph matching, inexact graph matching, error-tolerant graph matching, or error-correcting graph matching. In exact graph matching we are attempting to determine if two graphs are identical. Inexact graph matching implies we are attempting not to find a perfect matching, but rather a "best" or "closest" matching. Error-tolerant and error-correcting are special cases of inexact matching where the imperfections (*e.g.* missing nodes) in one of the graphs, called the data graph, are assumed to be the result of some errors (*e.g.* from transmission or recognition). We attempt to match the data graph to the most similar model graph in our database. Graph distance is a numeric measure of dissimilarity between graphs, with larger distances implying more dissimilarity. By graph similarity, we mean we are interested in some measurement that tells us how similar graphs are regardless if there is an exact matching between them.

1.1 Overview of Web Mining Methodologies

Web mining [ZLY02] is the application of machine learning (data mining) techniques to web-based data for the purpose of learning or extracting knowledge. Web mining encompasses a wide variety techniques, including soft computing [PTM00]. Web mining methodologies can generally be classified into one of three distinct categories: web usage mining, web structure mining, and web content mining [MBNL99]. For a survey of techniques used in these areas, see Ref. [KB00]. In *web usage mining* the goal is to examine web page usage patterns in order to learn about a web system's users or the relationships between the documents. For example, the tool presented by Masseglia *et al.* [MPC99] creates association rules from web access logs, which store the identity of pages accessed by users along with other information such as when the pages were accessed and by whom; these logs are the focus of the data mining effort, rather than the actual web pages themselves. Rules created by their method could include, for example, "70% of the users that visited page A also visited page B." Similarly, the method of Nasraoui *et al.* [NFJK99] also examines web access logs. The method employed in that paper is to perform a hierarchical clustering in order to determine the usage patterns of different groups of users. Beeferman and Berger [BB00] described a process they developed which determines topics related to a user query using click-through logs and agglomerative clustering of bipartite graphs. The transaction-based method developed in Ref. [Mer99] creates links between pages that are frequently accessed together during the same session. Web usage mining is useful for providing personalized web services, an area of web mining research that has lately become active. It promises to help tailor web services, such as web search engines, to the preferences of each individual user. For a recent review of web personalization methods, see Ref. [EV03].

In the second category of web mining methodologies, *web structure mining*, we examine only the relationships between web documents by utilizing the information conveyed by each document's hyperlinks. Like the web usage mining methods described above, the other content of the web pages is often ignored. In Ref. [KRRT99] Kumar *et al.* examined utilizing a graph representation of web page structure. Here nodes in the graphs are web pages and edges indicate hyperlinks between pages. By examining these "web graphs" it is possible to find documents or areas of interest through the use of certain graph-theoretical measures or procedures. Structures such as web rings, portals, or affiliated sites can be identified by matching the characteristics of these structures (*e.g.* we can identify portal pages because they have an unusually high out-degree). Graph models are also used in other web structure mining approaches. For example, in Ref. [CvdBD99] the authors' method examines linked URLs and performs classification using a Bayesian method. The graph is processed to determine groups of pages that relate to a common topic.

In this book we are concerned only with the third category of web mining, *web content mining*. In web content mining we examine the actual content of web pages (most often the text contained in the pages) and then perform some knowledge discovery procedure to learn about the pages themselves and their relationships. Most typically this is done to organize a group of documents into related categories. This is especially beneficial for web search engines, since it allows users to more quickly find the information they are looking for in comparison to the usual "endless" ranked list. There are several examples of web or text mining approaches [AHKV97] that are content-oriented and attempt to cluster documents for browsing. The Athena system of Agrawal *et al.* [AJS00] creates groupings of e-mail messages. The goal is to create folders (classes) for different topics and route e-mail messages automatically to the appropriate folders. Athena uses a clustering algorithm called C-Evolve to create topics (folders), while the classification of documents to each cluster is supervised and requires manual interaction with the user. The classification method is based on Naïve Bayes. Some notable papers that deal with clustering for web search include Ref. [BGG+99a], which describes 2 partitional methods, and Ref. [CH97], which is a hierarchical clustering approach. Nahm and Mooney [NM00] described a methodology where information extraction and data mining can be combined to improve upon each other; information extraction provides the data mining process with access to textual documents (text mining) and in turn data mining provides learned rules to the information extraction portion to improve its performance. An important paper that is strongly related to the current work is that of Strehl *et al.* [SGM00], which examined clustering performance of different clustering algorithms when using various similarity measures on web document collections. Clustering methods examined in the paper included k-means, graph partitioning, and self-organizing maps (SOMs). Vector-based representations were used in the experiments along with distance measures based on Euclidean distance, cosine similarity, and Jaccard similarity. One of the data sets used in this paper is publicly available and we will use it in our experiments.

1.2 Traditional Information Retrieval Techniques

Traditional information retrieval methods represent plain-text documents using a series of numeric values for each document. Each value is associated with a specific term (word) that may appear on a document, and the set of possible terms is shared across all documents. The values may be binary, indicating the presence or absence of the corresponding term. The values may also be a non-negative integers, which represents the number of times a term appears on a document (*i.e.* term frequency). Non-negative real numbers can also be used, in this case indicating the importance or weight of each term. These values are derived through a method such as the popular inverse document frequency (*tf·idf*) model [Sal89], which reduces the importance of terms that appear on many documents. Regardless of the method used, each series of values represents a document and corresponds to a point (*i.e.* vector) in a Euclidean feature space; this is called the vector-space model of information retrieval. This model is often used when applying machine learning techniques to documents, as there is a strong mathematical foundation for performing distance measure and centroid calculations using vectors.

1.2.1 *Vector-based distance measures*

Here we briefly review some of the most popular vector-related distance measures [Sal89][SGM00], which will also be used in the experiments we perform. First, we have the well-known Euclidean distance:

$$dist_{EUCL}(x, y) = \sqrt{\sum_{i=1}^{n}(x_i - y_i)^2}, \tag{1.1}$$

where x_i and y_i are the ith components of vectors $x = [x_1, x_2, \ldots, x_n]$ and $y = [y_1, y_2, \ldots, y_n]$, respectively. Euclidean distance measures the direct distance between two points in the space $\Re^n$.

For applications in text and document clustering and classification, the cosine similarity measure [Sal89] is often used. We can convert this to a distance measure by the following:

$$dist_{COS}(x, y) = 1 - \frac{x \bullet y}{\|x\| \cdot \|y\|}. \tag{1.2}$$

Here $\bullet$ indicates the dot product operation and $\|\ldots\|$ indicates the magnitude (length) of a vector. If we take each document to be a point in $\Re^n$ formed by the values assigned to it under the vector model, each value corresponding to a dimension, then the direction of the vector formed from the origin to the point representing the document indicates the content of the document. Under the Euclidean distance, documents with large differences in size have a large distance between them, regardless of whether or not the content is similar, because the length of the vectors differs. The cosine distance is *length invariant*, meaning only the direction of the vectors is compared; the magnitude of the vectors is ignored.

Another popular distance measure for determining document similarity is the extended Jaccard similarity [Sal89], which is converted to a distance measure as follows:

$$dist_{JAC}(x, y) = 1 - \frac{\sum_{i=1}^{n} x_i y_i}{\sum_{i=1}^{n} x_i^2 + \sum_{i=1}^{n} y_i^2 - \sum_{i=1}^{n} x_i y_i}. \tag{1.3}$$

Jaccard distance has properties of both the Euclidean and cosine distance measures. At high distance values, Jaccard behaves more like the cosine measure; at lower values, it behaves more like Euclidean. See Ref. [SGM00] for a comparison of the behavior of these distance measures.

1.2.2 *Special considerations for web documents*

Document clustering using the vector model has long been studied in the information retrieval field as a means of improving retrieval efficiency and corpus visualization [BYRN99][Sal89]. For example, in Ref. [CCA89] the application described by the authors uses the popular agglomerative hierarchical clustering method to create a cluster hierarchy for the entire document collection for the purpose of visualizing and browsing the document corpus. Another similar approach is that of Kohonen *et al.* [KKL+00], which uses self-organizing maps, a type of unsupervised neural network, to group documents in a collection. Like the application described in Ref. [CCA89], the Kohonen *et al.* system provides a environment where the results and groupings can be browsed. Early work on clustering documents retrieved by queries for the purpose of improving user navigation through the results is reported in Ref. [HP96].

A topic related to document clustering is that of document classification. The goal of such a task is to assign a label (or class) to a previously unseen document. This is different from document clustering, where the objective is to create groupings of a document collection. Document classification is a supervised learning task where example documents and their categories are available for learning in advance. Document classification is used for automated (rather than manual) categorization for documents. In Ref. [WAD+99], Weiss *et al.* studied the application of decision tree methods in order to categorize text documents. McCallum and Nigam [MN98] used a Bayesian (probabilistic) approach for document classification.

There are several reasons why information retrieval methods that deal with traditional text documents are not entirely suitable for web content mining. First, web documents contain additional markup elements (HTML tags) which are not found in plain-text documents. These elements can be a source of additional knowledge about the documents. As we saw above, there is a branch of web mining (web structure mining) that attempts to exploit the hyperlink information found in web documents. This information is not available for plain-text documents, so we must find ways to incorporate this information into our data representations during web mining. This is a major limitation of existing web content mining methods, as they either require discarding such information to arrive at traditional plain-text vector representations or they necessitate new or altered data mining procedures which explicitly take the additional information into account. Second, the web is highly heterogeneous, especially when compared to document corpora that are related to a single topic or field of interest. For example, the term "Amazon" can refer to many things on the Internet: an on-line book store, a rain forest, a river, or a person. Thus we may be unable to use specific domain knowledge (such as specialized stop word or synonym lists) that we could otherwise utilize in a system developed for a well-defined, homogeneous document collection. Additionally, web documents have a wide variation in size, style, layout, languages, *etc.* We must deal with these variations. Third, traditional information retrieval methods may not scale well to the size or dynamic nature of the Internet. Web pages tend to change often with time (they are updated, they are moved to another location, *etc.*) and thus techniques used in traditional information retrieval systems, such as those related to generation of indices or representatives of documents, can lead to out-of-date results. The web contains hundreds of millions of pages, some of which change frequently and must be re-examined periodically. These last two points are especially problematic for web document categorization methods, since creating an adequate training set to encompass all desired categories and updating it to deal with changing conditions is extremely difficult.

In contrast to the methods mentioned above, the work presented here represents the first time web document content itself has been modeled and retained using graphs in a web mining method. Note that, as we mentioned above, graph representations have been used for web mining (*e.g.* web graphs in web structure mining). However, the difference is that those graphs represent the documents (nodes) and their relationships through hyperlinks (edges). Our graphs represent the textual content of web documents through words (nodes) and adjacency information (edges), as will be discussed in detail in Chapter 3. Only recently have a few papers appeared in the literature that deal with representing the web documents themselves using graphs. Lopresti and Wilfong compared web documents using a graph representation that primarily utilizes HTML parse information, in addition to hyperlink and content order information [LW01][LW04]. In their approach they use graph probing, which extracts numerical feature information from the graphs, such as node degrees or edge label frequencies, rather than comparing the graphs themselves. In contrast, our representation uses graphs created solely from the content, and we utilize the graphs themselves to determine document similarity rather than a set of extracted features. Liang and Doermann represent the physical layout of document images as graphs [LD02]. In their layout graphs nodes represent elements on the page of a document, such as columns of text or headings, while edges indicate how these elements appear together on the page (*i.e.* they capture the spatial relationships). This method is based on the formatting and appearance of the documents when rendered, not the textual content (words) of a document as in our approach. Another recently reported approach [DG03][PG03] takes both the content and structure of web documents into account. Documents are initially represented by graphs according to either naturally occurring elements (*e.g.* pages, sections, paragraphs, *etc.*) or XML markup structure. However, rather than manipulating the graphs directly as data, as is done in our approach, probabilistic information is extracted to create Bayesian networks for retrieval or classification. Thus this method is more similar to a probabilistic learning model, rather than a purely graph-theoretical one.

1.3 Overview of Remaining Chapters

In this book we will be presenting important contributions that help improve the clustering and classification of web documents. This is accomplished by representing their content with a more versatile graph model, which can retain additional information that is not captured when using a vector representation. We will describe graph-theoretical extensions to existing, proven clustering and classification methods that for the first time allow them to deal with data represented by graphs rather than vectors. This approach has two main benefits. First, it allows us to keep the inherent structure of the original data by modeling web document content as a graph, rather than having to arrive at numeric feature vectors that contain only term frequency information. Second, we do not need to develop new algorithms or frameworks to deal with the graphs: we can simply apply straightforward extensions to go from classical data mining algorithms that use numerical vectors to those that can handle graphs. It is our contention that by using graphs to keep information that is usually lost we can improve clustering and classification performance over the usual vector model for the same algorithm. We will explore this contention through a series of experiments, using the well known k-means clustering and k-nearest neighbors (k-NN) classification algorithms. A surprising realization during our experiments is that, with careful selection of the graph representation model for an application, we can achieve polynomial time complexity for the graph similarity procedure. In the general case this is an NP-Complete problem. Note that these techniques are not limited to web documents or even text documents in general: they allow any data sets that are complex enough to require representation by graphs (*e.g.* software code, computer networks, maps, images, *etc.*) to now be clustered or classified using classical, popular methods without loss of the inherent structural information.

The remainder of this book is organized as follows. A review of graph similarity techniques as well as the mathematical definitions and notation needed for the methods we propose is presented in Chapter 2. We will review the maximum common subgraph approach, which is what we use for graph similarity in our web mining algorithms. We will also give introductions to some other related methods including graph isomorphism, graph edit distance, and median of a set of graphs. The five graph-theoretical distance measures we use will also be presented here.

In Chapter 3 we will show how web documents can be modeled as graphs using six different methods: *standard, simple, n-distance, n-simple-distance, absolute frequency,* and *relative frequency.* We also give some implementation details relating to the creation of document models from their content, such as stop word removal and stemming. The complexity analysis related to these representations is also given. We will describe the three web document data sets used for our experiments in this chapter as well.

In Chapter 4 we will describe an extension to the k-means clustering algorithm that allows the utilization of graphs instead of vectors [SLBK03b] and illustrate its usefulness by applying it to the problem of clustering a collection of web documents. We will define the clustering performance indexes that will be used to measure clustering performance in our experiments. We present experiments comparing our novel approach to the traditional vector methods when using different graph distance measures and graph representations of documents. The effect of graph size on the clustering performance is also investigated. We demonstrate how multidimensional scaling can be used with graphs to allow for visualization of the graph space and clusters of documents. Further, we will measure the performance of our clustering method when combined with the global k-means algorithm presented in [LVV03], which provides a deterministic method of finding "good" initial cluster center positions for k-means [SLBK03c]. Previous experimental results have shown that initialization with global k-means can lead to clustering performance which is as good or better than random initializations, and we will investigate whether this holds true for our methods and data sets as well. We also use this method to examine the question of the optimum number of clusters for the document collections. We will use the global k-means initializations for a range of different k values (numbers of clusters) and measure performance with additional cluster validity indexes.

In Chapter 5 we compare the traditional vector model representation to our new graph model in the context of the document classification task rather than clustering. We introduce a graph-based extension of the popular k-nearest neighbors (k-NN) classification algorithm [SLBK03a][SLBK04] and measure classification accuracy using the leave-one-out approach over all three web document collections. We select several values for the number of nearest neighbors, k, and look at the classification performance as a function of the size of the graphs representing each document. We also examine the effect of different graph-theoretical distance measures and graph representations on classification accuracy as in Chapter 4. Further, we compare execution times of both our graph-based approach and the traditional vector approach using cosine similarity or Jaccard similarity. Finally, we show how random node selection, a graph-theoretic analogue of the random feature subset selection method used with vector representations, can be used to build classifier ensembles that use both structural (graph-based) and statistical (vector-based) classifiers.

In Chapter 6 we describe a web search clustering system we developed within the graph-theoretic framework. This system takes a user's query, submits it to conventional web search engines, and then organizes the resulting web documents by a hierarchical clustering procedure. Each cluster is represented by a label describing the cluster contents. Our system originally used binary vector representations of web documents and cluster labels. We later upgraded our algorithms to use graph-representations. The most notable benefit of this change is that the cluster labels under the graph-based approach preserved the correct term ordering used in the phrases describing the clusters. An additional benefit is that the term co-occurrence information captured by the edges in the graphs allows for additional cluster organization, from independent terms (which are more general) to phrases (which are more specific). This chapter gives the reader an example of an actual, practical web mining system which utilizes graph-theoretic methods, including the details of migrating the system's algorithms from vectors to graphs, comparisons with similar systems, and examples of the system's output.

Concluding remarks and possible future extensions of the current work will be given in Chapter 7.

Chapter 2

Graph Similarity Techniques

We will use the concepts of graph similarity, graph distance, and graph matching in the following chapters as they form a basis for the novel approaches we have developed for performing clustering and classification tasks using graphs instead of more restrictive vectors. The purpose of the current chapter is to give a literature survey of the various methods that are used to determine similarity, distance and matchings between graphs as well as introduce the formal notation which will later be necessary to describe our algorithms. These topics are closely related to the topics of inexact graph matching or graph similarity, and several practical applications that utilize graph similarity or graph matching are represented in the literature, many of them in the field of image processing. Haris *et al.* performed labeling of coronary angiograms with graph matching [HEM+99]. In Ref. [PM99] a method for allocating tasks in multiprocessor systems using graphs and graph matching is described. In Ref. [HH99] Huet and Hancock describe a graph matching method for shape recognition in image databases. Another area where graph similarity and matching is popular is in chemistry, due to the natural representation of chemical structures (*e.g.* molecules) as graphs [Gro85][Owo88]. For a recent review of graph matching techniques used in pattern recognition, see Ref. [CFSV04].

In this book we are specifically interested in using graph techniques for dealing with web document content. Traditional learning methods applied to the tasks of text or document classification and categorization, such as rule induction [ADW94] and Bayesian methods [MN98], are based on a vector model of document representation or an even simpler Boolean model. Similarity of graphs in domains outside of information retrieval has largely been studied under the topic of graph matching. Under this model there exists a database of graphs and an input (or query) graph; the goal

13

is to find the graph in the database that most closely matches the input graph [LBV00]. In many applications the input graph is not expected to be an exact match to any database graph since the input graph is either previously unseen or assumed to be corrupted with some amount of noise. Thus we sometimes refer to this area as error-tolerant or inexact graph matching. As mentioned above, a number of graph matching applications have been reported in the literature, including the recognition of characters, graphical symbols, and two-dimensional shapes. For a recent survey see Ref. [Bun00]. We are not aware, however, of any graph matching applications that deal with content-based categorization and classification of web or text documents.

The remainder of this chapter is organized as follows. First, in Sec. 2.1, we give the mathematical notations and the definitions of graph and subgraph isomorphisms. If two graphs are isomorphic then there is an exact 1-to-1 matching between them; graph isomorphism was the basis for early (exact) graph matching methods. The other basic notation and definitions used in the book will also be given. In Sec. 2.2, we explain graph edit distance and how it provides a numeric dissimilarity between two graphs. In Sec. 2.3, we describe the maximum common subgraph approach and explain how it is related to graph edit distance. The state space search method is given in Sec. 2.4. In Sec. 2.5, we describe a probabilistic approach to matching graphs with errors. In Sec. 2.6, we recount a method based on distance preservation between graph nodes. We give some relaxed (sub-optimal) approaches to graph matching in Sec. 2.7. In Sec. 2.8, we give an account of mean and medians of a set of graphs; while not measurements of graph similarity per se, these concepts are related and very useful in certain applications. Summary remarks are given in Sec. 2.9.

2.1   Graph and Subgraph Isomorphism

In this section we describe graph and subgraph isomorphism. Before we give definitions for isomorphism, we first give definitions for graph and subgraph. A *graph* G [BJK00][WZC95] is a 4-tuple: $G = (V, E, \alpha, \beta)$, where V is a set of *nodes* (also called *vertices*), $E \subseteq V \times V$ is a set of *edges* connecting the nodes, $\alpha: V \to \Sigma_V$ is a function labeling the nodes, and $\beta: V \times V \to \Sigma_E$ is a function labeling the edges (Σ_V and Σ_E being the sets of labels that can appear on the nodes and edges, respectively). For brevity, we may abbreviate G as $G = (V, E)$ by omitting the labeling functions.

A graph $G_1 = (V_1, E_1, \alpha_1, \beta_1)$ is a *subgraph* [Bun97] of a graph $G_2 = (V_2, E_2, \alpha_2, \beta_2)$, denoted $G_1 \subseteq G_2$, if $V_1 \subseteq V_2$, $E_1 \subseteq E_2 \cap (V_1 \times V_1)$, $\alpha_1(x) = \alpha_2(x)$ $\forall x \in V_1$, and $\beta_1((x, y)) = \beta_2((x, y))$ $\forall (x, y) \in E_1$. Conversely, graph G_2 is also called a *supergraph* of G_1.

When we say that two graphs are *isomorphic*, we mean that the graphs contain the same number of nodes and there is a direct 1-to-1 correspondence between the nodes in the two graphs such that the edges between nodes and all labels are preserved. Formally, a graph $G_1 = (V_1, E_1, \alpha_1, \beta_1)$ and a graph $G_2 = (V_2, E_2, \alpha_2, \beta_2)$ are said to be *isomorphic* [Bun97], denoted $G_1 \cong G_2$, if there exists a bijective function $f \colon V_1 \to V_2$ such that $\alpha_1(x) = \alpha_2(f(x))$ $\forall x \in V_1$ and $\beta_1((x, y)) = \beta_2((f(x), f(y)))$ $\forall (x, y) \in V_1 \times V_1$. Such a function f is also called a *graph isomorphism* between G_1 and G_2.

There is also the notion of subgraph isomorphism, meaning a graph is isomorphic to a part of (*i.e.* a subgraph of) another graph. Given a graph isomorphism f between graphs G_1 and G_2 as defined above and another graph G_3, if $G_2 \subseteq G_3$ then f is a *subgraph isomorphism* [BJK00] between G_1 and G_3.

It is not known whether graph isomorphism is an NP-complete problem, however subgraph isomorphism is NP-complete [MKC01][MB98]. Clearly, as the number of nodes in the graphs increase the number of possible matchings to be checked increases combinatorally. A general procedure for determining subgraph isomorphism is given in Ref. [Ull76]. The naïve algorithm for graph isomorphism is to maintain a matrix which indicates which nodes in each graph are compatible; it can require all possible permutations of matchings to determine if there is an isomorphism. The procedure in Ref. [Ull76] improves the complexity by pruning the search space. Graph isomorphism tells us only that there exists an exact match between two graphs (*i.e.* that they are identical). It does not give us any indication of similarity between graphs, only that they are isomorphic or not. Subgraph isomorphism tells us if one graph appears as part of another graph. Formally, the similarity between two graphs G_1 and G_2, denoted $s(G_1, G_2)$, is a function that has the following properties:

(1) $0 \le s(G_1, G_2) \le 1$
(2) $s(G_1, G_2) = 1 \to G_1 \cong G_2$
(3) $s(G_1, G_2) = s(G_2, G_1)$
(4) if G_1 is more similar to G_2 than to G_3, then $s(G_1, G_2) \ge s(G_1, G_3)$

One problem with defining similarity in this way is that it is not clear what case causes $s(G_1, G_2) = 0$. This comes from the fact that we have no concept of an exact "opposite" of a graph. We do, however, have the idea of compliments of graphs. A *compliment* [CLR97] of a graph G, denoted $\overline{G}$, is the fully connected version of G such that the edges in G have been removed, $\overline{E} = \{(u, v)|(u, v) \notin E\}$.

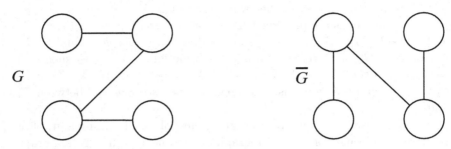

Fig. 2.1   A graph G and its compliment $\overline{G}$ may be isomorphic.

However, a graph may be isomorphic to its compliment (Fig. 2.1), so it does not necessarily hold that $s(G, \overline{G}) = 0$. Given this limitation, the usual method of determining numeric similarity between graphs is to use a distance measure. A distance metric [BJK00][BS98][FV01][WSKR01] between two graphs, denoted $d(G_1, G_2)$, is a function that has the following properties:

(1) *boundary condition*: $d(G_1, G_2) \geq 0$
(2) *identical graphs have zero distance*: $d(G_1, G_2) = 0 \rightarrow G1 \cong G2$
(3) *symmetry*: $d(G_1, G_2) = d(G_2, G_1)$
(4) *triangle inequality*: $d(G_1, G_3) \leq d(G_1, G_2) + d(G_2, G_3)$

We note that it is possible to transform a similarity measure into a distance measure, for example by:

$$d(G_1, G_2) = 1 - s(G_1, G_2). \tag{2.1}$$

It can be shown that this equation satisfies the various conditions above for similarity. Other equations are also possible for changing distance into similarity. Throughout the rest of this book we will see several proposed distance measures, some of which have been created from a similarity measure.

2.2 Graph Edit Distance

Edit distance is a method that is used to measure the difference between symbolic data structures such as trees [Tai79] and strings [WF74]. It is also known as the Levenshtein distance, from early work in error-correcting/detecting codes that allowed insertion and deletion of symbols [Lev66]. The concept is straightforward. Various operations are defined on the structures, such as deletion, insertion, and renaming of elements. A cost function is associated with each operation, and the minimum cost needed to transform one structure into the other using the operations is the distance between them. Edit distance has also been applied to graphs, as graph edit distance [SF83]. The operations in graph edit distance are insertion, deletion, and re-labeling of nodes and edges.

Formally, an editing matching function (or an error-correcting graph matching, *ecgm* [Bun97]) between two graphs G_1 and G_2 is defined as a bijective mapping function $M\colon G_x \to G_y$, where $G_x \subseteq G_1$ and $G_y \subseteq G_2$. The following six edit operations on the graphs, which are implied by the mapping M, are also defined:

(1) If a node $v \in V_1$ but $v \notin V_x$ then we delete node v with cost c_{nd}.
(2) If a node $v \in V_2$ but $v \notin V_y$ then we insert node v with cost c_{ni}.
(3) If $M(v_i) = v_j$ for $v_i \in V_x$ and $v_j \in V_y$ and $\alpha_1(v_x) \neq \alpha_2(v_y)$ then we substitute node v_i with node v_j with cost c_{ns}.
(4) If an edge $e \in E_1$ but $e \notin E_x$ then we delete edge e with cost c_{ed}.
(5) If an edge $e \in E_2$ but $e \notin E_y$ then we insert edge e with cost c_{ei}.
(6) If $M(e_i) = e_j$ for $e_i \in E_x$ and $e_j \in E_y$ and $\beta_1(e_x) \neq \beta_2(e_y)$ then we substitute edge e_i with edge e_j with cost c_{es}.

We note that there may be several functions M which edit graph G_1 into graph G_2. The *cost* [Bun97][Bun99] of a given an editing function M, denoted $\gamma(M)$, is defined as the sum of the costs c of all the individual edit operations implied by M. Usually the cost coefficients c are application dependant. In the error-correcting graph matching sense, they can be related to the probability of the operations (errors) occurring. We assume that the cost coefficients are non-negative and are invariant of the node or edge upon which they are applied (*i.e.* the costs are constant for each operation).

The edit distance between two graphs [Bun97], denoted $d(G_1, G_2)$, is defined as the cost of the mapping M that results in the lowest $\gamma(M)$.

More formally:

$$d(G_1, G_2) = \min_{\forall M}(\gamma(M)). \qquad (2.2)$$

Thus the distance between two graphs is the cost of an editing function which transforms one graph into the other via edit operations and which has the lowest cost among all such editing functions.

The advantage to the graph edit distance approach is that it is easy to understand and straightforward to apply. The disadvantage is that the costs for the edit operations (6 parameter values) need to be determined for each application. In Ref. [Bun99], Bunke gives an examination of cost functions for graph edit distance. He shows that an infinite number of equivalent cost classes exist under certain conditions; *i.e.*, it is the ratios between the different edit costs that differentiates sets of cost functions, rather than the individual cost values.

2.3   Maximum Common Subgraph / Minimum Common Supergraph Approach

Bunke has shown [Bun97] that there is a direct relationship between graph edit distance and the maximum common subgraph between two graphs. Specifically, the two are equivalent under certain restrictions on the cost functions. A graph g is a *maximum common subgraph (mcs)* [Bun97] of graphs G_1 and G_2, denoted $mcs(G_1, G_2)$, if: (1) $g \subseteq G_1$ (2) $g \subseteq G_2$ and (3) there is no other subgraph g' ($g' \subseteq G_1$, $g' \subseteq G_2$) such that $|g'| > |g|$. (Here $|g|$ is usually taken to mean $|V|$, *i.e.* the number of nodes in the graph; it is used to indicate the "size" of a graph.)

Similarly, there is the complimentary idea of minimum common supergraph. A graph g is a *minimum common supergraph (MCS)* [BJK00] of graphs G_1 and G_2, denoted $MCS(G_1, G_2)$, if: (1) $G_1 \subseteq g$ (2) $G_2 \subseteq g$ and (3) there is no other supergraph g' ($G_1 \subseteq g'$, $G_2 \subseteq g'$) such that $|g'| < |g|$.

Methods for determining the *mcs* are given in Refs. [Lev72][McG82]. The general approach is to create a compatibility graph for the two given graphs, and then find the largest clique within it. What Bunke has shown is that when computing the editing matching function based on graph edit distance (Sec. 2.2), the function with the lowest cost is equivalent to the maximum common subgraph between the two graphs under certain conditions on the cost coefficients. This is intuitively appealing, since the maximum common subgraph is the part of both graphs that is unchanged by deleting or inserting nodes and edges. To edit graph G_1 into graph G_2, one only needs to perform the following steps:

(1) Delete nodes and edges from G_1 that don't appear in $mcs(G_1, G_2)$
(2) Perform any node or edge substitutions
(3) Add the nodes and edges from G_2 that don't appear in $mcs(G_1, G_2)$

Following this observation that the size of the maximum common subgraph is related to the similarity between two graphs, Bunke and Shearer [BS98] have introduced a distance measure based on *mcs*. They defined the following distance measure:

$$d_{MCS}(G_1, G_2) = 1 - \frac{|mcs(G_1, G_2)|}{\max(|G_1|, |G_2|)}, \qquad (2.3)$$

where $\max(x, y)$ is the usual maximum of two numbers x and y, and $|\ldots|$ indicates the size of a graph (usually taken to be the number of nodes in a graph). The concept behind this distance measure is that as the size of the maximum common subgraph of a pair of graphs becomes larger, the more similar the two graphs are (*i.e.* they have more in common). The larger the maximum common subgraph, the smaller $d_{MCS}(G_1, G_2)$ becomes, indicating more similarity and less distance. If the two graphs are in fact identical, their maximum common subgraph is the same as the graphs themselves and thus the size of all three graphs is equal: $|G_1| = |G_2| = |mcs(G_1, G_2)|$. This leads to the distance, $d_{MCS}(G_1, G_2)$, becoming 0. Conversely, if no maximum common subgraph exists, then $|mcs(G_1, G_2)| = 0$ and $d_{MCS}(G_1, G_2) = 1$. This distance measure has been shown to be a metric, and produces a value in $[0, 1]$. This distance measure has four important properties [BJK00] (see Sec. 2.1 above). First, it is restricted to producing a number in the interval $[0, 1]$. Second, the distance is 0 only when the two graphs are identical. Third, the distance between two graphs is symmetric. Fourth, it obeys the triangle inequality, which ensures the distance measure behaves in an intuitive way. For example, if we have two dissimilar objects (*i.e.* there is a large distance between them) the triangle inequality implies that a third object which is similar (*i.e.* has a small distance) to one of those objects must be dissimilar to the other. The advantage of this approach over the graph edit distance method is that it does not require the determination of any cost coefficients or other parameters. However, the metric as it is defined in Eq. 2.3 may not be appropriate for all applications. Thus several other distance measures based on the size of the maximum common subgraph or minimum common supergraph have been proposed.

A second distance measure which has been proposed by Wallis *et al.* [WSKR01], based on the idea of graph union, is:

$$d_{WGU}(G_1, G_2) = 1 - \frac{|mcs(G_1, G_2)|}{|G_1| + |G_2| - |mcs(G_1, G_2)|}. \qquad (2.4)$$

By "graph union" we mean that the denominator represents the size of the union of the two graphs in the set theoretic sense; specifically adding the size of each graph ($|G_1| + |G_2|$) then subtracting the size of their intersection ($|mcs(G_1, G_2)|$) leads to the size of the union (the reader may easily verify this using a Venn diagram). This distance measure behaves similarly to MCS. The motivation for using graph union in the denominator is to allow for changes in the smaller graph to exert some influence over the distance measure, which does not happen with MCS. This measure was also demonstrated to be a metric, and creates distance values in $[0, 1]$.

A similar distance measure [Bun97] which is not normalized to the interval $[0, 1]$ is:

$$d_{UGU}(G_1, G_2) = |G_1| + |G_2| - 2 \cdot |mcs(G_1, G_2)|. \qquad (2.5)$$

Fernández and Valiente have proposed a distance measure based on both the maximum common subgraph and the minimum common supergraph [FV01]:

$$d_{MMCS}(G_1, G_2) = |MCS(G_1, G_2)| - |mcs(G_1, G_2)|, \qquad (2.6)$$

where $MCS(G_1, G_2)$ is the minimum common supergraph of graphs G_1 and G_2. The concept that drives this distance measure is that the maximum common subgraph provides a "lower bound" on the similarity of two graphs, while the minimum common supergraph is an "upper bound". If two graphs are identical, then both their maximum common subgraph and minimum common supergraph are the same as the original graphs and $|G_1| = |G_2| = |MCS(G_1, G_2)| = |mcs(G_1, G_2)|$, which leads to $d_{MMCS}(G_1, G_2) = 0$. As the graphs become more dissimilar, the size of the maximum common subgraph decreases, while the size of the minimum common supergraph increases. This in turn leads to increasing values of $d_{MMCS}(G_1, G_2)$. For two graphs with no maximum common subgraph, the distance will become $|MCS(G_1, G_2)| = |G_1| + |G_2|$. MMCS has also been shown to be a metric, but it does not produce values normalized to the interval $[0, 1]$, unlike the MCS or WGU. Note that if it holds that

$|MCS(G_1, G_2)| = |G_1| + |G_2| - |mcs(G_1, G_2)| \; \forall G_1, G_2$, we can compute $d_{MMCS}(G_1, G_2)$ as $|G_1| + |G_2| - 2|mcs(G_1, G_2)|$. This is much less computationally intensive than computing the minimum common supergraph

We can also create a version of this distance measure which is normalized to $[0, 1]$ as follows:

$$d_{MMCSN}(G_1, G_2) = 1 - \frac{|mcs(G_1, G_2)|}{\max(|MCS(G_1, G_2)|)}. \qquad (2.7)$$

For brevity we will refer to the distance measures of Eqs. 2.3–2.7 as MCS, WGU, UGU, MMCS, and MMCSN, respectively.

The distance metrics of Eqs. 2.3–2.7 are relatively new, and not much has been reported regarding their differences in performance for different problem domains. We will examine this issue in the coming chapters. Also, the graph size $|G|$ is typically defined simply as the number of nodes in the graph; the edge information is not (explicitly) captured in these distance measures.

Note that if the condition holds that $|MCS(G_1, G_2)| = |G_1| + |G_2| - |mcs(G_1, G_2)|$, then WGU and MMCSN are identical. Similarly, UGU and MMCS are identical. This can be verified by substituting this definition for $|MCS(G_1, G_2)|$ into Eqs. 2.6 and 2.7.

2.4 State Space Search Approach

In Sec. 2.2 we described the graph edit distance approach for determining graph similarity. In order to find the distance we need to find an edit matching function that has the lowest cost for the given cost coefficients. Depending on the size of the graphs and the costs associated with the edit operations, finding the lowest cost mapping may require an exhaustive examination of all possible matchings. If we allow the possibility of not having to determine the exact distance between graphs, we can perform other types of sub-optimal search. These searches may not find the global minimum cost function, but they can be performed more quickly (since we do not need to find all of the possible matching functions) and still yield acceptable results.

Each matching function we consider becomes a state in a search space. The cost $\gamma(M)$ for a state M becomes the value we attempt to minimize through the search. M is actually a graph isomorphism between subgraphs of the two graphs being matched; it specifies the operations needed to edit one graph into the other graph. Neighbors of a state M can be determined by adding/deleting nodes and edges to/from these subgraphs along with their corresponding isomorphic matching; these neighbor states indicate the creation (or removal) of a single matching between a node or edge in the two graphs (*i.e.* it specifies a change in the edit operations). Once the matching is represented in such a manner, many techniques become available for performing the search, including hill climbing, genetic algorithms, simulated annealing, and so forth. These searches may not find the optimal solution, but for some applications (such as graph matching for retrieval of images or documents) this may not be a concern. These techniques are also sensitive to initialization and parameter selection, so there can be a wide variety in performance.

For a more detailed description of this technique as well as experimental results comparing different search and initialization strategies, we refer the reader to Ref. [WZC95]. Early work in this area can be found in Ref. [EF84].

2.5   Probabilistic Approach

In this section we will give a summary of the approach proposed by Wilson and Hancock [WH97] which is based on probability theory. In the probabilistic method, we attempt to match a data graph G_D and a stored model graph G_M. These graphs are attributed graphs. An *attributed graph* [WH97] is a graph $G_y = (V, E, A)$, where A is a set of attributes associated with each node, $A = x_v^y, \forall v \in V$.

The attributes in the data graph are to be matched to those in the model graph, such that the matched nodes have the same or similar attributes. Edges may also have associated attributes in this model, but they are not considered in this approach. Next, we have the concept of super-clique of a node. A *super-clique* [WH97] of a node i in graph $G = (V, E)$ is defined as $C_i = i \cup \{j | (j, i) \in E\}$. In other words, the super-clique of a node i is the set of nodes which contains i and all nodes connected to it by edges. We attempt to match all super-cliques in the data graph with super-cliques in the model graph.

The set of all possible matches between super-clique C_i in the data graph G_D and super-cliques S_j in the model graph G_M is called a *dictionary* [WH97] and is denoted Θ_i. To cope with size differences between the data and model super-cliques we allow dummy (or null) nodes ϕ to be inserted into S_j so that both graphs have equal numbers of nodes. The function matching a node in C_i to a node in S_j is $f: V_D \to V_M \cup \phi$. The probability of matching errors (a node in the data graph is matched to the wrong node in the model graph) is denoted P_e and the probability of structural errors (a node in the data graph is matched to a dummy node in the model graph) is denoted P_ϕ. Given these definitions, some assumptions, and through application of Bayes' rule and other probability theoretic constructions, Wilson and Hancock arrive at a mathematical description for the probability of a super-clique matching between two graphs (denoted Γ_j for super-clique C_j):

$$P(\Gamma_j) = \frac{K_{C_j}}{|\Theta_j|} \sum_{S_j \in \Theta_j} \exp\{-(k_e H(\Gamma_j, S_i) + k_\phi[\psi(\Gamma_j, S_i) + \Psi(\Gamma_j)])\}, \quad (2.8)$$

where

$$K_{C_j} = [(1 - P_e)(1 - P_\phi)]^{|C_j|}, \quad (2.9)$$

$$k_e = \ln \frac{1 - P_e}{P_e}, \quad (2.10)$$

$$k_\phi = \frac{(1 - P_e)(1 - P_\phi)}{P_\phi}. \quad (2.11)$$

$H(\Gamma_j, S_i)$ is the Hamming distance between the super-clique of the data graph under the mapping f and the super-clique of the model graph, $\psi(\Gamma_j, S_i) = |C_j| - |S_i|$ (*i.e.* the number of null nodes inserted into S_i), and $\Psi(\Gamma_j)$ is the number of nodes in C_j which are mapped onto null nodes in S_i. The derivation of Eq. 2.8 is beyond the scope of this chapter, but the equation contains three parts which are fairly straightforward. First, the part associated with Eq. 2.9 is the probability of no errors occurring. Second, the part associated with Eq.. 2.10 is concerned with the probability of matching errors occurring. Third, the part associated with Eq.. 2.11 deals with the probability of structural errors occurring. For an in depth derivation of these equations, please refer to Ref. [WH97].

The authors then go on to derive rules which can be applied to update the matching function f under three different methods (null-labeling, constraint filtering, and graph edit operations). The methods use update rules of the form:

$$f(u) = \arg \max_{v \in V_M} \frac{P(u, v|x_u^D, x_v^M)}{P(u, v)} \sum_{j \in C_u} P(\Gamma_j). \quad (2.12)$$

Here $P(u, v)$ indicates the prior probability that node u in the data graph corresponds to node v in the model graph, while the other probability in the numerator is the conditional *a posteriori* probability given the corresponding attributes related with the nodes; approaches to determining these probabilities are application dependant. One method uses $P(\Gamma_j)$ as in Eq. 2.8, while the others use the form

$$P(\Gamma_j) = \sum_{S_i \in \Theta_j} e^{-k_e H(\Gamma_j, S_i)}. \qquad (2.13)$$

This form is obtained by setting the parameter $k_\phi = 0$, in other words ignoring the effect of mapping nodes in the data graph to null-labeled nodes in the model graph.

A benefit of this approach is that, under the simpler model of Eq. 2.13, there is only one parameter that must be adjusted. Another advantage of this framework is that it can be applied in many situations. For example, an extension of the work [WWH97] deals with multiple graph matching (compared to data-model graph matching of attributed graphs) through computations of fuzzy consistency matrices. In Ref. [FWH98], Finch *et al.* developed an energy function for graph matching based on the probabilistic framework of this section. A method using this approach for the fitness function in a genetic search for graph matching is described in Ref. [CWH97]. A similar probabilistic framework for hierarchical graphs is given in Ref. [WH99]. Myers *et al.* [MWH00] modified the approach described here to include graph edit distance; the new method achieves better complexity by removing the need to insert null nodes in the model graph.

2.6   Distance Preservation Approach

In Ref. [CKS98], Chartrand *et al.* describe an approach for graph distance calculation based on preserving the distance between nodes. The idea comes from the fact that when two graphs are isomorphic, the distances (meaning in this context the number of edges traversed) between every pair of nodes are identical in both graphs. Given a graph $G = (V, E)$, the distance between two nodes $x, y \in V$, denoted $d_G(x, y)$, is defined as the minimum number of edges that need to be traversed when traveling from x to y [CKS98]. Further, the ϕ-distance [CKS98] between two graphs

G_1 and G_2, denoted $d_\phi(G_1, G_2)$, is defined as

$$d_\phi(G_1, G_2) = \sum_{\forall x \forall y \in V_1} |d_{G_1}(x, y) - d_{G_2}(x, y)|, \qquad (2.14)$$

where ϕ is a 1-to-1 mapping (but not necessarily an isomorphism) between G_1 and G_2. Here $|\ldots|$ is the standard absolute value operation.

If ϕ is an isomorphism (*i.e.* $G_1 \cong G_2$), then $d_\phi(G_1, G_2) = 0$; if G_1 and G_2 are not isomorphic, then $d_\phi(G_1, G_2) > 0$. This leads to a definition of distance between two graphs, denoted $d(G_1, G_2)$, which is formally denoted

$$d(G_1, G_2) = \min_{\forall \phi} (d_\phi(G_1, G_2)), \qquad (2.15)$$

where $\min(\ldots)$ is the minimum function [CKS98].

Here again we see the idea of examining all the possible matching functions (ϕ, in the notation of the current method; M in the notation of graph edit distance) between two graphs in order to determine the distance between them. Eq. 2.15 above is directly comparable to Eq. 2.2 of Sec. 2.2, even though these two methods have different theoretical foundations. The authors also go on to show if the graphs meet certain requirements then we can make some other, less expensive calculations. For example, if G_1 and G_2 are connected graphs with equal numbers of nodes, then we can determine the lower bound on their distance by

$$d(G_1, G_2) \geq |td(G_1) - td(G_2)|, \qquad (2.16)$$

where

$$td(G) = \sum_{\forall u, v \in V} d(u, v). \qquad (2.17)$$

Or, in other words, the sum of distances between all pairs of nodes in a graph. Further theoretical contributions related to this approach can be found in Ref. [CKS98].

2.7 Relaxation Approaches

As we mentioned in Sec. 2.1, some early algorithms for determining exact graph matching (isomorphism) used a matching matrix (M) which indicates the compatibility of nodes in the two graphs being matched. If the ith row and jth column element of M, denoted M_{ij}, is a 1, then node i in

graph G_1 is matched with node j in graph G_2; otherwise there is no match
and $M_{ij} = 0$. There are constraints on the matrix M so that each row
has exactly one 1 and no column has more than one 1. Such a representation and the algorithms applied to it for determining graph matching are
straightforward, however they can require generating all the permutations
of possible node matchings over the matrix.

In order to improve time complexity, we can instead attempt to approximate the optimal solution by finding good sub-optimal solutions instead.
A method that is sometimes used to do this for graph matching problems
is called *relaxation* (or more specifically, *discrete relaxation*). Put simply,
discrete relaxation is a method of transforming a discrete representation
(such as the matrix M used for graph matching) into a continuous representation. Thus we can transform a discrete optimization problem (exact
graph matching using discrete matrix M) into a continuous optimization
problem. Compared to the state space search approach (Sec. 2.4), relaxation is a non-linear optimization approach. Gold and Rangarajan [GR96]
applied relaxation to the graph matching problem. They have posed the
problem of attributed graph matching in terms of an optimization problem:

$$E = -\frac{1}{2}\sum_{a=1}^{|V_1|}\sum_{i=1}^{|V_2|}\sum_{b=1}^{|V_1|}\sum_{j=1}^{|V_2|} M_{ai}M_{bj}\sum_{r=1}^{R} C_{aibj}^{(2,r)} + \alpha\sum_{a=1}^{|V_1|}\sum_{i=1}^{|V_2|} M_{ai}\sum_{s=1}^{S} C_{ai}^{(1,s)}.$$

$$(2.18)$$

Here M is the matching matrix as before, R is the number of edge types,
S is the number of node types, α is a weighting parameter, and the Cs are
compatibility measures between the edges of the two graphs. The goal is
then to minimize the objective function given in Eq. 2.18. The authors use
the graduated assignment algorithm to find an M which minimizes E. The
general procedure of the algorithm is as follows:

(1) Start with some valid initial matrix M^0.
(2) Determine a first order Taylor expansion of M^0 yielding:

$$Q_{ai} = -\frac{\partial E}{\partial M_{ai}^0} = \sum_{b=1}^{|V_1|}\sum_{j=1}^{|V_2|} M_{bj}^0 C_{aibj}.$$

$$(2.19)$$

(3) Use relaxation to create a continuous representation of M^0

$$M_{ai}^0 = e^{\beta Q_{ai}},$$

$$(2.20)$$

where β is a control parameter that is slowly increased as the procedure runs.

(4) Update the matrix M by a normalization procedure over both rows and columns.

(5) Repeat until convergence or iteration limit reached.

Medasani *et al.* [MKC01] gave a procedure based on fuzzy assignments and relaxation similar to the method just described. The objective function for this approach is

$$J(M,C) = \sum_{i=1}^{|V_1|+1} \sum_{j=1}^{|V_2|+1} M_{ij}^2 f(C_{ij}) + \eta \sum_{i=1}^{|V_1|+1} \sum_{j=1}^{|V_2|+1} M_{ij}(1 - M_{ij}), \quad (2.21)$$

where M is now a fuzzy membership matrix ($0 \leq M_{ij} \leq 1$) that relates the degree of match between nodes, C is a compatibility matrix between nodes (rather than edges as above), η is a control parameter, and

$$f(C_{ij}) = e^{-\beta C_{ij}}. \quad (2.22)$$

The summations in Eq. 2.21 are under the constraint that $(i,j) \neq (|V_1| + 1, |V_2| + 1)$; the extra nodes in the graphs are dummy nodes similar to slack variables. The authors then go on to derive the necessary update equations for M and C in order to minimize $J(M,C)$ and propose an algorithm which updates these matrices in an alternating fashion.

A drawback to these methods is that they can get stuck in local minima and are sensitive to initialization. The main benefit, as compared to state space search, is that the equations and algorithms for these methods are derived directly from the objective functions as opposed to performing a general search strategy or having to come up with some heuristics for the search.

2.8 Mean and Median of Graphs

In addition to the graph matching approaches we have described, we should also mention the concepts of mean and median of a set of graphs [GB02]. These do not explicitly give us an indication of graph similarity, but are useful in summarizing a group of graphs. This is useful in applications such as clustering, where we need to represent a group of graphs by some exemplar graph that represents the cluster.

The *mean of two graphs* [GB02] G_1 and G_2 is a graph g such that:

$$d(G_1, g) = d(G_2, g), \tag{2.23}$$

and

$$d(G_1, G_2) = d(G_1, g) + d(g, G_2). \tag{2.24}$$

In other words, a mean of two graphs G_1 and G_2 is a graph g that is equidistant from G_1 and G_2 and which is a distance from G_1 or G_2 equal to half the distance between G_1 and G_2. Clearly the mean will depend on the distance functions chosen, and there may be more than one graph satisfying these conditions; it is also possible that no mean exists for a given pair of graphs.

The *weighted mean of two graphs* [BGJ01] G_1 and G_2 is a graph g such that:

$$d(G_1, G) = \alpha(G_1, G_2), \tag{2.25}$$

and

$$d(G_1, G_2) = \alpha d(G_1, G_2) + d(g, G_2), \tag{2.26}$$

where $0 < \alpha < 1$. If $\alpha = 0.5$, then the same mean as in Eqs. 2.23 and 2.24 results.

An algorithm for finding the weighted mean of two graphs is given in Ref. [BGJ01]. The method involves finding a subset of editing operations (given the lowest cost editing function between the graphs) for the given α in order to determine the mean graph. In Ref. [BK00], a theoretical proof is given that any graph g such that $mcs(G_1, G_2) \subseteq g \subseteq G_1$ or $mcs(G_1, G_2) \subseteq g \subseteq G_2$ is a mean of G_1 and G_2. Thus the problem becomes finding a graph that is a supergraph of the maximum common subgraph, but a subgraph of one of the original graphs. Finally, we have the concept of the median of a set of graphs, which acts like a representative of the set. The *median of a set of graphs* S [BGJ01] is a graph $g \in S$ ($S = \{G_1, G_2, \ldots, G_n\}$) such that g has the lowest average distance to all elements in S:

$$g = \arg \min_{\forall s \in S} \left(\frac{1}{|S|} \sum_{i=1}^{|S|} dist(s, G_i) \right) \tag{2.27}$$

Since $g \in S$, it is straightforward (and relatively inexpensive) to simply compute the average distance to all graphs for each graph in S. Further, the median of a set of graphs always exists; it may or may not also be a mean.

2.9 Summary

In this chapter we have given a survey of the most popular methods for determining graph similarity that are represented in the literature. Graph isomorphism finds an exact 1-to-1 matching between identical graphs and was the earliest approach to graph matching. Unfortunately, it cannot handle inexact graph matching. Graph edit distance is a popular approach that can deal with inexact matching. It determines the cost of a sequence of edit operations needed to transform one graph into another; this cost is the distance between the two graphs. This is a straightforward method, but it requires the determination of several parameters (the costs of the various edit operations). The size of the minimum common subgraph of a pair of graphs has been shown to be related to the graph edit distance. Thus several distance measures that use the size of the minimum common subrgaph have been proposed. This technique has the advantage that edit costs do not need to be determined. However, the computation of the minimum common subgraph is NP-complete. Another method for calculating graph distance is a distance preservation approach that determines the minimum number of edges (distances) between every pair of nodes in each graph. If the graphs are the same, the distances will be identical for some matching of nodes. Otherwise, there will be a difference indicating the distance between the graphs. This method is only applicable to graphs with equal numbers of nodes and does not appear to be widely used.

Methods such as state space search and relaxation have also been applied to the problem of determining graph similarity. These techniques are often used to provide a sub-optimal approximation when the original problem is NP-complete or has a high potential for combinatorial explosion. For example, state space search can be used if we represent the matching or edit sequences between graphs as states, and then execute a search strategy for the state with the lowest cost. This results in a sub-optimal version of graph edit distance. Relaxation can be used to transform the discrete problem of node matching between graphs to a continuous representation, which then allows the application of non-linear optimization methods. This creates a sub-optimal version of the graph isomorphism approach. Drawbacks of these two methods are that they can be sensitive to initialization or become trapped at local optima. Another methodology which has been applied to the problem of matching attributed graphs is a probabilistic approach. There are several applications and extensions relating to this method, but the procedure is not straightforward and is only applicable to attributed graphs.

As we have seen, the approaches often have similarities with one another. For example, probability can be seen not just in the Bayesian approach described in Sec. 2.5, but also in the cost functions of graph edit distance (Sec. 2.2) and some state space search approaches (Sec. 2.4). Both state space representations and relaxation attempt to find good sub-optimal solutions. The idea of a function mapping (or transforming) one graph to another can be found in isomorphism, graph edit distance, state space representation, and minimum common subgraph.

There are also some open problems in the area of graph similarity. As we mentioned in Sec. 2.1, we have no concept of the opposite (inverse, negative, *etc.*) of a graph. Thus we have no definition of what it means to have 0 similarity between two graphs. A second area in need of improvement is the time complexity of some of the algorithms. These methods rely on solving NP-complete problems or have large potential for combinatorial explosion. Approximate and sub-optimal solutions have been proposed, however these are not guaranteed to reach the optimal solution and may require management of various extra parameters. A third problem: some of the approaches described in this chapter are applicable to determining similarity between two graphs at a time only. This is a problem when trying to match a large database of graphs to a single input graph. Messmer and Bunke [MB98] propose a method of decomposing large graphs into smaller components and then organizing these components into a network which indicates the relationship between the parts in order to deal with this issue. Finally, there have been no extensive cross-comparison experiments performed between these different methods. Most experimental results are in the area of stability analysis or in comparing performance within a certain framework for certain problem areas (*e.g.* within the state space search approach).

In the following chapters, we will be most interested in the minimum common subgraph approaches (Sec. 2.3), as we have discovered methods of overcoming this method's shortcomings while retaining its strengths. We will also make use of the graph median. In the next chapter we describe how we can use graphs to model web document content.

Chapter 3

Graph Models for Web Documents

In the previous chapter we reviewed various graph-theoretical techniques for determining graph similarity. Of particular interest to the work presented here are the distance measures based on the computation of the maximum common subgraph of a pair of graphs (Sec. 2.3) and the median of a set of graphs (Sec. 2.8). The distance measures based on maximum common subgraph (Eqs. 2.3–2.7) are straightforward in the sense that no space search or parameter value selection is required, but the drawback is that determining the maximum common subgraph is usually an NP-complete problem. However, for the proposed graph representations introduced here, the determination of the maximum common subgraph can be achieved in polynomial time, as we will see later in this chapter.

In this chapter we will describe several methods for representing web document content (or text documents in general) as graphs. These methods are named: *standard, simple, n-distance, n-simple distance, absolute frequency* and *relative frequency*. Each method is based on examining the terms on each web page and their adjacency. Terms are extracted by looking for runs of alphabetical characters separated by spaces or other types of common punctuation marks. Once the terms are extracted, we use several steps to reduce the number of terms associated with each page to some representative set. This is done to remove irrelevant terms and to reduce computation time.

3.1 Pre-Processing

When creating a graph model of a web document, we do not model the entire document as a graph. In order to reduce memory requirements and computation time, we perform a series of pre-processing steps to arrive at

31

a reduced set of the most important terms. First, we have a file of approximately 600 stop words, such as "the," "and," and "of," that contribute little information which we remove if they are present. The complete list of stop words is provided in Appendix B. We also perform some simple stemming in order to determine those word forms which should be considered to be identical (*e.g.* "test" and "tests"). Stemming is often used in information retrieval to reduce the size of term vectors by conflating those terms which are considered to be identical after the removal of their suffixes. The most common stemming algorithm is the one created by Porter [Por80]. Porter's algorithm is a fairly straightforward method that applies simple transformation rules in a series of steps in order to remove all the suffixes from a term, leaving only the "stem." Another approach to stemming besides using rules to remove suffixes is to create a database of words and their relationships. The WordNet system uses such a database [Mil95]. Lovins' algorithm [Lov68] is a mix of both the rule-based and database approaches. In Lovins' method, a list of approximately 260 suffixes is specified as a mini-database. Associated with each ending is a condition code that specifies some additional conditions that must be met to allow removal of the suffix. After the suffix is removed, some rules are applied to the remaining word to transform it to its final state.

The method of stemming we use is very simple. For each term, we look for plural forms by adding "-s" or "-es" and check to see if the plural form exists. Similarly for verbs ending in "-ing" we either add "-ing" (if the word does not end in "e") or by removing the trailing in "e" and then adding "-ing." If we determine that terms are alternate forms of each other, we conflate to the most frequently occurring form. This gives us good results; for example, when representing documents about "data mining," we conflate to "mining" and not "mine." After handling these cases, we select the most frequently occurring terms as nodes for the graph representing the document. This is very similar to the method described in Ref. [KRRT99] for extracting the index terms, except that we perform stemming.

We should also make some mention here of other approaches to reducing the number of terms that come from the information retrieval field. It has been noted before that when using the vector space model of information retrieval, performing calculations on vectors with a large number of elements (terms) can be very time consuming. A popular information retrieval technique for reducing the number of terms used is latent semantic indexing (LSI) [DDF+90]. This approach uses singular value decomposition, a statistical dimensionality reduction method, to arrive at a reduced set of terms.

LSI can achieve good results, but it is computationally expensive. It is also possible to simply drop terms with low weights (called truncation), as computed by some information retrieval metric, such as term frequency within a document. Experimental results have shown that reduced vectors (either by LSI or truncation) produce clusterings which are as good as using the original vectors, and are much faster to compute [SS97].

Stop word removal, stemming, and LSI are all related to the topic of information retrieval, or, more specifically, information extraction. The main goal of an information retrieval system is to provide users with relevant documents based on a query. We should emphasize that the methods presented in this book are not information retrieval systems. We do not select documents for retrieval; we are clustering or classifying them through the application of machine learning techniques. As mentioned in Chapter 1, a popular model used in information retrieval is the vector space model [Sal89]. In the vector space model, each document is represented in a Euclidean feature space $\Re^m$, where m is the number of terms (words) used as features. Each feature indicates the number of times a term appears in a document, or is a weight computed based on some statistical properties.

3.2 Graph Representations of Web Documents

We have several methods of creating graphs from web documents: standard, simple, n-distance, n-simple distance, absolute frequency and relative frequency. Previously, in Sec. 2.3, we stated that the usual "size" of a graph, $|G|$, is defined as the number of nodes in the graph. However, for our particular representations of web documents it is detrimental to ignore the contribution of the edges, which indicate the number of phrases (term adjacencies) identified in the content. Further, it is possible to have more than one edge between two nodes for certain representations. Thus we will use the following definition of graph size for all representations except the frequency representations (the size of a graph under the frequency representations will be described in detail below). Formally, the size of a graph $G = (V, E, \alpha, \beta)$, denoted $|G|$, is defined as:

$$|G| = |V| + |E|. \tag{3.1}$$

Thus we will take the size to be the sum of the number of vertices and edges in the graph.

Under the *standard representation* method each term after stop word removal and stemming becomes a vertex in the graph representing that document. Each node is labeled with the term it represents. Note that we create only a single vertex for each word even if a word appears more than once in the text. Thus each vertex in the graph represents a unique word and is labeled with a unique term not used to label any other node. Second, if word a immediately precedes word b somewhere in a "section" s of the document, then there is a directed edge from the vertex corresponding to term a to the vertex corresponding to term b with an edge label s. We take into account sentence terminating punctuation marks (periods, question marks, and exclamation points) and do not create an edge when these are present between two words. Sections we have defined for HTML documents are: *title*, which contains the text related to the document's title and any provided keywords (meta-data); *link*, which is text that appears in clickable hyper-links on the document; and *text*, which comprises any of the readable text in the document (this includes link text but not title and keyword text). Next, we remove the most infrequently occurring words on each document, leaving at most m nodes per graph (m being a user provided parameter). This is similar to the dimensionality reduction process for vector represen- tations [Sal89]. Finally, we perform a simple stemming method and conflate terms to the most frequently occurring form by re-labeling nodes and up- dating edges as needed. An example of this type of graph representation is given in Fig. 3.1. The ovals indicate nodes and their corresponding term labels. The edges are labeled according to title (TI), link (L), or text (TX). The document represented by the example has the title "YAHOO NEWS", a link whose text reads "MORE NEWS", and text containing "REUTERS NEWS SERVICE REPORTS". Note there is no restriction on the form of the graph and that cycles are allowed. This novel document representation takes into account additional web-related content information (specifically, the web document section where the terms appear is captured by the edge labels) which is not done in traditional information retrieval models. As we mentioned in Chapter 1, a problem with web content mining systems is that they discard or ignore this web-related information and fall back on the tra- ditional methods that deal only with plain-text documents. Other methods which take web-related information into account require new frameworks for dealing with the additional information, but our method allows us to de- fine different document representations, described below, without changing the basic data mining algorithms.

The second type of graph representation we will look at is what we call the *simple representation*. It is basically the same as the standard

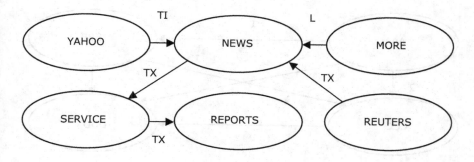

Fig. 3.1 Example of a standard graph representation of a document.

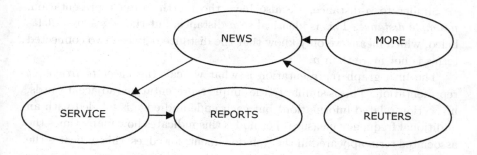

Fig. 3.2 Example of a simple graph representation of a document.

representation, except that we look at only the visible text on the page (no title or meta-data is examined) and we do not label the edges between nodes. Thus we ignore the information about the "section" where the two respective words appear together. An example of this type of representation is given in Fig. 3.2.

The third type of representation is called the *n-distance representation*. Under this model, there is a user-provided parameter, n. Instead of considering only terms immediately following a given term in a web document, we look up to n terms ahead and connect the succeeding terms with an edge that is labeled with the distance between them (unless the words are separated by certain punctuation marks). For example, if we had the following text on a web page, "AAA BBB CCC DDD", then we would have an edge from term AAA to term BBB labeled with a 1, an edge from term AAA to term CCC labeled 2, and so on. The complete graph for this example is shown in Fig. 3.3.

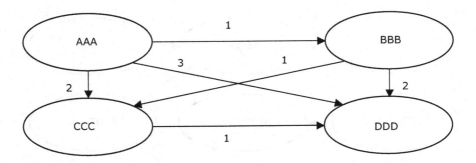

Fig. 3.3   Example of an *n*-distance graph representation of a document.

Similar to *n*-distance, we also have the fourth graph representation, *n-simple distance*. This is identical to *n*-distance, but the edges are not labeled, which means we only know that the distance between two connected terms is not more than *n*.

The fifth graph representation is what we call the *absolute frequency* representation. This is similar to the simple representation (adjacent words, no section-related information) but each node and edge is labeled with an additional frequency measure. For nodes this indicates how many times the associated term appeared in the web document; for edges, this indicates the number of times the two connected terms appeared adjacent to each other in the specified order. For this representation we modify our definition of graph size (Eq. 3.1). Under the absolute frequency representation the graph size is defined as the total of the node frequencies added to the total of the edge frequencies. Further, when we compute the maximum common subgraph we take the minimum frequency element (either node or edge) as the value for the *mcs*. For example, if we had two graphs that each had a node A, one with frequency of 10 and the other with frequency of 20, then node A in the *mcs* would have frequency of 10.

The final graph representation is the *relative frequency representation*, which is the same as the absolute frequency representation but with normalized frequency values associated with the nodes and edges. The absolute frequency representation uses the total number of term occurrences (on the nodes) and co-occurrences (edges). A problem with this representation is that large differences in document size can lead to skewed distances, similar to the problem encountered when using Euclidean distance with vector representations. Under the relative frequency representation, instead of associating each node with the total number of times the corresponding term appears in the document, a normalized value in $[0, 1]$ is assigned by dividing each node frequency value by the maximum node frequency value that occurs in the graph; a similar procedure is performed for the edges. Thus each node and edge has a value in $[0, 1]$ associated with it, which indicates the relative frequency of the term (for nodes) or co-occurrence of terms (for edges).

In Appendix A some examples of graphs created from web documents using the standard representation are provided for inspection, along with the original HTML code of the documents and their appearance as when rendered in a web browser.

These forms of knowledge representation are a type of semantic network, where nodes in the graph are objects and labeled edges indicate the relationships between objects [RN95]. The conceptual graph is a type of semantic network sometimes used in information retrieval [Lu90]. With conceptual graphs, terms or phrases related to documents appear as nodes. The types of relations (edge labels) include synonym, part-whole, antonym, and so forth. Conceptual graphs are used to indicate meaning-oriented relationships between concepts, whereas our method indicates structural relationships that exist between terms (content) in a web document. Our method of document representation is somewhat similar to that of directed acyclic word graphs (DAWGs) [CV97], which is most commonly used for compact dictionary representation. However, in our representations nodes represent words rather than letters, we allow for cycles and multiple edges between nodes, and the edges in our graphs are labeled. It is important to note that while our representations appear superficially similar to the bi-gram, trigram, or N-gram models [TWL02], those are statistically-oriented approaches based on word occurrence probability models. Our method does not require or use the computation of term probabilities.

3.3 Complexity Analysis

Calculating the distance between two graphs (Eqs. 2.3–2.7) requires the computation of the maximum common subgraph of the pair of graphs. The determination of the maximum common subgraph in the general case is known to be an NP-complete problem[MB98]. (Methods for computing the *mcs* are presented in Refs. [Lev72][McG82].) However, with our graph representation for documents each node in a graph has a unique label (representing a unique term) that no other node in the graph has [DBDK03].

Thus the maximum common subgraph, G_{mcs}, of a pair of graphs, G_1 and G_2, can be created by the following procedure:

(1) Find the nodes V_{mcs} by determining the subset of node labels that the original graphs have in common with each other and create a node for each common label.

(2) Find the edges E_{mcs} by examining all pairs of nodes from step (1) and introduce edges that connect pairs of nodes in both of the original graphs.

We see that the complexity of this method is $O(|V_1| \cdot |V_2|)$ for step (1), since we need only compare each node label from one graph to each node label of the other and determine whether there is a match or not. Thus the maximum number of comparisons is $|V_1| \cdot |V_2|$, and since each node has a unique label we only need to consider each combination once. The complexity is $O(|V_{mcs}|^2)$ for step (2), since we have $|V_{mcs}|$ nodes and we look at all combinations of pairs of nodes to determine if an edge should be added between them or not:

$$\binom{|V_{mcs}|}{2} = \frac{|V_{mcs}|!}{(|V_{mcs}| - 2)! \cdot 2!} = \frac{|V_{mcs}| \cdot (|V_{mcs}| - 1)}{2} < |V_{mcs}|^2. \qquad (3.2)$$

Thus the overall complexity is $O(|V_1| \cdot |V_2| + |V_{mcs}|^2) \leq O(|V|^2 + |V_{mcs}|^2) = O(|V|^2)$ if we substitute $V = \max(|V_1|, |V_2|)$.

3.4   Web Document Data Sets

In order to evaluate the performance of our methods we will perform several experiments using three different collections of web documents, called the F-series, the J-series, and the K-series [Bol98][BGG+99a][BGG+99b]. These three data sets were selected because of two major reasons. First, all of the original HTML documents are available for these data sets, which is necessary if we are to represent the web documents using graphs; many other document collections only provide a pre-processed vector representation, which is unsuitable for use with our method. Second, ground truth assignments are provided for each data set, and there are multiple classes representing easily understandable groupings that relate to the content of the documents. Some web document collections are not labeled or are presented with some other task in mind than content-related classification or clustering (*e.g.* building a predictive model based on user preferences).

The F-series originally contained 98 documents belonging to one or more of 17 sub-categories of four major category areas: *manufacturing, labor, business & finance,* and *electronic communication & networking.* Because there are multiple sub-category classifications from the same category area for many of these documents, we have reduced the categories to just the four major categories mentioned above in order to simplify the problem. There were five documents that had conflicting classifications (*i.e.,* they were classified to belong to two or more of the four major categories) which we removed, leaving 93 total documents. The J-series contains 185 documents and ten classes: *affirmative action, business capital, information systems, electronic commerce, intellectual property, employee rights, materials processing, personnel management, manufacturing systems,* and *industrial partnership.* We have not modified this data set. The K-series consists of 2,340 documents and 20 categories: *business, health, politics, sports, technology, entertainment, art, cable, culture, film, industry, media, multimedia, music, online, people, review, stage, television,* and *variety.* The last 14 categories are sub-categories related to entertainment, while the entertainment category refers to entertainment in general. These were originally news pages hosted at Yahoo (http://www.yahoo.com). Experiments on this data set are presented in Ref. [SGM00]. These three data sets [Bol98][BGG⁺99a][BGG⁺99b] can be downloaded at ftp://ftp.cs.umn.edu/dept/users/boley/PDDPdata/.

Data for the vector-based experiments we will perform comes from preprocessed term–document matrices obtained from the same web site that hosts these document collections. The number of dimensions (terms) used for the vector representation of each data set is 332 (F-series), 474 (J-series) and 1,458 (K-series).

Chapter 4

Graph-Based Clustering

In this chapter we will introduce a new method of clustering where the data to be clustered will be represented by graphs instead of vectors or other models. Specifically, we will extend the classical k-means clustering algorithm to work with graphs that represent web documents. We wish to use graphs because they can allow us to retain information which is often discarded in simpler models. For example, when representing web documents by graphs instead of vectors we can keep information such as the term appearance order or where in the document the terms appear. This in turn can possibly lead to an improvement in clustering quality, and we will investigate this experimentally.

Clustering with graphs is well established in the literature. However, the traditional paradigm in those methods has been to treat the entire clustering problem as a graph: nodes represent the items to be clustered and weights on edges connecting two nodes indicate the distance (dissimilarity) between the objects the nodes represent. The usual procedure is to create a minimum spanning tree of the graph and then remove the remaining edges with the largest weight in the minimum spanning tree until the number of desired clustered (connected components) is achieved [JMF99][TK99][Zah71]. After applying the algorithm the connected components indicate which objects belong to which clusters: objects whose nodes are connected by edges are in the same cluster. Recently there has been some progress with performing clustering directly on graph-based data. For example, an extension of self-organizing maps (SOMs) which allows the procedure to work with graphs has been proposed [GB02]; graph edit distance and weighted mean of a pair of graphs were introduced to deal with graph-based data under the SOM algorithm. Clustering of shock trees using tree edit distance has also been considered [LRKT+01]. Both

41

of these methods have in common that they use graph (or tree) edit distance for their graph distance measures. One drawback of this approach is that the edit cost functions must be specified for each application. Sanfeliu *et al.* have investigated clustering of attributed graphs using their own function-described graphs as cluster representatives [SSA00]. However, their method is rather complicated and much more involved than our straightforward extension of a classical, simple clustering algorithm.

In Sec. 4.1 we describe our extended *k*-means algorithm. The clustering performance measures we will use to compare the clusterings produced by each method are introduced in Sec. 4.2. Initial comparisons of our method to previously published results using vector representations are given in Section 4.3. Section 4.4 details the results of various experiments using different graph representations and graph-theoretic distance measures. We compare the performance of different well-known clustering algorithms when clustering graph-based data in Sec. 4.5. In Sec. 4.6 we show how the document clusters can be visualized graphically using multidimensional scaling, even when the documents themselves are represented by graphs. Finally, in Sec. 4.7 we give a graph-based version of the global *k*-means algorithm and perform experiments relating to the performance of global *k*-means compared with random initialization. We also explore the issue of finding the optimal number of clusters automatically under global *k*-means with cluster validity measures.

4.1 The Graph-Based *k*-Means Clustering Algorithm

With our formal notation for graphs (Chapter 2) we are ready to describe our framework for extending the classical *k*-means clustering method. The extension is surprisingly simple. First, any distance calculations between data items is accomplished with a graph-theoretical distance measure, such as those of Eqs. 2.3–2.7. Second, since it is necessary to compute the distance between data items and cluster centers, it follows that the cluster centers (centroids) must also be graphs. Therefore, we compute the representative "centroid" of a cluster as the median graph of the set of graphs in that cluster (Eq. 2.27).

The *k*-means clustering algorithm is a simple and straightforward method for clustering data [Mit97]. The basic algorithm is given in Fig. 4.1. This method is applicable to purely numerical data when using Euclidean distance and centroid calculations. The usual paradigm is to represent each

Inputs:	the set of n data items and a parameter, k, defining the number of clusters to create
Outputs:	the centroids of the clusters and for each data item the cluster (an integer in $[1,k]$) it belongs to
Step 1.	Assign each data item randomly to a cluster (from 1 to k).
Step 2.	Using the initial assignment, determine the centroids of each cluster.
Step 3.	Given the new centroids, assign each data item to be in the cluster of its closest centroid.
Step 4.	Re-compute the centroids as in Step 2. Repeat Steps 3 and 4 until the centroids do not change.

Fig. 4.1 The traditional k-means clustering algorithm.

Inputs:	the set of n data items (represented by graphs) and a parameter k, defining the number of clusters to create
Outputs:	the centroids of the clusters (represented by median graphs) and for each data item the cluster (an integer in $[1,k]$) it belongs to
Step 1.	Assign each data item randomly to a cluster (from 1 to k).
Step 2.	Using the initial assignment, determine the median of the set of graphs of each cluster.
Step 3.	Given the new medians, assign each data item to be in the cluster of its closest median, using a graph-theoretic distance measure.
Step 4.	Re-compute the medians as in Step 2. Repeat Steps 3 and 4 until the medians do not change.

Fig. 4.2 The graph-based k-means clustering algorithm.

data item, which consists of m numeric values, as a vector in the space $\Re^m$. In this case the distances between two data items are computed using the Euclidean distance in m dimensions and the centroids are computed to be the mean or weighted mean of the data in the cluster. However, now that we have a distance measure for graphs (Eqs. 2.3–2.7) and a method of determining a representative of a set of graphs (the median, Eq. 2.27) we can apply the same method to data sets whose elements are graphs rather than vectors by: 1. replacing the distance measure used in Step 3 with a graph-theoretical distance measure and 2. replacing the centroid computed in Step 2 with the median of a set of graphs. The graph-based version of the k-means algorithm is given in Fig. 4.2.

As mentioned in Sec. 3.3, for general graphs the computation of the maximum common subgraph is NP-complete. However, for the graph representations of web documents presented in Sec. 3.2, the computation of the maximum common subgraph is $O(m^2)$, with m being the number of nodes, due to the existence of unique node labels in the graph representations (i.e. we need only examine the intersection of the nodes, since each node has a unique label) [DBDK03]. For vector-based k-means, the complexity is $O(knm)$ per iteration, where n is the number of items to be clustered and m is the number of dimensions. For graph-based k-means it is $O(knm^2) + O(k^{-1}n^2m^2)$; here m is the number of nodes in the graphs. The first term represents Step 2 in the k-means algorithm (determination of the closest cluster center for each item), while the second term corresponds to Step 3 (computation of the median graphs). To determine the closest cluster representative, we calculate the distance between each data item, of which there are n, and each center, of which there are k. Thus there are kn distance calculations, which are $O(m^2)$. So the overall complexity of Step 2 is $O(knm^2)$. Recall that the median graph, Eq. 2.27, requires the computation of graph distance $|S|^2$ times, where $|S|$ is the number of graphs in a cluster. On average, $|S| = n/k$, thus we have the complexity to compute k medians:

$$O(k|S|^2m^2) = O(k(n/k)^2m^2) = O(k^{-1}n^2m^2) \qquad (4.1)$$

Note that the graph-based k-means method, as we have described it above, is known as k-medoids [KR90] when using a vector representation, due to the fact that we use medians to represent clusters rather than means.

4.2 Clustering Performance Measures

We will evaluate clustering performance in our experiments using the following three clustering performance measures. The first two indices measure the matching of obtained clusters to the "ground truth" clusters (*i.e.* accuracy), while the third index measures the compactness and separation of the clusters. The first index is the *Rand index* [KM95][Ran71], which is defined as:

$$R_I = \frac{A}{A + D} \qquad (4.2)$$

where A is the number of "agreements" and D is the number of "disagreements" (described below). We compute the Rand index by performing a pair-wise comparison of all pairs of objects in the data set after clustering. If two objects are in the same cluster in both the "ground truth" clustering and the clustering we wish to measure, this counts as an agreement. If two objects are in different clusters in both the ground truth clustering and the clustering we wish to investigate, this is also an agreement. Otherwise, there is a disagreement. Thus the Rand index is a measure of how closely the clustering created by some procedure matches ground truth (*i.e.* it is a measure of clustering accuracy). It produces a value in the interval $[0, 1]$, with 1 representing a clustering that perfectly matches ground truth. The second performance measure we use is *mutual information* [CT91][SGM00], which is defined as:

$$\Lambda^M = \frac{1}{n} \sum_{l=1}^{k} \sum_{h=1}^{g} n_l^{(h)} \log_{k \cdot g} \left(\frac{n_l^{(h)} \cdot n}{\sum_{i=1}^{k} n_i^{(h)} \sum_{i=1}^{g} n_l^{(i)}} \right) \qquad (4.3)$$

where n is the number of data items, k is the desired number of clusters, g is the actual number of "ground truth" categories, and is the number of items in cluster i classified to be category j. Note that k and g may not necessarily be equal, which would indicate we are attempting to create more (or fewer) clusters than those that exist in the ground truth clustering. Mutual information represents the overall degree of agreement between the clustering and the categorization provided by the ground truth with a preference for clusters that have high purity (*i.e.* are homogeneous with respect to the classes of objects clustered). Higher values indicate better performance.

The third performance measure we use is the *Dunn index* [Dun74], which is defined as:

$$D_I = \frac{d_{min}}{d_{max}} \qquad (4.4)$$

where d_{min} is the minimum distance between any two objects in different clusters and d_{max} is the maximum distance between any two items in the same cluster. The numerator captures the worst-case amount of separation between clusters, while the denominator captures the worst-case compactness of the clusters. Thus the Dunn index is an amalgam of the overall worst-case compactness and separation of a clustering, with higher values being better. It does not, however, measure clustering accuracy compared to ground truth as the other two methods do. Rather it is based on the basic underlying assumption of any clustering technique: items in the same cluster should be similar (*i.e.* have small distance, thus creating compact clusters) and items in separate clusters should be dissimilar (*i.e.* have large distance, thus creating clusters that are well separated from each other).

4.3   Comparison with Previously Published Results

In order to perform an initial investigation into the performance and possible benefits of our graph-based approach, we performed experiments that apply the extended k-means clustering algorithm using graphs to the K-series document collection. We selected this data set primarily because we wished to compare the performance of our method to previously reported results. In Ref. [SGM00] Strehl *et al.* compared the performance of different vector-based clustering methods for the K-series data set, presenting results for a variety of standard clustering methods, including classical k-means. The authors used various similarity measures and mutual information (Eq. 4.3) as a performance metric.

In an attempt to adhere to the methodology of the experiments of Strehl *et al.*, which used the vector model approach, we have selected a sample of 800 documents from the total collection of 2,340 and have fixed the desired number of clusters to be $k = 40$ (two times the number of categories), which is the same number of clusters used in the original experiment. Strehl *et al.* used this number of clusters "since this seemed to be the more natural number of clusters as indicated by preliminary runs and visualisation" [SGM00]. The results for our method using different numbers of maximum nodes per graph and the original results from Strehl *et al.* for vector-based k-means and a random baseline assignment are given in Table 4.1 (higher mutual information is better). Each row gives the average of 10 experiments using the same 800 item data sample. The variation in results between runs comes from the random initialization in the first step of the k-means algorithm. For these experiments we used the MCS distance measure (Eq. 2.3) and the standard representation described in Chapter 3.

The same performance data is plotted graphically in Fig. 4.3. In Fig. 4.4 we show the execution times for performing a single clustering of the document collection when using 5, 50, 100, and 150 nodes per graph. These results were obtained on a 733 MHz single processor Power Macintosh G4 with 384 megabytes of physical memory running Mac OS X. The clustering took 7.13 minutes at 5 nodes per graph and 288.18 minutes for 150 nodes per graph. Unfortunately, no execution time data is available for comparison from the original experiments in Strehl *et al.*

From Fig. 4.3 we see that the mutual information generally tends to increase as we allow larger and larger graphs. This makes sense since the larger graphs incorporate more information. On the figure we indicated the values of mutual information from the original experiments for three

Table 4.1 Results of our experiments compared with results from Strehl *et al.*.

method	maximum nodes/graph	Λ^M (average)
Graphs	150	0.2218
Graphs	120	0.2142
Graphs	90	0.2074
Graphs	75	0.2045
Graphs	60	0.1865
Extended Jaccard Similarity	—	0.1840
Pearson Correlation	—	0.1780
Cosine Measure	—	0.1780
Graphs	45	0.1758
Graphs	30	0.1617
Graphs	15	0.1540
Graphs	5	0.1326
Random (baseline)	—	0.0660
Euclidean	—	0.0460

out of the five methods from Table 4.1. Euclidean is the classical k-means with a Euclidean distance measure (Eq. 1.1). Random baseline is simply a random assignment of data to clusters; it is used to provide a baseline for comparison. We would expect any algorithm to perform better than Random, but we see the Euclidean k-means did not. Finally, Jaccard is k-means using the extended Jaccard similarity (Eq. 1.3). It was the best performing of all the k-means methods reported in the original experiment so we have omitted cosine similarity and Pearson correlation on the chart for clarity.

It is not a surprising result to see Euclidean distance perform poorly when using the vector model for representing documents, as it does not have the property of vector length invariance. Because of this, documents with similar term frequency proportions but differences in overall total frequency have large distances between them even though they are supposed to be considered similar. For example, if we were interested in the topic "data mining", a document where the terms "data" and "mining" each appeared 10 times and a document where both terms each appeared 1,000 times are considered to be identical when we have the length invariance property (*i.e.* their distance is 0). It is only the relative proportion between the terms that is of interest when determining the documents content, since there are often large variances in total term frequency even for documents related to the same topic. Here both documents contain an equal proportion of the terms "data" and "mining". If the term "mining" occurred much more

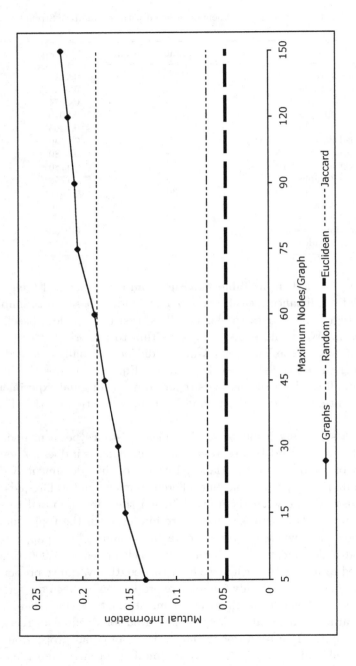

Fig. 4.3 Mutual information as a function of the maximum number of vertices per graph.

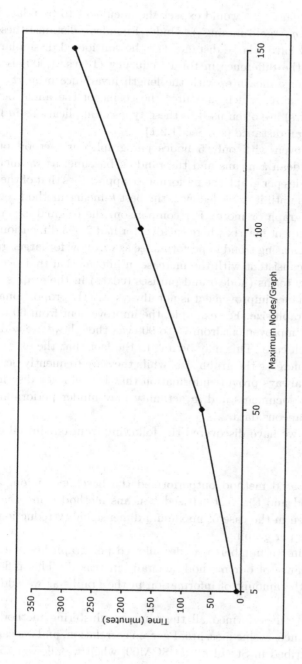

Fig. 4.4 Clustering time as a function of the maximum number of vertices per graph.

frequently than "data", we would expect the document to be related to a different topic (*e.g.*, "gold mining"). Under Euclidean distance these two documents would have a large distance (*i.e.* be considered dissimilar) due to the fact that the difference in total frequency (10 vs. 1,000) is large. This is why distance measures with the length invariance property (such as the cosine measure, which measures the cosine of the angle between two feature vectors) are often used in these types of applications in lieu of standard Euclidean distance (see Sec. 1.2.1).

We see that even with only 5 nodes per graph our method outperforms both Euclidean k-means and the random baseline; as we increased the number of nodes per graph the performance approaches that of the other k-means methods until it exceeded even the best k-means method reported at 75 nodes per graph or more. For comparison, the original experiment used a term-document matrix where each vector had 2,903 dimensions. We note a general increasing trend in performance as we allow for larger graphs, which would be consistent with the increase in information that occurs as we introduce new terms (nodes) and phrases (edges) in the graphs. However, the performance improvement is not always strictly proportional with the increase in graph size. For example, the improvement from 60 to 75 is greater than the improvement from 75 to 90 even though we are adding 15 new nodes in each case. This may be due to the fact that the extra nodes added when we increase the graph size, while they are frequently occurring terms, may not always provide information that is useful for discriminating between the documents and in actuality may hinder performance by introducing extraneous data.

In summary, we have discovered the following from our initial experiments:

(1) Our graph-based method outperformed the baseline random assignment method and the vector-based k-means method using Euclidean distance, even in the case of maximum dimensionality reduction using only 5 nodes per graph.

(2) As the maximum number of nodes allowed per graph became larger, the performance of our method generally increased. This reflects an increase in the amount of information in the graphs as we add nodes and edges.

(3) Our method outperformed all the k-means clustering methods (Euclidean distance, cosine measure, Pearson correlation, and Jaccard similarity) described in Strehl *et al.* [SGM00] when we allowed 75 nodes

per graph or more. We believe this reflects the information retained by the graph representation which is not present when using the vector model approach.

Based on these initial results, we proceed to investigate further experiments in the following sections.

4.4 Comparison of Different Graph-Theoretical Distance Measures and Graph Representations for Graph-Based Clustering

In this section we will investigate the performance of our graph-based clustering method based on k-means as compared with the traditional approach of using vector representations. We will examine the effect of different graph-theoretic distance measures (Sec. 4.4.1) and graph representations (Sec. 4.4.2). We will use the following methodology for the experiments presented in this section. For each experiment, whether based on our graph method or a traditional vector method, we will perform ten separate trials each using a random initialization. We will report the average of the ten trials as the performance for that experiment in order to account for the variance between runs due to the random initialization of the clustering algorithm. The vector representation experiments will use the vector-based distance measures (Eq. 1.1–1.3) we described previously. The experiments related to our graph-based methods will be run for a range of maximum graph sizes (the parameter m described in Sec. 3.2). We will apply the clustering algorithms to our three data sets (Sec. 3.4) and we will measure clustering performance using the Rand index (Eq. 4.2), mutual information (Eq. 4.3), and the Dunn index (Eq. 4.4). For the experiments in Sec. 4.4.1 we will use the MCS, WGU, UGU, MMCS, and MMCSN distance measures (Eqs. 2.3–2.7) with the standard graph representation. Concerning the experiments in Sec. 4.4.2, we will use the graph representations (standard, simple, n-distance, n-simple distance, absolute frequency and relative frequency) defined in Chapter 3 with the MCS distance measure. For the distance related graph representations, namely n-distance and n-simple distance, we will use $n = 5$ (*i.e.* 5-distance and 5-simple distance). Note that for the non-frequency graph representations and graph sizes we have defined, $|MCS(G_1, G_2)| = |G1| + |G2| - |mcs(G_1, G_2)|$ and thus WGU and MMCSN are identical, as are UGU and MMCS (see Chapter 2). Any differences between the identical distance measures reflected in the results below come from the random initialization of the k-means algorithm.

4.4.1   *Comparison of distance measures*

The results of our experiments for the F-series documents are given in Fig. 4.5 for Rand index, Fig. 4.6 for mutual information, and Fig. 4.7 for Dunn index. The results of the vector-model clusterings are shown by horizontal lines. The results for our graph-based method are given for graph sizes ranging from 10 to 100 nodes per graph. Similarly, the results of our experiments for the J-series documents are given in Figs. 4.8–4.10 for graph sizes of 10 to 60 nodes per graph. Results for the K-series, utilizing 70 nodes per graph for each graph-theoretic distance measure, are presented in Table 4.2.

Table 4.2   Distance measure comparison for the K-series.

distance measure	Rand index	mutual information	Dunn index
vector (cosine)	0.8537	0.2266	0.0348
vector (Jaccard)	0.8998	0.2441	0.0730
MCS	0.8957	0.1174	0.0284
WGU/MMCSN	0.8377	0.1019	0.0385
UGU/MMCS	0.1692	0.0127	0.0649

We see that the graph-based methods that use normalized distance measures performed as well or better than vector-based methods using cosine similarity or Euclidean distance. Distance measures that were not normalized to the interval $[0, 1]$ performed poorly, particularly when the maximum allowed graph size became large. To see why this occurs, we have provided the following example.

Example 4.1   Let $|G_1| = 10$, $|G_2| = 10$, $|mcs(G_1, G_2)| = 0$, $|G_3| = 20$, $|G_4| = 20$, and $|mcs(G_3, G_4)| = 5$. Clearly graphs G_3 and G_4 are more similar to each other than graphs G_1 and G_2 since G_1 and G_2 have no common subgraph whereas G_3 and G_4 do. However, the distances computed for these graphs are $d_{MCS}(G_1, G_2) = 1.0$, $d_{MCS}(G_3, G_4) = 0.75$, $d_{UGU}(G_1, G_2) = 20$ and $d_{UGU}(G_3, G_4) = 30$.

So we have the case that the distance for un-normalized graph union (UGU) is actually greater for the pair of graphs that are more similar. This is both counter-intuitive and the opposite of what happens in the cases of

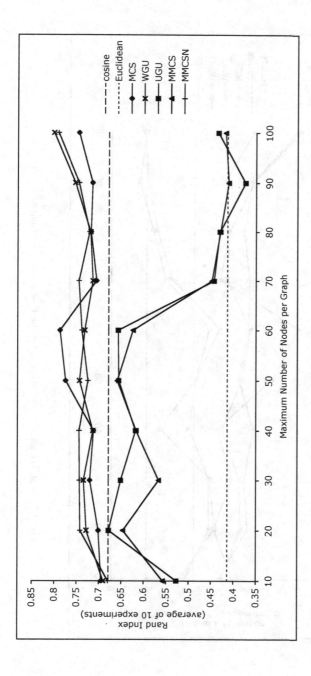

Fig. 4.5 Distance measure comparison for the F-series data set (Rand index).

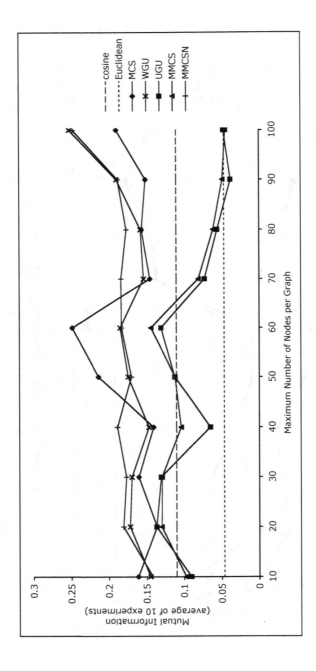

Fig. 4.6 Distance measure comparison for the F-series data set (mutual information).

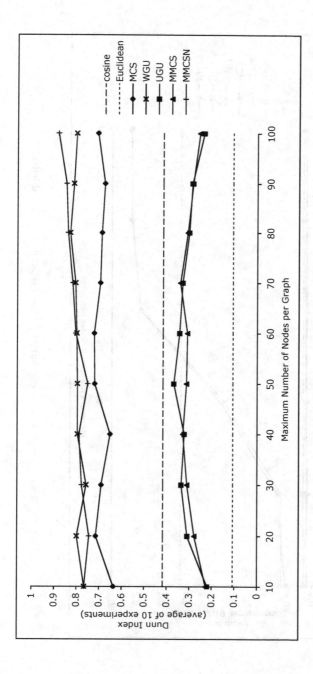

Fig. 4.7 Distance measure comparison for the F-series data set (Dunn index).

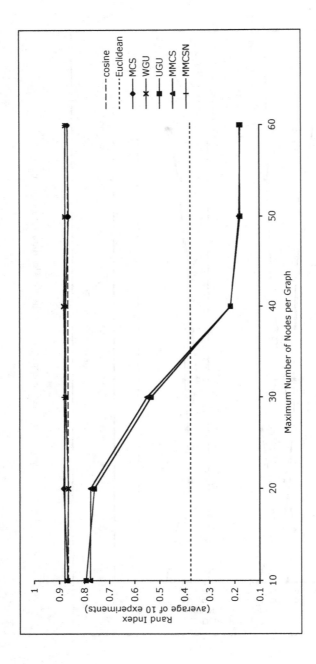

Fig. 4.8   Distance measure comparison for the J-series data set (Rand index).

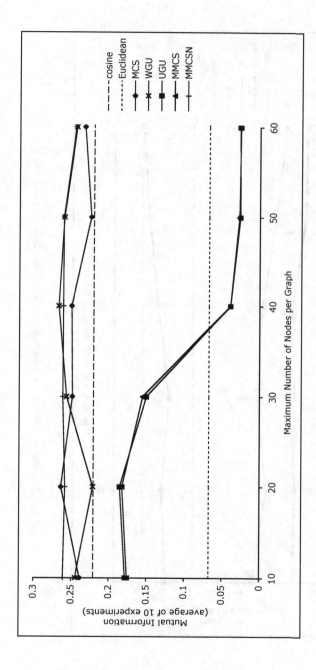

Fig. 4.9 Distance measure comparison for the J-series data set (mutual information).

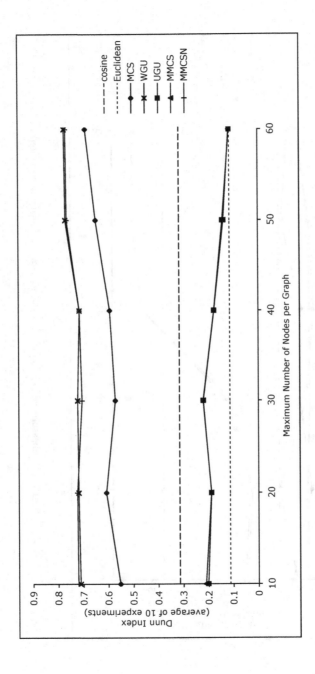

Fig. 4.10   Distance measure comparison for the J-series data set (Dunn index).

the normalized distance measures. Thus this phenomenon leads to the poor clustering performance. Since the size of the graph includes the number of edges, which can grow at a rate of $O(|V|^2)$, we can see that the potential size variance which causes this phenomenon becomes more pronounced as we increase the number of nodes per graph (*i.e.* as $|V|$ increases).

We see from the experimental results that the quality of clustering as measured by the Dunn index is more or less constant with the size of the graphs, with the distance measure seeming to have more effect than the data representation itself. We note similar behavior between mutual information and Rand index. For these two indices we see performance peaking at certain graph sizes but otherwise the performance is fairly constant. This could be due to the fact that the terms selected for those graph sizes provide particularly good discriminating information on the pre-defined set of categories. For larger graphs that indicate a decline in performance, it may be the case that we have polluted the graphs with unimportant terms which hurt the performance of the clustering algorithm. We also see that the results for each distance measure under all three performance indices are consistent across all three data sets. The fact that the graph-based methods performed as well or better than the vector-based method, even when the size of the graphs was relatively small, is encouraging and may indicate the quality of the added structural information that is captured in the graphs but not in the vector representations. Further, with the graph model there is also a potential for computational and space savings in terms of the data represented. For example, if we wish to add a new term to a document in a vector model representation, all documents must have their dimensionality increased by one (and thus the dimensionality of the feature space increases by one). However, if we want to add a new term to a document with a graph representation, we need only add the new node and edges to that particular graph, and the distance calculations between other graphs remains unaffected.

4.4.2 *Comparison of graph representations*

From our experimental results that compare our methods of representing web documents by graphs (Chapter 3), which are presented in Figs. 4.11–4.13 and 4.14–4.16 as a function of the maximum number of nodes allowed in a graph for the F-series and the J-series, respectively, we see that the various graph representations can perform as well or better than the conventional vector model approach in terms of clustering accuracy (Rand

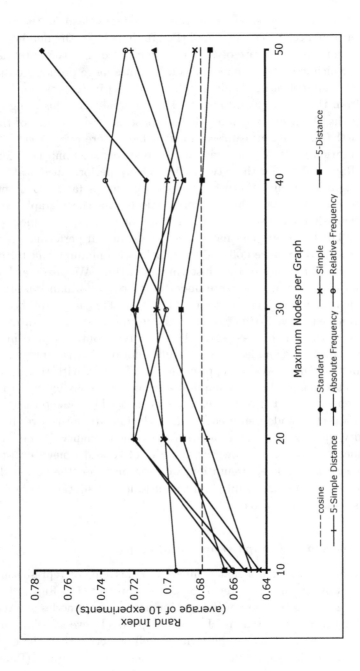

Fig. 4.11 Graph representation comparison for the F-series data set (Rand index).

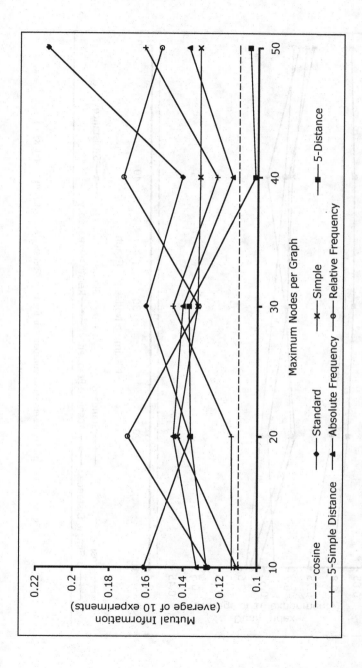

Fig. 4.12 Graph representation comparison for the F-series data set (mutual information).

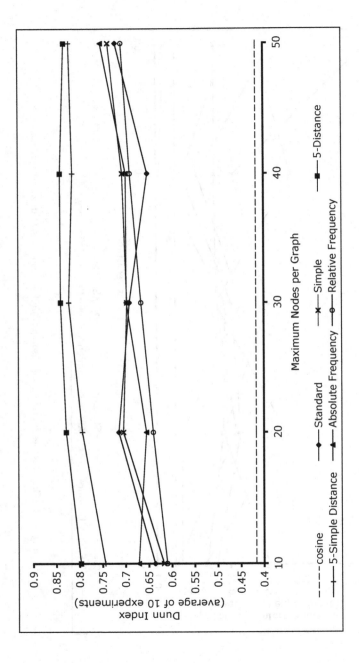

Fig. 4.13   Graph representation comparison for the F-series data set (Dunn index).

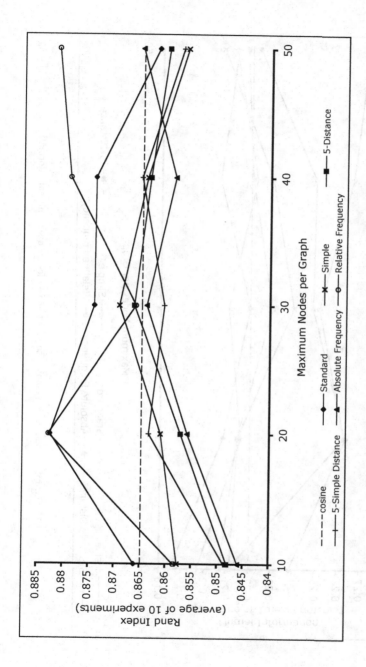

Fig. 4.14 Graph representation comparison for the J-series data set (Rand index).

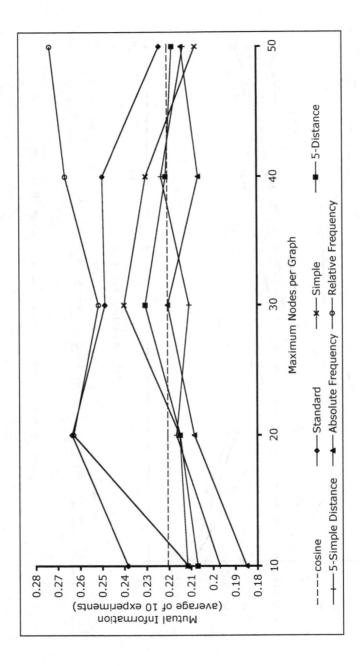

Fig. 4.15   Graph representation comparison for the J-series data set (mutual information).

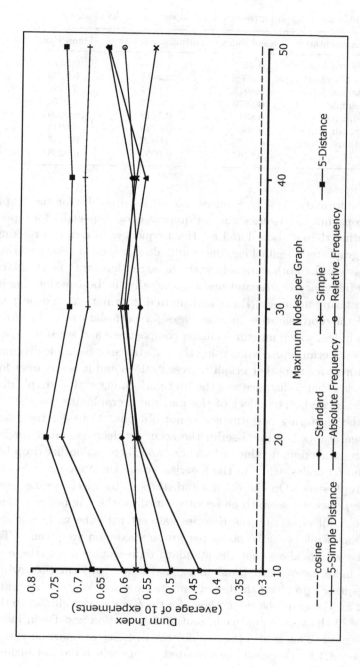

Fig. 4.16 Graph representation comparison for the J-series data set (Dunn index).

Table 4.3   Graph representation comparison for the K-series.

graph representation	Rand index	mutual information	Dunn index
vector (cosine)	0.8537	0.2266	0.0348
vector (Jaccard)	0.8998	0.2441	0.0730
standard	0.8957	0.1174	0.0284
simple	0.8870	0.0972	0.0274
5-distance	0.8813	0.1013	0.0206
5-simple distance	0.8663	0.0773	0.0234
absolute frequency	0.8770	0.0957	0.0335
relative frequency	0.8707	0.0992	0.0283

and mutual information). The F-series showed good results for the graph representations, but the J-series was not quite as good, especially for representations other than standard and relative frequency. In terms of ranking the various graph representations, the results do not show a clear ordering that is consistent for both data sets with the exception that the standard and relative frequency representations are generally the best performing in terms of clustering accuracy (Rand and mutual information) and outperform the vector representation in most cases for both data sets. In terms of the Dunn index, which measures cluster compactness and separation, we obtain the best performance when using the n-distance or n-simple distance representations over the other graph representations and it is apparent for the Dunn index that 5-distance was the best performing with 5-simple distance a close second. The effect of the maximum graph size (number of nodes) on the clustering performance is not obvious. Consider the standard representation. For the J-series the accuracy decreases at 30 nodes after reaching a maximum value at 20 nodes and there is another drop between 40 and 50 nodes, while in the F-series we see the opposite behavior for those graph sizes. On the other hand, the quality of clustering itself (Dunn index) does not seem to be sensitive at all to the number of nodes.

The results for clustering the K-series data set with the various graph representations while using 70 nodes per graph maximum are given in Table 4.3. The results show that the standard representation was the best performing in terms of both Rand index and mutual information, while absolute frequency provided the best Dunn index score. We see that while Rand index for the graph-based methods for the K-series was similar to the performance of the vector approach, mutual information and Dunn index were not as good. This is also the case for the distance comparison experiments in Sec. 4.4.1 It is possible we created graphs which did not include enough terms (nodes) for this data set, to compensate for the increase in both the number of documents and the number of clusters. In Table 4.4 we give the results of performing k-means on the K-series data set for a variety of graph sizes using the standard representation and MCS distance.

Table 4.4 Clustering performance comparison for the K-series.

method	Rand index	mutual information	Dunn index
vector (cosine)	0.8537	0.2266	0.0348
vector (Jaccard)	0.8998	0.2441	0.0730
graph (40 nodes/graph)	0.8563	0.0752	0.0240
graph (70 nodes/graph)	0.8957	0.1174	0.0284
graph (100 nodes/graph)	0.8888	0.1310	0.0298
graph (200 nodes/graph)	0.9053	0.1618	0.0307

We observe that the performance of all three measures continued to increase with larger graph sizes, so it seems likely that larger graph sizes are needed with this data set. This fact is also reflected in the vector representation, which uses over three times as many dimensions as the J-series and four times as many dimensions as the F-series. Due to the time requirements for clustering the K-series (2,340 documents with graphs of more than 200 nodes) under each graph representation and distance measure for a range of graph sizes, we omit these experiments. Further results concerning the K-series data set are given in Chapter 5.

The experiments in this section relied on a random initialization of the k-means algorithm, which is the conventional way the algorithm is applied. However, using a random initialization has drawbacks. First, the initialization may be poor and lead the algorithm to converge on a bad final clustering of the data. Second, the fact that each clustering created using the same algorithm may be different leads to difficulty in comparing experimental results. The usual methodology is to perform a series of experiments and report the average, as was done here. However, this is time consuming as the same experiment must be performed repeatedly. Recently a new method of deterministically arriving at a good initialization state for the k-means algorithm has been reported. In Sec. 4.7 we will create a graph-based version of this method and apply it to our web data sets for the purpose of examining the effect it has on clustering performance.

4.5   Comparison of Clustering Algorithms

In this section we will compare the clustering performance of several different classical clustering algorithms when using data represented by graphs. As we saw above, it has been shown that the graph representation scheme under the k-means algorithm compares favorably with the vector approach in terms of clustering performance. We have already investigated the effects of various graph distance measures and graph representations on clustering performance. However, the impact of changing the underlying clustering algorithm when clustering data represented by graphs has not been examined. Given graph-theoretic distance and cluster representative definitions, we can adapt many different clustering algorithms to work with graph-based data in addition to k-means.

We examine clustering with graph-based data using the hierarchical agglomerative, graph partitioning, and fuzzy c-means algorithms. The application of hierarchical agglomerative clustering [Sal89] to graphs is straightforward. We need only determine the pair-wise distance between the graphs using some graph theoretic distance measure. Once we have a distance matrix, we can directly apply the method. The same applies to the graph partitioning algorithm. For the fuzzy c-means algorithm, which is a partitional clustering algorithm that assigns fuzzy membership values in the interval $[0, 1]$ to each item in a data set, we need to make some modifications over the usual case. The typical fuzzy c-means algorithm works as follows [KY95]. First, a fuzzy partition matrix A is generated randomly. Entry a_{ij} in matrix A indicates the membership of data item i in cluster j. From this fuzzy matrix cluster centers v_j are calculated by the following equation:

$$v_j = \frac{\sum_{k=1}^{n}[A_j(x_k)]^m x_k}{\sum_{k=1}^{n}[A_j(x_k)]^m} \tag{4.5}$$

where x_k is the vector representing the kth data item (out of n total data items) and m is a user provided parameter that controls the behavior of the algorithm. Next the fuzzy matrix A is updated from the new cluster centers by:

$$A_{ij} = \left[\sum_{k=1}^{c} \left(\frac{d(x_j, v_i)}{d(x_j, v_k)} \right)^{\frac{1}{m-1}} \right]^{-1} \tag{4.6}$$

where c is the number of clusters and $d(x, v)$ is the distance between data item x and cluster center v (usually defined as the Euclidean distance). The cluster centers and fuzzy partition matrix are alternately recomputed using the same procedure, until the maximum change in successive fuzzy matrices is less than or equal to some user provided value ε. At that point the algorithm is terminated and the matrix A contains the induced fuzzy partition that represents the clustering of the data set. The main challenge with adapting fuzzy c-means for graphs lies in creating a method of computing the cluster representatives. Under fuzzy c-means the cluster centers are computed with a weighted averaging that takes into account the membership values of each data item. Thus the graph median cannot be directly used as was done with k-means. We propose the following method of determining cluster centers for graph-based data. For each cluster j, use deterministic sampling [KY95] to compute the number of copies of each graph i to use, $e_j(i)$, which is defined as:

$$e_j(i) = \left[n \frac{a_{ij}}{\sum_{\forall i} a_{ij}} \right] \tag{4.7}$$

Here n is the total number of items in the data set. We then create a set of graphs consisting of $e_j(i)$ copies of graph i and compute the median graph of this set to be the representative of cluster j. This procedure replaces Eq. 4.5 above.

The clustering performance results for the F-series and the J-series for the various graph-based clustering algorithms are given in Figs. 4.17 and 4.18, respectively. The charts show the performance of each algorithm as a group of four columns. From left to right the algorithms compared are: k-means, fuzzy c-means, hierarchical agglomerative clustering (single link), hierarchical agglomerative clustering (complete link), and graph partitioning. These experiments use the standard representation and the MCS distance measure.

As before, we varied the maximum number of nodes allowed per graph. Within each group of columns, the white (leftmost) bar indicates using 30 nodes per graph maximum. The grey bars correspond to using 50 nodes per graph maximum, while the black bars are the results when using 70 nodes per graph maximum. The rightmost (striped) bars represent the performance of the traditional vector-based approach using a distance measure based on Jaccard similarity. Nondeterministic clustering algorithms that use random initializations (k-means and fuzzy c-means) are represented by the average of ten experiments.

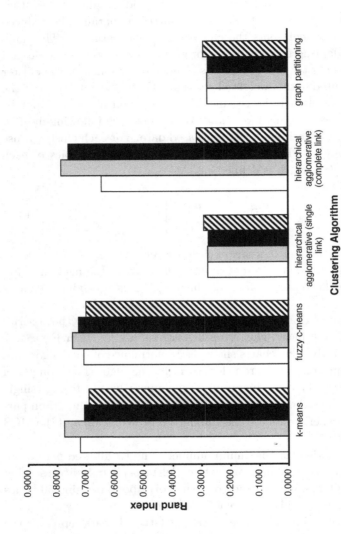

Fig. 4.17 Algorithm comparison for the F-series data set (Rand index).

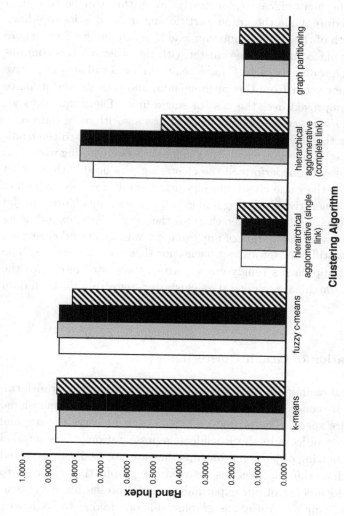

Fig. 4.18 Algorithm comparison for the J-series data set (Rand index).

The results indicate that the single link hierarchical clustering algorithm and the graph partitioning algorithm both performed poorly for all graph sizes and both data sets. Their similar performance is not surprising, as both methods take a similar approach of examining pairs of minimum distance objects; the hierarchical agglomerative algorithm can be seen as a bottom-up procedure while the graph partitioning method is its top-down counterpart. Both of these algorithms can lead to a "chaining effect" where most objects are placed in one large cluster with the other clusters containing only one or a few objects each. Complete link hierarchical agglomerative clustering does not suffer from this phenomenon, and thus its performance is considerably improved over the case of single link. The graph sizes we selected did not have a consistent influence across algorithms or data sets.

In comparing the performance of the graph-based methods to the traditional vector-based clustering, we see that in most cases clustering with data represented by graphs outperformed the clustering produced with a vector representation for the same clustering algorithm. Only for the single link hierarchical agglomerative clustering and graph partitioning algorithms did the vector approach perform better than all the graph-based experiments in the group; however, the margin of improvement was slight and clustering performance was still poor for all approaches for these two algorithms. The graph clustering approach strongly outperformed the vector model for the complete link hierarchical agglomerative clustering algorithm for both data sets.

4.6   Visualization of Graph Clustering

Multidimensional scaling [CC94] is a mathematical technique for transforming spaces that are complex or not well understood into a lower dimensional Euclidean feature space. The procedure attempts to preserve the original distances between objects in the Euclidean representation. This method is useful for visualizing object relationships that are not easily represented graphically, such as the relationships between the graphs that are used to represent web documents in our experiments. By representing web documents (or other complex entities) as graphs and then taking the pair-wise distance between the graphs using one of the graph-theoretical distance measures we can apply multidimensional scaling to arrive at a representation of the graphs in $\Re^2$. This allows the graphs to be plotted graphically as points on an $x-y$ plane, which is not possible for the original untransformed space.

We have performed multidimensional scaling on our data sets using the standard representation and MCS distance to create graphs from the web pages. The results of the scaling are shown in Fig. 4.19 for the F-series, Fig. 4.20 for the J-series, and Fig. 4.21 for the K-series. For the F and J-series, the left side shows the results when using 10 nodes per graph; the right side utilizes 30 nodes per graph. For the K-series the left side is 70 nodes per graph while the right is 100 nodes per graph. Each graph is plotted as a point in a two-dimensional Euclidean space; the symbol of each point is given by the ground truth cluster the graph belongs to. The ellipses give an indication of cluster shape and size (they are fit to cover all the points of each cluster while minimizing the area).

The F-series plot clearly shows the four clusters of this data set. Though there is some overlap towards the center of the plot, many of the data points can be easily differentiated. Looking at the change between the left and right plots, we see cluster compactness and separation improves as we add more nodes to the graphs. For example, the bottom right cluster (pluses) is smaller and no longer overlaps the center cluster (triangles) or middle left cluster (crosses). Similarly, the top right cluster (circles) is also more compact and no longer overlaps the middle or middle left clusters. This is an intuitively appealing result. The J-series is more difficult to view since it contains many overlapping clusters. However, we see the data points become much more evenly distributed as we increase the graph size (on the left plot many of the points are concentrated in the top left area). This allows for easier differentiation between clusters. We should note that with multidimensional scaling there is some information loss due to the reduction of the number of dimensions; thus the plots here will not correspond exactly to actual clustering performance as performed in the graph domain. However, the apparent increase in cluster compactness and separation with larger graph sizes seems reasonable. The K-series contains more than ten times the number of documents of the J-series, making it more difficult to view individual web documents. However, two well-separated clusters are clearly visible on the figures: the bottom left cluster (the triangles) and the top middle cluster (circles). The effect of increasing the number of nodes per graph is less dramatic than in the other two data sets. This is probably due either to the amount of information added by going from 70 to 100 nodes per graph being less than the increase in information when going from 10 to 30 in the other data sets, or that this data set is simply to complex (too large, too many clusters) to visualize well.

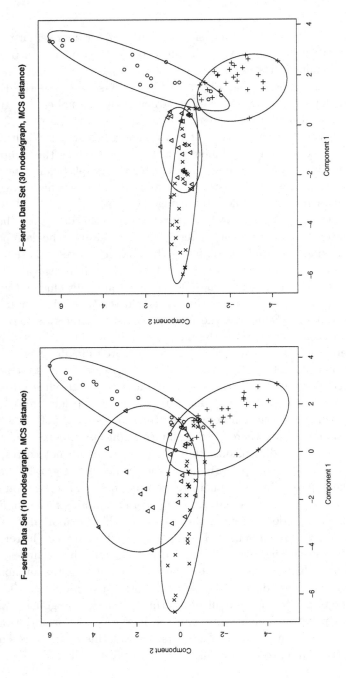

Fig. 4.19   F-series data set represented by graphs scaled to two dimensions using 10 nodes/graph (left) and 30 nodes/graph (right).

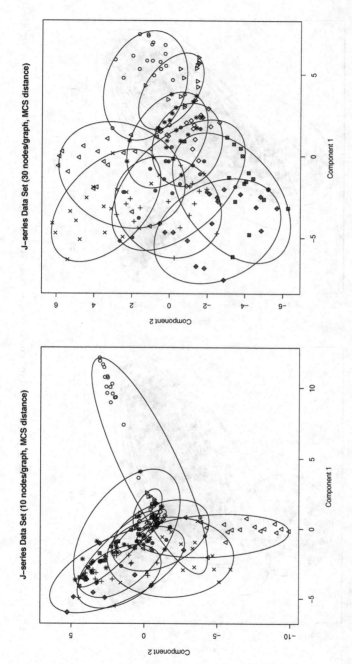

Fig. 4.20 J-series data set represented by graphs scaled to two dimensions using 10 nodes/graph (left) and 30 nodes/graph (right).

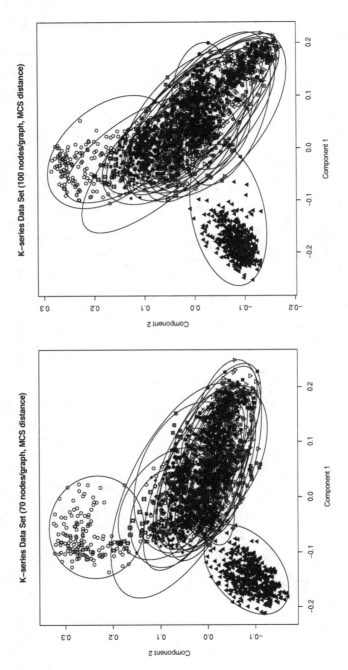

Fig. 4.21   K-series data set represented by graphs scaled to two dimensions using 70 nodes/graph (left) and 100 nodes/graph (right).

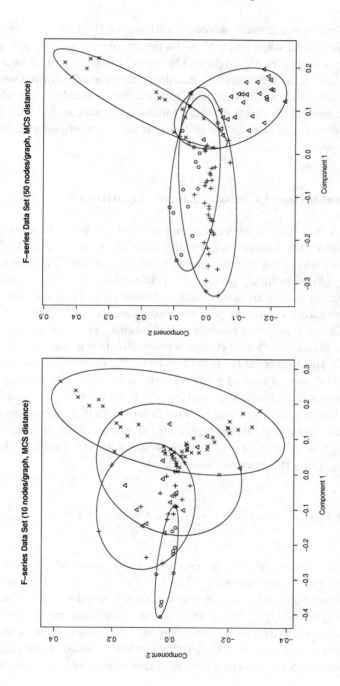

Fig. 4.22 Multidimensional scaling performed on the F-series data set with 10 nodes per graph maximum (left) and 50 nodes per graph maximum (right).

Fig. 4.22 shows two clusterings created with our method for the F-series data set: one produced when using 10 nodes per graph maximum (left) and one using 50 nodes per graph (right). The mutual information measured for the clustering on the left is 0.1242. Similarly, the mutual information of the clustering depicted on the right side of the figure is 0.1981. Note that the increase in mutual information, which indicates a better match with the ground truth clustering, is reflected in the plot as better organized, more compact, clusters.

4.7   The Graph-Based Global k-Means Algorithm

In our previous experiments with clustering we used random initializations at the first step of the k-means algorithm. Recently Likas *et al.* [LVV03] have introduced what they call the global k-means method. This method provides a way of determining "good" initial cluster centers for the k-means algorithm, without having to use random initializations. Their experimental results have shown clustering performance under global k-means which is as good or better than using random initializations. The basic procedure is an incremental computation of cluster centers. Starting at the case of one cluster ($k = 1$), the cluster center is defined to be the centroid of the entire data set. For the general case of k clusters, the centers are determined by taking the centers from the $k - 1$ clusters problem and then determining the optimum location of a new center. This is accomplished by considering each data item as the new cluster center and then executing the k-means algorithm with that particular set of cluster centers and determining which data point minimizes the error as defined by:

$$E(m_1, \ldots, m_M) = \sum_{i=1}^{N} \sum_{k=1}^{M} I(x_i \in C_k) \|x_i - m_k\|^2, \qquad (4.8)$$

where N is the number of data items, M is the number of clusters, x_i is data item i, m_k is cluster center k, and $I(X) = 1$ if X is true and 0 otherwise. A problem with this approach is that it requires execution of the k-means algorithm $O(N \cdot M)$ times. For many applications this will be too time-consuming. With this in mind, the authors have also proposed a "fast" version of global k-means. Under this method, instead of running k-means when considering each data item as a new cluster center candidate, we calculate the following:

$$b_n = \sum_{j=1}^{N} \max(d_{k-1}^j - \|x_n - x_j\|^2, 0), \qquad (4.9)$$

where d_{k-1}^j is the distance between data item x_j and its closest cluster center for the $k-1$ clustering problem. We then select the new cluster center to be data item x_i where:

$$i = \arg\max_n b_n. \qquad (4.10)$$

It is this "fast" version of the global k-means method that we have implemented and that we will use for our experiments in this section. Specifically we will apply the global k-means method to our graph-based k-means algorithm to see if there is any improvement over the previous cases that used random initializations [SLBK03c]. Further, due to the incremental nature of the global k-means method, where determining the initial centers for k clusters implies we must also determine the initial centers for 1 to $k-1$ clusters, this provides an opportunity to examine the question of automatically determining the optimum number of clusters. Many clustering methods, including k-means, require the user to specify in advance the number of clusters to create. With a method that automatically determines the number of clusters we do not have to do this, which is beneficial if the number of clusters is not known a priori. In Sec. 4.7.1 we will give experimental results which compare clustering performance under global k-means as compared with random initialization. In Sec. 4.7.2 we will look at the problem of automatically determining the best number of clusters; we will run both the global k-means and random methods for a range of k values and calculate various performance indices for each case.

Cluster validity has long been studied and several approaches are represented in the literature. In Ref. [FK96], Frigui and Krishnapuram present a clustering algorithm based on fuzzy c-means which determines the optimal number of clusters by merging similar clusters, thus eliminating unimportant or spurious clusters. In Refs. [KP99][NK98] interesting methods of finding the number of clusters with a procedure based on scale-space persistence are presented. In general terms, an ever-expanding neighborhood is examined. When the neighborhood is at a minimum, every data point is in its own separate cluster. As the neighborhood expands clusters are merged until eventually there is one giant cluster comprising the entire data set. This can be seen as "zooming" in or out on the data, effectively looking at different levels of granularity. By performing this zooming over a range of fixed increments, we can look at how many clusters exist at each increment. The optimum number of clusters is then the one that persisted over the largest range of increments. Hardy investigates seven methods of determining the number of clusters in [Har96]. One of his observations is that since every clustering method has an underlying implicit cluster characteristic that it prefers, we must be sure to choose an algorithm that matches the structure of the data. Cluster validity using graph-theoretic concepts in place of traditional validity indices was investigated in Ref. [PB97]. New cluster validity methods for the fuzzy *c*-means algorithm have been proposed in Refs. [RLR98][ZLE99]. New clustering algorithms which explicitly take into account cluster validity are given in Refs. [WCS01][ZALE99].

4.7.1   *Global k-means vs. random initialization*

We performed a series of experiments on the F-series and J-series data sets; we omit the K-series due to computational time concerns. The results are presented in Tables 4.5–4.8 for values of k equal to the number of clusters present in ground truth ($k = 4$ for F-series, $k = 10$ for J-series). We compared our usual graph-based method using MCS distance and the standard representation to the vector-based method using distance based on Jaccard similarity. The results show that in all cases, whether graph or vector related, the global k-means method outperformed the corresponding random method. Here random denotes the average of ten experiments each using a random initialization. This reaffirms the original experimental results of Ref. [LVV03]. The results also show that, except for the case of F-series data set when using 10 nodes per graph, our graph-based method outperformed the vector method. The execution times for the experiments are also given in Tables 4.9 and 4.10. All experiments were carried out on the same system under the same operating conditions: an un-loaded 296 MHz Sun UltraSPARC-II with 1,024 megabytes of memory. As expected, the execution time for global k-means is much greater than random, due to the need to compute the cluster centers. We also see the potential for a time savings over the vector case when using small graphs. For the J-series, not only was using the graph-based method with a maximum graph size of 10 nodes better performing than the vector case, it was faster by nearly four and a half hours.

Table 4.5 Results for F-series data set (Rand index).

graph size	global k-means		random	
	Jaccard	graphs	Jaccard	graphs
10	0.7057	0.7281	0.6899	0.6730
20	0.7057	0.7976	0.6899	0.7192
30	0.7057	0.7838	0.6899	0.7394

Table 4.6 Results for F-series data set (mutual information).

graph size	global k-means		random	
	Jaccard	graphs	Jaccard	graphs
10	0.1914	0.1653	0.1020	0.1498
20	0.1914	0.2274	0.1020	0.1638
30	0.1914	0.2336	0.1020	0.1793

Table 4.7 Results for J-series data set (Rand index).

graph size	global k-means		random	
	Jaccard	graphs	Jaccard	graphs
10	0.8809	0.9049	0.8717	0.8689
20	0.8809	0.9065	0.8717	0.8819
30	0.8809	0.9056	0.8717	0.8758

4.7.2 *Optimum number of clusters*

Previously we have used three indices to measure clustering performance: Rand index, mutual information, and Dunn index. Both Rand and mutual information compare the clustering produced by an algorithm to the actual ground truth clustering. For the problem of determining the optimum number of clusters automatically, we cannot assume that a ground truth clustering is available for evaluation. In this case we need a cluster validation index, which is a measure of clustering quality that is not dependent on knowing the ground truth clustering. The Dunn index (Eq. 4.4) is one such index, however it is sensitive to noise and outliers. Some other notable indices have been reported in the literature, and we present some of them

Table 4.8   Results for J-series data set (mutual information).

graph size	global k-means		random	
	Jaccard	graphs	Jaccard	graphs
10	0.2787	0.3048	0.2316	0.2393
20	0.2787	0.3135	0.2316	0.2597
30	0.2787	0.3188	0.2316	0.2447

Table 4.9   Execution times using random initialization (in seconds).

data set	graphs – 10	graphs – 20	graphs – 30	Jaccard
F-series	84.4	126.1	205.3	24.5
J-series	173.1	396.4	550.2	214.9

Table 4.10   Execution times using global k-means (in minutes).

data set	graphs – 10	graphs – 20	graphs – 30	Jaccard
F-series	11.87	24.88	38.68	14.57
J-series	239.55	545.92	818.47	507.55

here. First we have the *C index* [HS76], which is defined as:

$$C = \frac{S - S_{min}}{S_{max} - S_{min}} \qquad (4.11)$$

where S is the sum of all distances of pairs of items in the same cluster. We define l to be the number of these pairs used to compute S. S_{min} and S_{max} are the sum of the l smallest and largest distances, respectively. The smaller the value of C, the better the clustering.

Another validity index is the *Davies-Bouldin index* [DB79], defined as:

$$DB = \frac{1}{M} \sum_{i=1}^{M} \max_{j=1,\ldots,M; j \neq i} (d_{ij}), \qquad (4.12)$$

where M is the number of clusters and

$$d_{ij} = \frac{r_i + r_j}{d(c_i, c_j)}. \qquad (4.13)$$

Here r_i is the average distance of all data items in cluster i to their cluster center and $d(c_i, c_j)$ is the distance between the centers of clusters i and j. d_{ij} measures, similar to the Dunn index, the compactness (numerator) and separation (denominator) of cluster pairs. A small value of the Davies-Bouldin index is desirable.

Finally, we have the *Goodman-Kruskal index* [GK54], which is somewhat similar to the Rand index. In the Goodman-Kruskal method we examine all quadruples of data items (q, r, s, t) and look to see if they conform to one of the following cases:

(1) $d(q, r) < d(s, t)$; q and r in the same cluster; s and t in different clusters
(2) $d(q, r) > d(s, t)$; q and r in different clusters; s and t in the same cluster
(3) $d(q, r) < d(s, t)$; q and r in different clusters; s and t in the same cluster
(4) $d(q, r) > d(s, t)$; q and r in the same cluster; s and t in different clusters

If we have case (1) or case (2), this is called concordant and indicates that pairs of items that are in the same cluster should have a smaller distance than pairs of items that are in different clusters. Similarly, cases (3) and (4) are called discordant. Let S^+ be the number of concordant quadruples and S^- be the number of discordant quadruples. The Goodman-Kruskal index is then given by

$$GK = \frac{S^+ - S^-}{S^+ + S^-} \qquad (4.14)$$

A large value for GK indicates a good clustering (*i.e.* high concordance). A problem with this method is immediately evident, however: the complexity of computing GK is $O(n^4)$, where n is the number of items in the data set. Thus computing this index can be more time consuming than performing the clustering itself.

We performed experiments for values of k varying from 2 to 10 for both the F-series and the J-series data sets when using both global k-means or a random initialization. Here random initialization is accomplished as before by randomly assigning each data item to a cluster. Note that it is not possible to re-use the same random initialization for different values of k, thus each experiment has a separate random initialization. Our graphs were created using the standard representation and a maximum of 10 nodes/graph; the distance measure used was MCS. The results are presented in Tables 4.11–4.14. The "best" number of clusters is determined from Rand index and mutual information, which indicate the performance as compared to ground truth.

Table 4.11   Results for F-series data set using global k-means.

number of clusters	Dunn	DB	GK	C	Rand	MI
2	0.6667	1.8567	0.3431	0.2451	0.5304	0.0978
3	0.6667	1.8665	0.5163	0.3687	0.6604	0.1231
4	0.6667	1.7833	0.6161	0.4188	0.7281	0.1653
5	0.6667	1.7785	0.6795	0.4391	0.7578	0.1868
6	0.6667	1.7091	0.7207	0.4028	0.7665	0.2156
7	0.6667	1.6713	0.7588	0.3745	0.7775	0.2186
8	0.6667	1.7688	0.7557	0.3780	0.7695	0.2090
9	0.6667	1.6971	0.7956	0.3385	0.7761	0.2205
10	0.6667	1.6560	0.8109	0.3236	0.7779	0.2229

Table 4.12   Results for F-series data set using random initialization.

number of clusters	Dunn	DB	GK	C	Rand	MI
2	0.6667	1.8567	0.3431	0.2451	0.5304	0.0978
3	0.6667	1.8660	0.5440	0.3480	0.6676	0.1317
4	0.6667	1.7983	0.6202	0.4173	0.7169	0.1530
5	0.6667	1.9934	0.5629	0.4889	0.7057	0.1423
6	0.6818	1.7981	0.6980	0.4244	0.7644	0.1844
7	0.6667	1.8774	0.6772	0.4545	0.7634	0.2017
8	0.6471	1.9110	0.6615	0.4763	0.7695	0.2160
9	0.6667	1.6304	0.7472	0.4011	0.7831	0.2154
10	0.6667	1.7314	0.7086	0.4610	0.7751	0.2127

We see from the results that these two indices agreed on (*i.e.*, were optimal for) the same value for k for the experiments that used global k-means. For the experiments using random initialization, there was not an agreement and consequently we cant decide definitively on the "best" number of clusters in these cases. The next observation regarding the results is that both Davies-Bouldin and Goodman-Kruskal always agreed on the same k value. Further, the agreement of these two performance indices also coincides with the optimal values for Rand index and mutual information determined using global k-means. Dunn and C index do not seem very useful in terms of finding the correct k value. We see that only in the case of global k-means with the F-series did Dunn agree with the other indices, and even then the Dunn index had identical values for all k. C index fared slightly better, agreeing with the other indices for global k-means for the J-series; although the optimal value was at $k = 2$ for global k-means with the F-series, its second best value was at the correct k value. We note that

Table 4.13   Results for J-series data set using global *k*-means.

number of clusters	Dunn	DB	GK	C	Rand	MI
2	0.4286	1.9427	0.2376	0.2950	0.4850	0.0911
3	0.6250	1.8845	0.4544	0.3987	0.6830	0.1435
4	0.6500	1.8174	0.5328	0.4338	0.7618	0.1848
5	0.6000	1.7792	0.5797	0.4122	0.7986	0.2041
6	0.6000	1.7768	0.6612	0.3610	0.8471	0.2480
7	0.6000	1.7653	0.6692	0.3612	0.8638	0.2599
8	0.6154	1.7453	0.7300	0.3177	0.8833	0.2819
9	0.6154	1.7612	0.7543	0.2947	0.8978	0.2978
10	0.6154	1.7379	0.7686	0.2855	0.9049	0.3048

Table 4.14   Results for J-series data set using random initialization.

number of clusters	Dunn	DB	GK	C	Rand	MI
2	0.4286	1.9427	0.2376	0.2950	0.4850	0.0911
3	0.4286	1.9337	0.1970	0.4466	0.5818	0.0724
4	0.5833	1.8693	0.3849	0.4830	0.7205	0.1472
5	0.6500	1.7627	0.5727	0.4123	0.7907	0.2078
6	0.5714	1.8642	0.5313	0.4680	0.7772	0.1768
7	0.6000	1.9639	0.6046	0.4043	0.8360	0.2279
8	0.5833	1.8532	0.6180	0.4138	0.8617	0.2332
9	0.5833	1.9477	0.6163	0.4066	0.8581	0.2347
10	0.5714	1.8726	0.6063	0.4800	0.8659	0.2215

global *k*-means was clearly much better in terms of agreement between cluster performance indices than random: for both F and J-series five out of six indices agreed for global *k*-means, whereas random only achieved three out of six agreements (F-series) or two out of six agreements (J-series). Finally, we see that for the F-series, a larger number of clusters is indicated than is present in ground truth. This could be due to the fact that the F-series data set originally contained many more classes (see Sec. 3.4). Recall that we altered the ground truth to four larger clusters which subsumed the more specific topics. It is possible that this structure is still apparent in the data, even though we are using only a maximum of 10 terms per graph. Another possibility is that the indices we are using are sometimes skewed towards a larger number of clusters. For example, when the number of clusters equals the number of data items (*i.e.* each data item is its own cluster), indices that measure clustering performance as a function of the distance of data items from their cluster centers become maximized.

We have explored content-based clustering of web documents using k-means and global k-means. In the next chapter we turn towards performing supervised classification of the web document sets using the k-nearest neighbor algorithm.

Chapter 5

Graph-Based Classification

Automated classification techniques, where new, previously unseen data items are categorized to a predefined class of similar items, has been an active research area in pattern recognition, machine learning, and data mining. Manual classification can be costly due to the large number of instances to be checked, their complexity, or an insufficient amount of expert domain knowledge required to perform the classification. The benefit of automated systems in application domains where this occurs is obvious. Classification of natural language documents, such as web documents, is one such domain. Because the number of documents being produced now is more than ever before, especially when we consider the Internet with its massive amount of heterogeneous documents, manual classification and categorization can be extremely difficult.

Classification is different than the clustering procedures we previously examined for two major reasons. First, classification is a supervised learning task, meaning the classifier is first trained by exposing it to a set of labeled example data. Only after sufficient training is the classifier ready to be used for classification. Second, classification assigns a label to each data item (web document). In contrast clustering creates a series of groupings of the data. Thus the performance of clustering and classification algorithms is measured in different ways.

In this chapter we introduce a graph-based extension of the popular k-nearest neighbors (k-NN) classification algorithm. The leave-one-out approach will be used to compare classification accuracy over our three document collections. We will select several values for the number of nearest neighbors, k, and will also look at the performance as a function of the size of the graphs representing each document. We will also compare the performance of different graph theoretical distance measures and the various methods of representing the web documents using graphs described in Chapter 3, much as we did for k-means. These issues will be addressed in Sec. 5.1. In Sec. 5.2 we will describe a method of creating classifier ensembles using both graph-based (structural) and statistical (vector-based) classifiers. The goal of combining multiple classifiers is to improve accuracy over the case of using a single classifier. Our method uses random node selection, a method analogous to random feature subset selection used for vector-based classifiers, to create graph-based classifiers. We will present results of experiments performed with this approach.

5.1   The k-Nearest Neighbors Algorithm

5.1.1   *Traditional method*

In this section we describe the k-nearest neighbors (k-NN) classification algorithm and how we can easily extend it to work with graph-based data. The basic k-NN algorithm is given as follows (see Fig. 5.1) [Mit97]. First, we have a data set of training examples (sometimes also called training instances). In the traditional k-NN approach these will usually be numerical vectors in some real-valued Euclidean feature space. Each of these training instances is associated with a label which indicates to what class the instance belongs. Given a new, previously unseen instance, called a query or input instance, we attempt to estimate which class it belongs to. Under the k-NN method this is accomplished by looking at the k training instances closest (*i.e.* with least distance) to the input instance. Here k is a user provided parameter and distance is usually defined to be the Euclidean distance. Once we have found the k nearest training instances using some distance measure, such as one of those defined in Eqs. 1.1–1.3, we estimate the class by the majority among the k instances. This class is then assigned as the predicted class for the input instance. If there are ties due to more than one class having equal numbers of representatives amongst the nearest neighbors we can either choose one class randomly or we can break the tie with some other method, such as selecting the tied class which has the minimum distance neighbor. For the experiments in this chapter we will use the latter method, which in our experiments has shown a slight improvement over random tie breaking in nearly all cases. k-NN is classified as a lazy, instance-based learning algorithm. Lazy meaning learning is not actually performed until a new query instance is encountered, and instance-based meaning the knowledge utilized by the method is stored as the instances themselves rather than as rules, tables, or some other format.

Inputs:	a set of pre-classified training instances, a query instance q, and a parameter k, defining the number of nearest neighbors to use
Outputs:	a label indicating the class of the query instance q
Step 1.	Find the k closest training instances to q according to a distance measure
Step 2.	Select the class of q to be the class held by the majority of the k nearest training instances

Fig. 5.1   The basic k-nearest neighbors algorithm.

5.1.2   *Graph-based approach*

The extension to using graphs as data for the k-NN algorithm is straightforward: we simply represent the data as graphs (Chapter 3) and use a graph-theoretical distance measure (Eqs. 2.3–2.7) in lieu of traditional vector-based distance measures such as Euclidean distance. Otherwise the algorithm remains unchanged from its usual form. As discussed in the next section, we have implemented the k-NN algorithm for both the traditional case of representing data as numeric vectors and our approach where we represent data as graphs.

For k-NN, the complexity for the vector case is $O(nm) + O(n \log n)$, where m is the number of dimensions and n is the number of training examples. The first term is the complexity of calculating the distance between the input instance and each training example. The second term represents the complexity of sorting these distances to find the nearest neighbors. For graphs, the complexity is $O(nm^2) + O(n \log n)$, m in this case being the number of nodes per graph. This follows directly from the vector complexity, substituting the graph distance complexity, $O(m^2)$, in place of the vector distance complexity. In this case, only the first step, distance calculation, is affected; using graphs does not affect the complexity of the sorting stage.

5.1.3   *Experimental results*

For our graph-based experiments we used several values of maximum graph size to examine the effect of graph size on performance. Classification accuracy was measured by the leave-one-out method. In this method we iterate over all n documents, using $n - 1$ documents as training instances and then classifying the remaining instance. Accuracy is reported as the number of documents classified correctly divided by n. As we mentioned in Sec. 3.4, the F-series contains four classes: manufacturing, labor, business & finance, and electronic communication & networking; the J-series contains ten classes: affirmative action, business capital, information systems, electronic commerce, intellectual property, employee rights, materials processing, personnel management, manufacturing systems, and industrial partnership; and the K-series has 20 classes: business, health, politics, sports, technology, entertainment, art, cable, culture, film, industry, media, multimedia, music, online, people, review, stage, television, and variety.

The results for the F-series, the J-series, and the K-series are given in Figs. 5.2, 5.3, and 5.4, respectively. The graphs show the classification accuracy as a function of k, the number of nearest neighbors to use. We used values of 1, 3, 5, and 10 for k. The dotted lines in the figures indicate the performance of the vector model approach when using the cosine distance measure (Eq. 1.2) or extended Jaccard distance measure (Eq. 1.3), which we take here to be benchmarks against which our novel graph-based method is compared. The graph-based methods in these figures use the MCS distance measure (Eq. 2.3) and the "standard" graph representation (see Chapter 3).

We see that in the F and J-series graphs of as few as 10 nodes usually outperformed the vector-based methods, regardless of the number of nearest neighbors. We also see that the performance continued to improve as we created larger graphs, with graphs using up to 20 or 30 nodes outperforming the usual vector methods in nearly all cases. The K-series, however, needed larger graph sizes to attain an improvement in accuracy over the vector model. We attribute this to the greater number of classes and documents used in this data set (twice as many classes as the J-series, and more than ten times the number of documents). In order to properly differentiate between classes a larger number of terms is necessary. This is also reflected in the vector model, which uses a much higher dimensionality for the K-series than the other two data sets (1,458 terms for K versus 332 for F and 474 for J). For the K-series we used graph sizes of 40, 70, 100 and 150 nodes per graph maximum. At 40 nodes per graph our method performed similarly to but slightly better than the vector approach using cosine distance (comparing the best case performance for each method). With 70 nodes per graph the best performance using graphs was similar to the best performance using Jaccard. With 100 nodes per graph the graph method outperformed both of the vector methods for values of $k \geq 3$ (three out of four cases). In all three document collections, the graph representations that outperformed the vector model were based on a significantly smaller

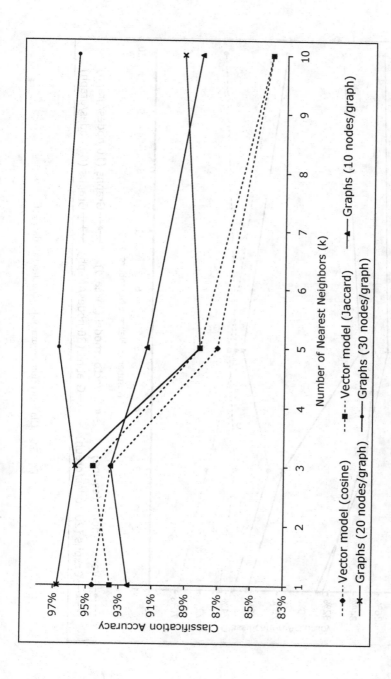

Fig. 5.2   Classification accuracy for the F-series data set.

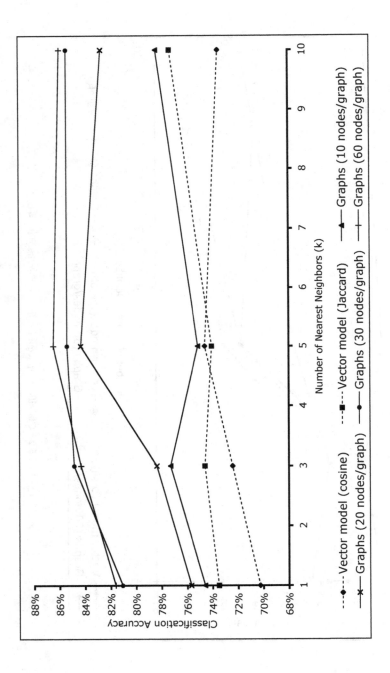

Fig. 5.3   Classification accuracy for the J-series data set.

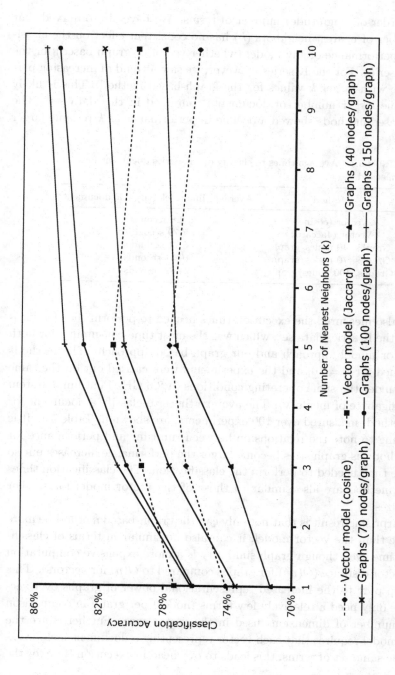

Fig. 5.4 Classification accuracy for the K-series data set.

(by an order of magnitude) number of terms. We have also observed that the number of nearest neighbors (k) has no consistent effect on the classification performance of any model (whether vector or graph based) for the F and J-series. For the K-series, however, we saw a trend of increasing performance with larger k values for the graph-based method. This is likely due to the larger number of documents contained in this data set. The vector-based methods showed a decline in performance as k became larger than 5.

Table 5.1   Average times to classify one K-Series document for each method.

Method	Average time to classify one document
Vector (cosine)	7.8 seconds
Vector (Jaccard)	7.79 seconds
Graphs, 40 nodes/graph	8.71 seconds
Graphs, 70 nodes/graph	16.31 seconds
Graphs, 100 nodes/graph	24.62 seconds

We also measured the execution times needed to perform the classification for the K-series data set, which was the most time-consuming, for both the vector model approach and our graph-based approach. The methods were timed for $k = 10$, and the experiments were carried out on the same system under the same operating conditions (a 2.6 GHz Pentium 4 system with 1 gigabyte of memory). The average times to classify a document for each method, measured over 100 experiments, are shown in Table 5.1. It is interesting to note the relationship between run time and performance for our method: as graph sizes become larger the performance increases but so does the time needed to perform the classification. The classification times for our method are also similar to those of the vector model for smaller graph sizes.

A surprising result is that not only can the graph-based method be more accurate than the vector model, it can also be similar in terms of classification time even though graph similarity is a more expensive computation than vector distance ($O(n^2)$ for graphs compared to $O(n)$ for vectors). This is due in part to the increased representational power of graphs over vectors: we only need a relatively few terms (nodes) per graph in comparison to the number of dimensions used in the vector case. Further, since the vector model requires that each vector representing a document include exactly the same set of terms, this leads to overhead in execution time for the distance comparison of all documents whether or not each term is actually useful for every document (*i.e.* incorporating a new term always increases the dimensionality of all vectors by one). In contrast, our graph-based method allows us to define specific terms for only a select group of graphs by simply adding relevant nodes and edges to those graphs while leaving the others unchanged. Consequently, n graphs each with m nodes can contain information relating to up to $n \cdot m$ distinct terms, while n equal-size vectors with m dimensions in a term–document matrix refers to m terms only. Given this observation it may be possible to attain even better time savings by selecting the group of terms modeled in each graph more carefully. We could, for example, allow hard-to-classify documents to be represented by larger graphs while using a minimal representation for others.

In Figs. 5.5–5.7 we show the comparison of different graph distance measures when classifying the F, J, and K-series, respectively. The MCS distance, which was used in Figs. 5.2–5.4, is shown as a dotted line. The results of each distance measure are based on the same set of best performing graphs (30 nodes per graph maximum for F and J; 100 for K) for each data set. We see that the graph-based methods that use normalized distance measures performed well, while distance measures that were not normalized to the interval $[0, 1]$ performed poorly. This same behavior was also noted in Chapter 4 for clustering performance.

In Figs. 5.8–5.10 we give the results of the comparison of the different graph representations we proposed for the F, J, and K-series, respectively. The dotted line indicates the standard representation, which was what was used in Figs. 5.2–5.4. We use the same graph sizes as we used previously in the distance measure comparison (Figs. 5.5–5.7). Here, as before, we use $n = 5$ for our distance related representations, *i.e.* 5-distance and 5-simple distance. There are some interesting trends that are apparent in these graphs. We see that while the standard representation performed well in many cases, in the F and J data sets the simple representation produced the best performance of all the methods (at $k = 3$ for the F-series and $k = 5$ for the J-series) while for the K-series the absolute frequency representation was clearly the best for all values of k. For the F and J-series this could indicate that the simple representation can be just as good or better than the standard representation, but is more sensitive to the value of k. Note that in both cases (F and J) the standard representation outperformed the simple representation for $k = 1$, which suggests that the standard method actually creates a representation that is better when we compare two data items in the pair-wise sense; *i.e.* the standard method creates graphs that

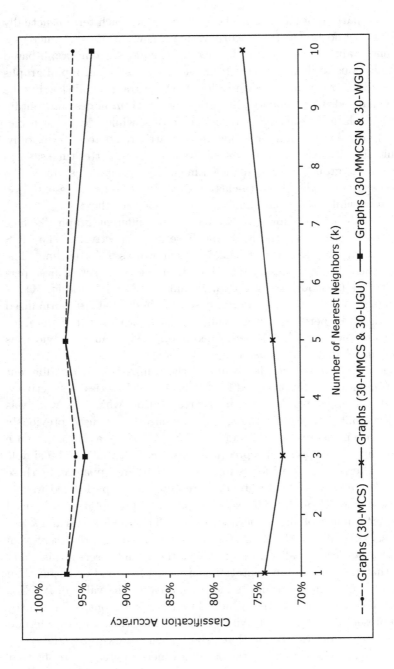

Fig. 5.5   Distance measure comparison for the F-Series data set.

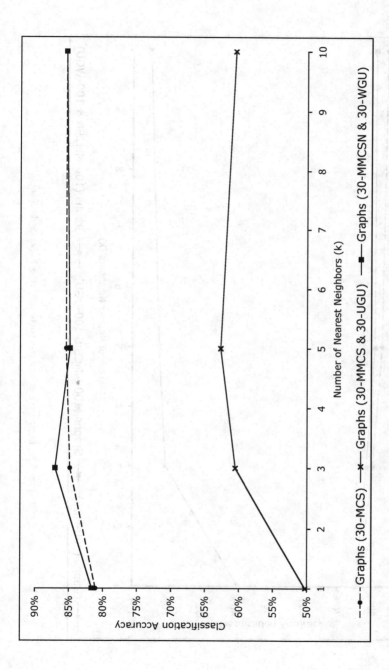

Fig. 5.6 Distance measure comparison for the J-Series data set.

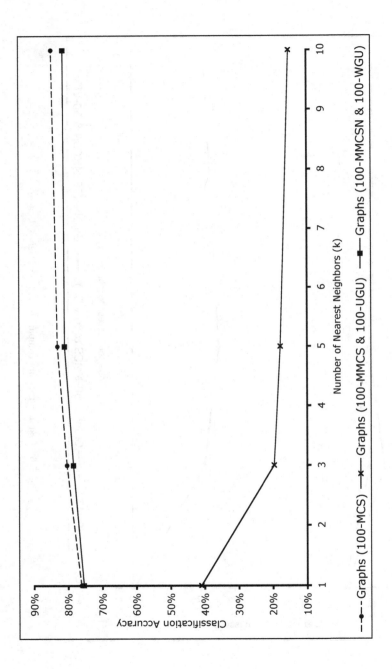

Fig. 5.7 Distance measure comparison for the K-Series data set.

when compared to each other provide a more accurate distance value, and it is only when we introduce larger neighborhoods of graphs that the simple representation can be more effective than the standard. The relative frequency representation performed well for the F-series at $k = 1$, but its performance declined with larger k values. For the J-series, the opposite trend was present for relative frequency: larger values of k lead to increasingly better performance.

For the K-series, the superior performance of the absolute frequency representation is possibly due to the fact that this is a highly homogeneous data set. Compared to the F and J-series data sets, whose documents are authored by different people and contain variations in style, layout, and structure, the K-series documents have similar layout, structure and size due to being formatted and hosted by a single source (Yahoo). Every document contains an identical subset of terms (*e.g.* "news", "sports", *etc.*) that comes from elements such as menus and navigation links. Using the absolute frequency representation may help differentiate document content under these conditions. For example, the term "news" may appear on every document because it appears as a navigational link, but if it appears twenty times instead of three this may be significant for classification purposes. Alternatively, a term such as "news" appearing on a document may have a low frequency due to it coming from a navigational link. Thus the importance of such terms when calculating document similarity is less than other terms with higher frequency (those that are content-related). This information is captured in the frequency-related representations but not the other graph representations. The relative frequency representation did not perform as well as absolute frequency for the K-series, indicating that normalization of frequency values was not necessary for this homogeneous data set.

In the experimental results above we saw that while the MCS distance and standard representation were consistently among the top performing methods in many cases, for the J-series the WGU/MMCSN distance measure (Fig. 5.6, 87.03% for $k = 3$) and simple graph representation (Fig. 5.9, 85.95% for $k = 5$) were the best performing overall (the best performance overall being indicated by the data point that appears highest in the chart). In order to determine if we could obtain an even better performance for the J-series, we considered the case where we combine the best overall performing distance measure (WGU/MMCSN) and the best overall performing graph representation (simple). Note that for both the F-series and the K-series the best overall distance measure was MCS, and the results

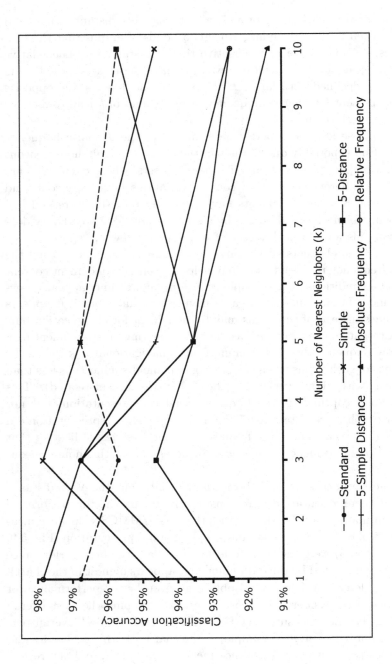

Fig. 5.8   Graph representation comparison for the F-Series data set.

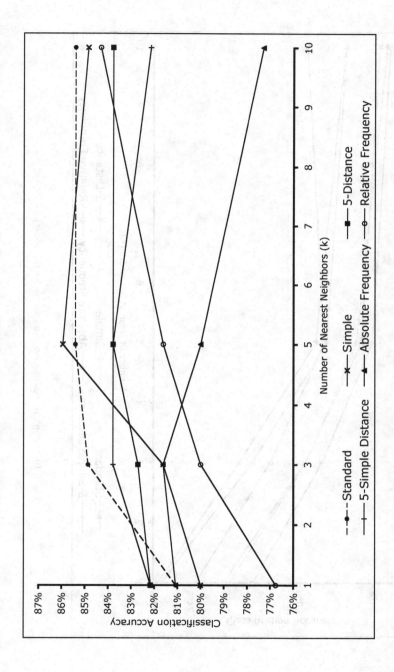

Fig. 5.9   Graph representation comparison for the J-Series data set.

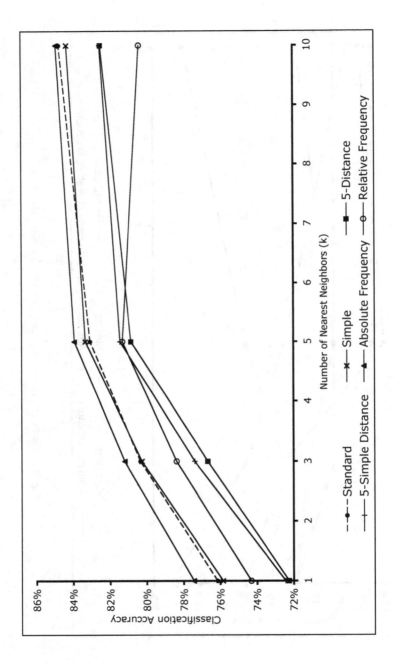

Fig. 5.10   Graph representation comparison for the K-Series data set.

of combining the MCS distance measure with the various representations is already given in Figs. 5.8 and 5.10. The outcome of combining the WGU/MMCSN distance measure with the simple representation for the J-series is given in Fig. 5.11. We see that we obtained a slightly better result than the combination of MCS and standard for $k = 5$ (86.49%), which was also the best overall performance for the J-series for $k = 5$. However, neither of the two combinations has a consistent advantage over the other one.

5.2 Graph-Based Multiple Classifier Ensembles

5.2.1 *Basic algorithm*

In order to further improve classifier accuracy over the case of a single classifier, the idea of creating classifier ensembles has been proposed [KHDM98][Die00]. This methodology involves combining the output of several different (usually independent) classifiers in order to build one large, and hopefully more accurate, multiple classifier system. Several approaches have been proposed to create classifier ensembles. Bagging, for instance, creates classifiers by randomly selecting the group of training examples to be used for each classifier [Bre96]. A similar idea is that of random feature subset selection [Ho98]. In this method, we randomly select the features (dimensions) to be used for each feature vector to create a group of classifiers.

Below we introduce a technique for creating graph-based classifier ensembles using random node selection. To our knowledge, this is the first time such an approach has been taken to build structural classifier ensembles. We will consider ensembles that include both structural, *i.e.* graph-based, and statistical, *i.e.* feature vector-based, classifiers. In Ref. [MRS03] such an approach, using one statistical and one structural classifier, has been proposed. However, the classifiers used in Ref. [MRS03] were both designed by hand. By contrast, our method allows for automatic ensemble generation out of one single structural base classifier. We will perform experiments in order to test the accuracy of the classifier ensembles created with our novel procedure.

As mentioned above, the goal of creating an ensemble of classifiers is to achieve a higher overall accuracy than any single classifier in the ensemble by combining the output of the individual classifiers. The classifiers used in our ensembles perform the k-nearest neighbors method described

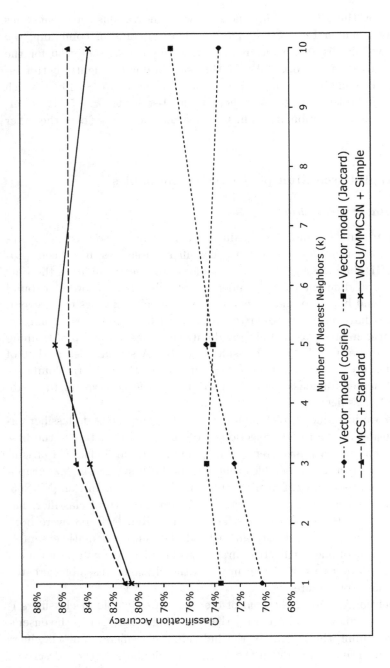

Fig. 5.11 Combining WGU/MMCSN distance measure and simple representation for the J-Series.

in Sec. 5.1. Different graph-based classifiers are generated by randomly removing nodes (and their incident edges) from the training graphs until a maximum number of nodes is reached for all graphs. We create several graph-based classifiers using this method, and each becomes a classifier in the ensemble.

For each classifier, we output the three top ranked classification labels. The ranked outputs from each classifier are then combined using a Borda count [HHS92]. The first ranked class receives a vote of 3, the second a vote of 2, and the third a vote of 1. Using the Borda count we select the class with the highest total vote count as the predicted class for the ensemble, with ties broken arbitrarily.

5.2.2 *Experimental results*

In order to evaluate the performance of our proposed method of creating classifier ensembles using random node selection, we performed experiments on the J-series data set. For our experiments, we created graphs using the standard representation and used the MCS distance measure to find the nearest neighbors. For the parameter m, which indicates the maximum number of the most frequent nodes to retain in each graph (see Sec. 3.2), we used a value of 100 for our experiments. In addition to the graph-based classifiers, we also include a single vector-based k-NN classifier in the ensemble. For the vector-based classifiers, we used the term–document matrix of 474 dimensions that was provided with the data set and distance based on the Jaccard similarity (Eq. 1.3) for the vector-based classifiers.

The experimental results are given in Table 5.2. Each row indicates an experiment with different parameter values, which are shown in the three leftmost columns. The parameters are NN, the maximum number of nodes to randomly be included in each prototype graph; NC, the number of classifiers in the ensemble; and k, which is the parameter k used in the k-NN algorithm (the number of nearest neighbors). Note that in a given ensemble there will be $NC - 1$ graph-based classifiers created through random node selection and a single vector-based classifier.

The results of each experiment are shown in the next six columns as classification accuracy measured by leave-one-out. *Min* is the accuracy of the worst single classifier in the ensemble. Similarly, *Max* is the accuracy of the best single classifier in the ensemble. *Ens* is the accuracy of the combined ensemble using Borda count as described above. *Oracle* is the accuracy if we assume that when at least one individual classifier in the ensemble correctly classifies a document the ensemble will also correctly classify the document; this gives us an upper bound on the best possible accuracy of the ensemble if we were able to find an optimal combination method but leave the classifiers themselves as they are. *BL (G)* (baseline graph-based classifier) gives the accuracy of a single graph-based classifier using the standard k-NN method with the full sized training graphs ($m = 100$) for a baseline comparison; similarly, *BL (V)* (baseline vector-based classifier) gives the accuracy of the vector-based k-NN classifier used in the ensemble. The final column, *Imp*, is the difference between *Ens* and *BL (G)*, which indicates the performance improvement realized by the ensemble over the baseline graph-based classifier. The average of each column is shown in the bottom row of the table.

Table 5.2   Experimental results for the multiple classifier ensemble for the J-series.

NN	NC	k	Min	Max	Ens	Oracle	BL (G)	BL (V)	Imp
50	3	1	73.51%	73.51%	84.32%	90.81%	80.00%	73.51%	4.32%
50	3	3	74.59%	78.92%	81.62%	92.97%	81.62%	74.59%	0.00%
50	3	5	74.05%	76.76%	81.62%	89.73%	83.24%	74.05%	-1.62%
50	5	1	72.43%	76.76%	84.32%	92.97%	80.00%	73.51%	4.32%
50	5	3	74.59%	78.92%	84.32%	94.59%	81.62%	74.59%	2.70%
50	5	5	74.05%	80.54%	84.32%	95.14%	83.24%	74.05%	1.08%
50	10	1	68.65%	78.38%	81.62%	95.14%	80.00%	73.51%	1.62%
50	10	3	70.81%	78.92%	80.00%	94.05%	81.62%	74.59%	-1.62%
50	10	5	69.19%	80.00%	80.54%	96.22%	80.00%	73.51%	0.54%
75	3	1	73.51%	77.84%	84.32%	90.27%	80.00%	73.51%	4.32%
75	3	3	74.59%	82.16%	81.62%	91.89%	81.62%	74.59%	0.00%
75	3	5	74.05%	80.54%	83.24%	90.81%	83.24%	74.05%	0.00%
75	5	1	73.51%	79.46%	84.86%	93.51%	80.00%	73.51%	4.86%
75	5	3	74.59%	81.08%	84.32%	94.59%	81.62%	74.59%	2.70%
75	5	5	74.05%	82.70%	84.32%	94.05%	83.24%	74.05%	1.08%
75	10	1	73.51%	78.92%	82.70%	93.51%	80.00%	73.51%	2.70%
75	10	3	74.59%	81.08%	83.78%	94.59%	81.62%	74.59%	2.16%
75	10	5	74.05%	84.86%	84.86%	95.68%	83.24%	74.05%	1.62%
Average			73.24%	79.52%	83.15%	93.36%	81.44%	74.02%	1.71%

The first thing we observe from the results is that, in every case but one, the accuracy of the ensemble (*Ens*) was greater than the best single classifier in the ensemble (*Max*). Additionally, the ensemble accuracy (*Ens*) was always greater than the baseline vector classifier (*BL (V)*). We note also that the best accuracy attained by our ensemble method was 84.86% (for $NN = 75$, $NC = 5$, $k = 5$), while the best accuracy achieved by the graph-based baseline classifiers ($BL\ (G)$) was 83.24% (for $k = 5$); out of $BL\ (G)$, $BL\ (V)$, and *Ens*, *Ens* attained both the highest average and highest maximum accuracy. Note that the performance of $BL\ (G)$ and $BL\ (V)$ is dependent only on the parameter k. The results furthermore show that the ensemble was an improvement over the baseline graph-based classifier in 13 out of 18 cases; conversely, $BL\ (G)$ was better than *Ens* in 2 out of 18 cases. However, *Oracle*, in all cases, was much better than *Ens* (the maximum oracle accuracy was 96.22%). This suggests one should look at improving the combination scheme. This could be done, for example, by altering our current method of Borda ranking to include more rankings or better tie breaking procedures. Alternatively we could introduce a weighted voting scheme, where classifier weights are determined by methods such as genetic algorithms [LHS97]. One could also take the distances returned by our k-NN classifiers into account. The number of classifiers (NC) and the parameter k did not seem to affect ensemble accuracy in any specific way.

Chapter 6

The Graph Hierarchy Construction Algorithm for Web Search Clustering

The goal of web search clustering, a type of web content mining system, is to organize the results of a search into groups of topics. As mentioned in Chapter 1, this is done in order to allow the user to more easily find the desired web pages from among the results by displaying them by topic area rather than as a ranked list. In this chapter we give the details of such a system which we have created. Our system initially used a binary vector representation for web pages and cluster labels, but we upgraded it in a straightforward manner to work with graphs instead, as we will describe below.

Web page clustering as performed by humans was examined by Macskassy *et al.* [MBDH98]. Ten subjects were involved in the experiments, and each was asked to manually cluster the results of five different queries submitted to a web search engine at Rutgers University. The queries were selected from the most popular submitted to this particular web search engine: accounting, career services, employment, library, and off campus housing. All subjects received the pages' URLs and titles, however four of the ten subjects were also given the full text of each page for each query. The subjects then clustered the group of documents associated with each query. The investigators examined the size of clusters created, the number of clusters created, the similarity of created clusters, the amount of cluster overlap, and documents not clustered. The results indicated that the size of clusters was not affected by access to the full text of each document and that there was no preference for a specific cluster size. As to number of clusters, the subjects who had access to the full text of the web pages tended to create more clusters than those who did not.

There are some important papers that deal specifically with the clustering of web search results using automated systems. One of the earliest such papers is that of Zamir and Etzioni [ZE98], which gives some of the first experimental evaluations of clustering methods as applied to web search results. In that paper the authors introduced a clustering algorithm called suffix tree clustering (or STC) in order to cluster web search results. STC works by creating a tree of words encountered in the web documents such that documents that share words or strings of words also share a common parent node in the tree. The nodes in this tree are then scored according to the number of documents represented by the node multiplied by a weighting factor. Based on this score a cluster similarity is determined, which is used to determine cluster overlap and the merging of overlapping clusters. The result is a group of clusters which have terms or phrases related with them. STC was used in the authors' Grouper system to implement a system for clustering web search results. STC was also used in a recently reported system called Carrot[2], which was used to cluster both English and Polish documents [SW03]. A similar web search system, called MSEEC, was introduced in Ref. [HKN99]. MSEEC uses the LZW compression algorithm to generate a tree similar to that of STC. An interesting feature of MSEEC is that it can utilize multiple search engines. This can be useful if, for example, the search engines cover different sets of documents. Another web search clustering system is described by He *et al.* [HDZS01]. This system uses a hybrid web structure/web content mining approach to clustering, by creating a graph of web pages based on their hyperlinks and then performing a graph partitioning method. Textual information from the pages, in the form of vector representations, is used to determine the weight of edges in the graph. Co-citation, where we assume that when many pages link to the same target pages this implies that the target pages are related, is also used in the calculation of edge weights. This system was not available to the public, nor was the data used in the experiments. Organizing web search results using classifiers has also been studied [DC00], however these methods require supervised learning using a fixed group or hierarchy of clusters. If new topics are to be created, as often happens with the highly dynamic nature of the Internet, the classifier training process must be repeated.

A group of Carnegie Mellon University researchers headed by Dr. Raul Valdes-Perez have recently developed a commercial meta-search engine called Vivísimo [Viv]. In response to a user query, Vivísimo presents "clustered results," which are categorized groupings of web pages organized by conceptually related topics. Vivísimo is an online search system and thus the quality of its results depends entirely on the quality of the snippets stored by other search engines. The hierarchy of topics created by Vivísimo always has a single topic at its root node. The user can control the total number of returned web pages (100, 200 or 500), but not the size and the structure of the clustering hierarchy.

In this chapter we will describe our Cluster Hierarchy Construction Algorithm (CHCA) and Graph Hierarchy Construction Algorithm (GHCA): novel hierarchical clustering algorithms which we have implemented in a system that clusters search results obtained from conventional web search engines. We gave our original descriptions of this system in Refs. [SLK01a][SLK01b][SLKar]. The basic operation of our search clustering system is to take a user provided search string, pass it on to a web search engine (or group of engines), examine the results from those engines, then finally display to the user a group of hierarchically arranged clusters (topics) related to the search subject. Clusters are displayed by printing the list of terms associated with the cluster, which are derived from either the vector (CHCA) or graph (GHCA) representing the cluster. Web pages found by the search engines are assigned to these clusters. The major benefit of our web content mining system over conventional search engines is the differentiation of results based on the related topics and sub-topics. Conventional search engines usually return a large ranked list that is not organized according to topic. Thus users of our system can focus on only the specific areas they are interested in when viewing the results, potentially increasing the speed with which the desired web pages are found. A second benefit is that the collection of topics and their organization provides the user with additional knowledge about the search query topic and how it is related to similar topics. Other benefits of our system include the ability to perform analysis on the full text of the actual documents, when operated in asynchronous (off-line) mode.

There are a number of different algorithms for performing clustering, including hierarchical clustering algorithms which create clusters arranged as a hierarchy rather than partitions. The most well known of these that is widely used for information retrieval is the agglomerative hierarchical clustering method [Sal89]. We will give some details about this algorithm and compare it to our method later in the chapter. An overview of many clustering algorithms and their related issues is given in Ref. [JD88]. More recent surveys of clustering can be found in Refs. [JMF99][Mir96]. However, unlike other clustering methods, which do not label clusters according to topic, the interesting features of applying GHCA is not so much the separation of documents into clusters, but rather the cluster labels and the knowledge representation [LS93][RN95] induced by the hierarchy of topics.

This chapter is organized as follows. In Sec. 6.1 we give the Cluster Hierarchy Construction Algorithm, and early vector-based version of GHCA, and describe how it works in detail. In Sec. 6.2, we describe the relevant implementation details of the search result processing system we created. In Sec. 6.3 we give results of using our system for different query topics as well as comparisons with other similar systems. The GHCA algorithm, a version of CHCA that works with web documents represented by graphs rather than vectors, is given in Sec. 6.4. Some final remarks are presented in Sec. 6.5.

6.1   Cluster Hierarchy Construction Algorithm (CHCA)

In this section we give the details of the Cluster Hierarchy Construction Algorithm (CHCA), an early form of GHCA that was vector-based, and compare it to similar existing clustering algorithms. We also give a classification of this clustering method based on its characteristics. First we give a review of the concept of inheritance, which is the mechanism used by CHCA and GHCA to create the parent/child cluster relationship.

6.1.1   *A review of inheritance*

Inheritance is a technique of creating new, more specialized entities by defining them in terms of existing entities. This terminology and method of creating specialization from existing models comes from the subject object-orientation, which is a software engineering technique that promotes code re-use. In the context of the current work we will apply inheritance to clusters for the purpose of creating new, more specialized clusters that are related to previously existing clusters. Each cluster we create is associated with a topic relating to a web search and is defined by a list of terms that indicate the topic's meaning. When a cluster (called a child cluster or sub-cluster) inherits from another cluster (called a parent cluster or super-cluster) the child receives the terms associated with its parent. Usually, the child cluster will also define new terms of its own. For example, if the parent contains three terms (A, B and C) then its child will have terms A, B and C as well as new terms (*e.g.* D and E). It is possible for a cluster to have more than one parent, which is called multiple inheritance. Clusters that are not defined using inheritance (*i.e.* those that have no parents) are called *base clusters*. Clusters created in this way form a structure called a hierarchy, where children are connected to their parents.

Consider the following example which illustrates the concept. We have a base cluster with a single term: STUDENT. It has two child clusters: UNDERGRADUATE STUDENT and GRADUATE STUDENT. The cluster GRADUATE STUDENT in turn has children MASTERS GRADUATE STUDENT and PH.D. GRADUATE STUDENT. The cluster MASTERS GRADUATE STUDENT is a specialization (*i.e.* more specific form) of the cluster GRADUATE STUDENT, which in turn is a specialization of the cluster STUDENT. Similarly, STUDENT is a generalization (*i.e.* less specific form) of the cluster UNDERGRADUATE STUDENT. As we traverse downward through the hierarchy, the clusters become more specific (specialized) and as we move upward they become more general. Observe that in many natural languages, such as English, more specificity is created when more terms are used to describe an entity. Similar to the example above, we see that, for example, "master's degree seeking full-time student" is much more specific than simply "student" when describing a person. We make use of this observation in our search clustering system, as clusters with more terms associated with them tend to be specializations of more general clusters.

6.1.2 *Brief overview of CHCA*

Before we describe our algorithm in detail, we present in this sub-section a brief overview of how CHCA works. The algorithm takes a binary matrix (a table) as input. The rows of the table correspond to the objects we are clustering. In this case we are dealing with web pages, but the method is applicable to other domains as well. The columns correspond to the possible attributes that the objects may have (terms appearing on the web pages for this particular application). When row i has a value of 1 at column j, it means that the web page corresponding to i contains term j. From this table, which is a binary representation of the presence or absence of terms for each web page, we create a reduced table containing only rows with unique attribute patterns (*i.e.*, duplicate rows are removed). Using the reduced table, we create a cluster hierarchy by examining each row, starting with those with the fewest terms (fewest number of 1's); these will become the most general clusters in our hierarchy. The row becomes a new cluster in the hierarchy, and we determine where in the hierarchy the cluster belongs by checking if any of the clusters we have created so far could be

B	the set of row vectors remaining to be processed by the algorithm (the "before set")
$\vec{c}$	a row vector that is the current candidate for becoming a new cluster
$\vec{d}$	any cluster (row vector) in the "current set" K
$\vec{d}'$	any cluster (row vector) in the "done set" D
D	the set of row vectors already processed by the algorithm (the "done set")
K	the set of parents of the current cluster candidate $\vec{c}$
m	the number of columns in the membership table X (the number of terms)
n	the number of rows in the membership table X (the number of web pages)
$\tilde{n}$	the number of rows in the reduced membership table X (number of distinct rows)
$\vec{r}$	a row vector from X, representing the terms appearing on a particular web page
$\vec{x}$	a cluster in the hierarchy created by the algorithm
X	the membership table with n rows and m columns
$\tilde{X}$	the reduced membership table, created from X, with m columns and $\tilde{n}$ rows
MCT	a user defined parameter, the Maximum Cluster Threshold, which determines the maximum number of clusters to create
MPT	a user defined parameter, the Minimum Pages Threshold, which determines the minimum number of pages each cluster can contain
MDT	a user defined parameter, the Maximum Distance Threshold, which determines the maximum difference in terms to consider when adding new clusters
$\vec{\phi}_m$	a row vector with m components, all of which are 0 (the empty cluster)
$-$	the difference operation between vectors defined above (in Step 3e only, we use this operator as a shorthand for the set theoretic removal of an element from a set)

Fig. 6.1 Summary of notation used in CHCA.

parents of the new cluster. Potential parents of a cluster are those clusters which contain a subset of the terms of the child cluster. This comes from the notion of inheritance discussed above. If a cluster has no parent clusters, it becomes a base cluster. If it does have a parent or parents, it becomes a child cluster of those clusters which have the most terms in common with it. This process is repeated until all the rows in the reduced table have been examined or we create a user specified maximum number of clusters, at which point the initial cluster hierarchy has been created. The next step in the algorithm is to assign the web pages to clusters in the hierarchy. In general there will be some similarity comparison between the terms of each web page (rows in the original table) and the terms associated with each cluster, to determine which cluster is most suitable for each web page. Once this has been accomplished, the web pages are clustered hierarchically. In the final step we remove any clusters with a number of web pages assigned to them that is below a user defined threshold and re-assign the web pages from those deleted clusters.

6.1.3 *CHCA in detail*

We will now introduce the formal notation that will be used in the detailed description of the CHCA algorithm as well as the algorithm itself. Let $\vec{a}$ be a binary vector, which is defined as a vector whose components have two possible values: 0 or 1. In other words, a vector composed of bits. $|\vec{a}|$ is defined as the number of 1 bits in the vector $\vec{a}$, *i.e.* the Hamming Weight. Let $\vec{a_i}$ and $\vec{a_j}$ be x-bit vectors, *i.e.* bit vectors with x dimensions or components. Let $\vec{a_i} \bullet \vec{a_j}$ be the bitwise (component by component) ANDing of two x-bit vectors, resulting in a new x-bit vector. $\vec{a_i} - \vec{a_j}$ is defined as $abs(|\vec{a_i}| - |\vec{a_j}|)$, where $abs(\ldots)$ is the standard absolute value operation. Let $\vec{\phi}_x$ be the bit vector of length x with all 0 entries, which is called the *empty cluster*. Let $\times$ be the standard scalar multiplication operator. Below we present the CHCA algorithm (a summary of notations and variables used in the algorithm is given in Fig. 6.1):

Step 1. Given n sets representing n entities (in the context of the current work, web pages returned by a search engine) each with attributes from a common set with m elements (the common set of terms appearing on all the pages) we create a binary membership table X with n rows and m columns. The entries in each cell of the table will be either 1 or 0. If the element j from the common set is a member of set i, then $X_{ij} = 1$; otherwise $X_{ij} = 0$. For convenience, each row of the table can be interpreted as an m-bit vector that we call a "row vector," denoted by $\vec{r}$. In this first step we are basically creating a data structure (the membership table X), which will help us describe and perform the algorithm. The table is a binary representation of the relationships between each web page and each term and is the primary input to the algorithm. The table will have a number of rows corresponding to the number of web pages and a number of columns equal to the total number of terms which appear on at least one page. If page i contains the jth term, then at row i and column j in the membership table (denoted X_{ij}) there will be a 1; otherwise there will be a 0. In the vector space model of information retrieval, this table is called a document–term matrix or an attribute matrix [GF98][MBK00]. We use the term "membership table" to clarify that this table is used for clustering and not for an information retrieval task.

Step 2. Construct a reduced membership table $\tilde{X}$ by removing duplicate row vectors, leaving only $\tilde{n}$ ($\leq n$) distinct row vectors. This new data structure $\tilde{X}$ will be used in the next step of the algorithm which actually creates the hierarchy. Since we only consider each unique row vector, we only need the smaller $\tilde{X}$ table to create the hierarchy. This step can be viewed as a pre-processing step which reduces the memory requirements and running time of the main part of the algorithm.

Step 3. Create the cluster hierarchy from $\tilde{X}$ using user provided values for parameters *MCT, MDT,* and *MPT* (which we will describe in detail after the presentation of the algorithm). The description for the procedure is as follows:

Let B, the "before set," be the set of row vectors not yet assigned to any cluster. It initially contains all the row vectors of $\tilde{X}$, namely $\{\vec{r}_1, \ldots, \vec{r}_{\tilde{n}}\}$. Set D, the "done set," is the set of clusters created by the algorithm so far. D is initially set to $\{\vec{\phi}_m\}$. While $B \neq \varnothing$ (*i.e.* nonempty, there are still candidates to process) and $|D| \leq MCT + 1$ do the following steps:

Step 3a. Let $\vec{c}$ be a row vector from set B such that for all $\vec{a}_i \in B$, $|\vec{c}| \leq |\vec{a}_i|$. In other words, $\vec{c}$, the "candidate vector," is a row vector from set B which has a minimum number of terms (1 bits). If there is more than one row with the same minimum number of terms, select one at random for $\vec{c}$.

Step 3b. Find a set of clusters $K \subseteq D$ such that $\vec{c} - \vec{d} \leq \vec{c}' - \vec{d}'$ and $\vec{c} \bullet \vec{d} = \vec{d}$ for all $\vec{d} \in K$ and $\vec{d}' \in D$. That is, determine the subset K of cluster(s) in D (*i.e.* in the existing cluster hierarchy) that are parent(s) of the candidate row vector $\vec{c}$. The parent clusters in set K must satisfy the following two conditions simultaneously:

(1) *Subsethood.* The terms of the row vector(s) in K are subsets of the terms of row $\vec{c}$. $\vec{c} \bullet \vec{d} = \vec{d}$ states that K only consists of those clusters such that the attributes of the parent clusters (those in K) are a subset of those of the child cluster. This is in-line with the notion of inheritance: the child cluster has all the terms of its parents, plus some newly defined terms. Thus a parent cluster's terms are a subset of those of its children.

(2) *Minimum Distance.* When using the vector difference operation we defined above, *i.e.* $abs(|\vec{c}| - |\vec{d}|)$, with vectors that satisfy the subsethood condition just described, the opera-

tion gives the number of terms that differ between parent and child clusters; the number of common terms is given by $|\vec{c}|$. The condition $\vec{c} - \vec{d} \leq \vec{c'} - \vec{d'}$ means the direct parents of $\vec{c}$ are those clusters that have the least "distance" (difference in terms) from the child (or, put another way, the parents of are those clusters with the most terms in common). This is needed to enforce a proper ordering among the clusters. For example, consider the following hierarchy that should nominally be created: cluster a is the parent of cluster b and cluster b is the parent of cluster c. If we do not enforce some kind of ordering, we could instead have both cluster b and c as a direct children of a, since by transitivity cluster a's attributes are a subset of both b's and c's. Further, the empty cluster $\vec{\phi}_m$ is by definition a subset (parent) of every cluster. Without this second condition we could end up with all clusters inheriting from the empty cluster and becoming base clusters. Using the minimum distance condition we attach child clusters only to their most similar parent(s).

Step 3c. If the minimum of $\vec{c} - \vec{d}$ for all $\vec{d} \in K \leq MDT$ or K contains $\vec{\phi}_m$ (*i.e.* $\vec{c}$ is a base cluster), then candidate vector becomes the child of all clusters in K by inheritance (or multiple inheritance if K has more than one element). Otherwise, skip to Step 3e. Clusters with $\vec{\phi}_m$ (the empty cluster) as a parent are base clusters. Each child cluster inherits the terms from its parent cluster(s) and adds its new terms.

Step 3d. $D = D \cup \vec{c}$. In other words, add the row vector corresponding to $\vec{c}$ to the set D (the "done set").

Step 3e. $B = B - \vec{c}$. That is, remove the row vector corresponding to $\vec{c}$ from the set B (the "before set").

Step 4. After the loop in Step 3 ends, the initial cluster hierarchy has been created. However the web pages have not yet been assigned to clusters. For each web page (row) in the original membership table X, assign the web page to a cluster using the distance measure:

$$Dist(r, i) = \frac{1}{m} \sum_{j=1}^{m} Y_{ij} \cdot (Y_{ij} - X_{rj}) \qquad (6.1)$$

where m is the number of terms (number of columns), X_{rj} is the jth term in row r of the original membership table, and Y_{ij} is the jth term of cluster i in the hierarchy (the vector corresponding to the cluster). In other words, the distance is the average number of terms in the cluster i that are missing in the web page r (the "extra" terms are ignored). If all the cluster terms appear in the page, the distance is zero. If the page contains none of the terms in the cluster, the distance attains its maximum value (1.0). Otherwise, it takes some value in $[0, 1]$ that is proportional to the compatibility of a web page and a cluster. The distance of any document to the empty cluster is zero. We assign each web page to the cluster with the smallest distance. In case of a tie, we prefer clusters with the most terms (*i.e.* those that are most specific). If we tie again on that criteria, we choose a cluster from among those tied clusters with the fewest number of assigned web pages to try to balance out the number of pages per cluster.

Step 5. Starting with the clusters farthest down in the hierarchy, remove those clusters that have a number of web pages assigned to them less than MPT. Reassign the pages from the deleted clusters to the remaining clusters. Repeat this process until no cluster has fewer than MPT pages. Give children of deleted parents updated parents using the subsethood and minimum distance criteria given in Step 3b above.

The CHCA algorithm includes 3 user specified parameters to control the results. The first parameter is a threshold for the maximum number of clusters to create (MCT, maximum cluster threshold). Without this constraint, CHCA will create a cluster for each row in the reduced membership table. However, this can be a large number of clusters, especially if the number of columns is large. So for clarity in interpreting and viewing the cluster hierarchy we limit the number of clusters to be created. Note the check is for $MCT + 1$ in Step 3 due to the fact that D contains the empty cluster in addition to the clusters created and thus its cardinality is always 1 greater than the actual number of clusters created so far. Another parameter is a maximum distance threshold between parent and child clusters (MDT, maximum distance threshold). When a new cluster is added to the hierarchy, it adds a certain number of new terms to its parent's terms (even if the cluster is a base cluster and its parent is the empty cluster). Depending on the application, we may wish to avoid adding those clusters which add too many new terms in one step (they overspecialize). For example, consider a cluster with 2 terms: A, B. There are two possible child clusters of this cluster: one with terms A, B, C and one with terms A, B, D, E, G, H, K. The distance between the former and its parent is 1 term. The distance between the latter and its parent is 5 terms. By changing this parameter we can control the size of the "jumps" we wish to allow (base clusters are exempt from the check). The final parameter is the minimum allowed pages per cluster (*MPT*, minimum pages threshold). It may be that some clusters are initially assigned only a few web pages. The minimum pages threshold allows us to specify the minimum number of pages a cluster should have. If after creating the hierarchy there are clusters that are assigned less than this number of pages, we delete those clusters, starting with the clusters at the lowest levels of the hierarchy. As we delete each cluster that has less than *MPT* pages, we reassign the deleted cluster's web pages using the same method just described in Step 4. After all the clusters with a number of pages below *MPT* are deleted, we update the hierarchy structure by giving parents to orphaned clusters whose original parents were deleted, using the same method as in Step 3b.

Each cluster has associated with it a bit vector, which indicates its related terms. When we display the topic (label) of each cluster in the hierarchy to the user, we print out the list of corresponding terms which have a 1 bit for that cluster's vector; *e.g.* if cluster 5 has a 1 bit at columns 17 and 24, we print out the terms associated with columns 17 and 24 when displaying cluster 5. The terms are printed in alphabetical order, since no ordering information is preserved in the vector representation (*i.e.* we do not know which term comes first on a given web page). Later, we will show how GHCA uses graphs to preserve the ordering information.

We will now discuss the computational complexity of the algorithm. n is the number of rows in the original membership table (the number of web pages) and m is the number of columns (the total number of terms). Note that the worst case occurs when the reduced membership table and the original table are identical in size ($n = \tilde{n}$). We start with Step 2, as Step 1 is basically a description of how to prepare the input to CHCA. For Step 2, the complexity is $O(n^2 m)$. This is due to the fact that we need to compare each of the n vectors with the others, and each comparison consists of checking m bits of the vector. In Step 3a, the complexity of a single iteration is $O(nm)$, since we check m bits each in at most n vectors in the worst case. For Step 3b, it is $O(nm)$ for a single iteration. Steps 3c, 3d, and 3e are each $O(1)$. Step 3 is executed n times in the worst case (when $MCT \geq n$), thus the overall complexity for Step 3 in $O(n^2 m)$. For Step 4, we have $O(n^2 m)$ for the worst case, since the distance measure will make comparisons for all m vector components. For Step 5, we have a maximum of n checks or deletions of clusters (since the maximum number of clusters in the worst case is n). Each deletion requires the reassignment of at most $O(MPT) = O(1)$ web pages, which in turn requires $O(nm)$ computations. So the overall complexity for Step 5 is $O(n^2m)$. Thus the time complexity for CHCA is $O(n^2m)$ in the worst case.

Table 6.1   Simple example to illustrate concepts of CHCA.

	Has High Performance Engine	Works on Land	Can Fly	Floats
BOAT	0	0	0	1
SPEED BOAT	1	0	0	1
CAR	0	1	0	0
RACE CAR	1	1	0	0

6.1.4   *CHCA: An example*

A simple example is in order to clarify the ideas and terminology of CHCA that we introduced above. The following is just a general example of creating the hierarchy and is not necessarily related to processing web search results. For brevity we will omit the steps which deal with assigning web pages to clusters (Step 4 and Step 5); this is an example of creating a cluster hierarchy only. For this example, let us consider the domain of vehicles. The membership table X for this example is given in Table 6.1. Here we have 4 entities ($n = 4$ rows): BOAT, SPEED BOAT, CAR, and RACE CAR. We also have 4 possible attributes that each entity could have, and thus $m = 4$ columns. In this case, each row is unique and thus there is no reduced membership table (it is already reduced). Assume $MCT = 4$ and $MDT = 4$.

We initialize B as the set of row vectors of $\tilde{X}$, $B = \{[0001], [1001], [0100], [1100]\}$ and set $D = \{\vec{\phi}_4 = \{[0000]\}$. Next we select the row vector from B with the minimum Hamming Weight, which is either BOAT [0001] or CAR [0100] since both have a weight of 1, to be the new candidate vector $\vec{c}$. Since there is a tie, we arbitrarily select BOAT, so $\vec{c} = [0001]$. After that we determine which clusters in D can be parents of $\vec{c}$. So far there is only element in D, the empty cluster [0000]. Thus BOAT becomes a base cluster since the empty cluster is its parent, and we update B and D by adding $\vec{c}$ to D and removing it from B. Note that we skip the distance (MDT) check since $\vec{c}$ is a base cluster (*i.e.* K contains $\vec{\phi}_4$). B is now $\{[1001], [0100], [1100]\}$ and D is updated to $\{[0000], [0001]\}$.

We repeat the process since B is not empty and $|D| = 2 < MCT + 1$. We will select CAR [0100] since it has minimum weight. It will also be a base cluster and now $B = \{[1001], [1100]\}$ and $D = \{[0000], [0001], [0100]\}$. Another iteration through the loop, we can select either SPEED BOAT or RACE CAR from B since their weights are equal at 2. We choose SPEED BOAT. This time, K will be $\{[0001]\}$ as [0001] is the subset of [1001] that has minimum distance: $[1001] - [0001] = 1$ whereas $[1001] - [0000] = 2$. Thus the cluster SPEED BOAT becomes the child of the cluster BOAT, since the distance (1) is less than MDT (4). The algorithm performs one more iteration and the resulting cluster hierarchy is shown in Fig. 6.2. The results seem intuitive: a hierarchy where we move from the general cases to the specific as we travel downwards has been created.

In Sec. 6.2, we will describe some important implementation details of our web search processing system. In order to get good results in our application we have added another parameter related to pre-processing the input to CHCA. We will discuss this parameter as well as the values we selected for MCT, MDT, and MPT for our application in the next section.

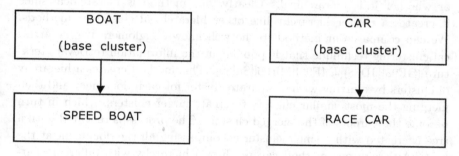

Fig. 6.2   Cluster hierarchy created from the example in Table 6.1.

6.1.5   *Examination of CHCA as a clustering method*

In Refs. [JD88][JMF99], Jain *et al.* give various characteristics which all clustering methods have, in order to differentiate and classify them. In this sub-section we will attempt to classify our clustering algorithm, CHCA, using those criteria. We will also mention clustering algorithms which are similar to CHCA that have been reported in the literature.

The first criteria is whether CHCA is exclusive or non-exclusive. Exclusive means each object belongs to exactly one cluster. Non-exclusive means an object can belong to more than one cluster. As we have described the actual implementation above, CHCA is exclusive. However, it need not be, as the cluster hierarchy creation process is separate from the process that assigns web pages to clusters. We could easily assign a page to more than one cluster, for example, if the distance measure between the page and several clusters were equal. In fact, the graph-based extension of CHCA, GHCA, which we introduce later is non-exclusive. The best we can say on the subject is that it is implementation specific: CHCA is neither specifically exclusive or non-exclusive.

The next issue is whether our method is intrinsic or extrinsic. Intrinsic means the clustering method is unsupervised, whereas extrinsic implies the method learns from prepared examples. CHCA is clearly an intrinsic method as we do not provide labeled training examples. The algorithm clusters only on the basis of the data provided. Indeed, with the Internet comprising nearly every subject imaginable it is intractable to create training sets for them all.

Another important issue is whether CHCA is a partitional method, or whether it is hierarchical. Clearly, our method is hierarchical since it creates a cluster hierarchy like other hierarchical clustering methods. We can compare our method to the well known agglomerative hierarchical clustering technique that is popular in the information retrieval literature [GF98][JD88][JMF99][Mir96][Sal89]. This method creates a hierarchy of clusters by starting with a separate cluster for each document and then merging the most similar clusters to create larger clusters, which in turn become the parents of the merged clusters. The process is repeated until a tree is created with a single cluster encompassing all the document at the root. Although our method can produce a hierarchy with different characteristics than the agglomerative method (*e.g.* we allow for multiple root nodes and for multiple inheritance), the graphical interpretation of the resulting hierarchy structure is the same as in the agglomerative hierarchical method. Nodes in the hierarchy are either clusters or the objects that are being clustered (web pages). Web pages appear only as leaf nodes, while the internal nodes are clusters. Links indicate a parent/child relationship (in the case both nodes are clusters) or a "belongs to" relationship (where one node is a web page). In our method we allow a child cluster to have more than one parent, unlike the agglomerative method where every child cluster has exactly one parent. Similarly, if we allow documents to be linked to more than one cluster we arrive at the non-exclusive version of the algorithm. There are also divisive hierarchical clustering algorithms. In those approaches, all objects start out in a single cluster. The idea is to split large clusters into smaller clusters, forming a hierarchy. However, in the literature the agglomerative method is most prevalent.

CHCA cannot be classified as either agglomerative or divisive, since we neither split or join clusters. Instead we should consider CHCA as an iterative method, as it constructs the hierarchy by adding new clusters one at a time (see Ref. [Gor96]). It is important to note the difference between conventional hierarchical clustering methods and CHCA in terms of the information provided by the hierarchy that is created. With conventionally created hierarchies, a measure of similarity (such as a distance measure) is used to compare the objects in clusters in order to determine when clusters should be merged into a parent or split into children. This leads to a hierarchy whose characteristic is differentiation between siblings (children of the same cluster). The information imparted by such a hierarchy is the series of nested partitionings which indicate the clustering of the objects and their nesting order. In comparison, CHCA uses the idea of inheritance to create the parent/child relationship. A child cluster must contain all the attributes of its parent. This is different from the notion of similarity used in the conventionally created hierarchies. Thus, the characteristic of a cluster hierarchy created by CHCA is that child clusters are specializations of their parents. In other words, a child cluster contains all the attributes of its parent in addition to other attributes which distinguish it from its parents and siblings. Conversely, parent clusters are generalizations of their children: they contain a subset of the child's essential attributes. The information conveyed by an hierarchy created by CHCA includes which clusters are specializations or generalizations of others (the parent/child relationship), which clusters share a common set of elements but also have other differences (the sibling relationship), which terms are most general (those shared between parents and children), and which terms are used to differentiate and specialize the clusters (those terms found in children but not parents).

A similar method of determining parents through subsets of terms is also used in the MSEEC system [HKN99]. One of the main differences between that method and CHCA is that we allow for multiple inheritance (multiple parents) whereas MSEEC uses trees (single parents). Thus MSEEC must break ties for multiple valid parents, which it does by selecting the cluster with the most documents assigned. The other phases of MSEEC, such as controlling the number of clusters and generating their associated terms are quite different from ours (*e.g.* we eliminate small clusters and re-assign the documents whereas MSEEC merges similar clusters). The STC method used in Carrot[2] [SW03] and Grouper [ZE98] also arranges terms in a tree like structure from general (less terms) to specific (more terms). However, STC creates a purely partitional clustering, not a hierarchical one. Collocation networks [MV03] are another similar method for extracting terms and their relationships from documents; this method uses frequency of term occurrence and mutual information (see Sec. 4.2) to generate a visualization of a document.

A method similar to CHCA, but which has not been used for web mining, is the hierarchical biclustering HICLAS system described in Ref. [BR88][RMB96]. Like CHCA, HICLAS performs hierarchical clustering on a matrix with binary entries. It also uses the set theoretic notion of subsets to order the clusters, just as CHCA does. But there are several important differences between HICLAS and CHCA. The first difference is that HICLAS performs a sequence of Boolean decompositions on binary matrices in order to create cluster hierarchies. Thus HICLAS is more akin to a direct optimization approach, as it is attempting to optimize the "goodness of fit" of the created hierarchy on the input data [Gor96]. In contrast, CHCA is an iterative approach, as discussed above. A second difference is HICLAS creates two separate cluster hierarchies, one for the objects (rows) and one for the attributes (columns), and then associates clusters in these two hierarchies. CHCA creates a single cluster hierarchy in terms of the attributes (terms) into which objects (web pages) are classified. By assigning web pages to clusters (groups of terms) we are in effect creating a hierarchy incorporating both the terms themselves (the clusters) and the web pages. The hierarchy of terms (*i.e.* the cluster hierarchy) is created directly in Step 3 of the algorithm, and the hierarchy of web pages is created indirectly by assigning them to clusters in Steps 4 and 5. A third difference is that the subset ordering in our approach is the reverse of the one used in HICLAS. In CHCA, the top level clusters have the fewest associated attributes (*i.e.* are most general) while those in the lower levels have more; in HICLAS, the top level clusters have the most attributes (*i.e.* are most specific). CHCA is more in line with the inheritance paradigm, as we discussed above in Sec. 6.1.1.

In summary, CHCA is an intrinsic, iterative, hierarchical clustering method which can be either exclusive or non-exclusive (depending on the implementation) and uses the idea of inheritance rather than a traditional measure of similarity to create the cluster hierarchy.

6.2 Application of CHCA to Search Results Processing

With the explosion of content on the Internet it is becoming increasingly more difficult for users to find the exact pages containing the information they want to view. Conventional search engines can return hundreds or thousands of pages for a single query. Clearly it is not a good use of the user's time to manually sift through all of the results [KKL+00][ZE98]. Our approach to improving this situation is to perform an unsupervised hierarchical clustering of the pages returned by a conventional search engine and organize the topics related to the search in a hierarchy. We note that supervised classification methods are difficult to use for web searches due to the fact that the number of topics (clusters) on the web is very large and highly dynamic and such systems require prior training on a known group of topics. This is one of the reasons we use CHCA for web search clustering, as it is unsupervised and does not require training examples. CHCA has the further benefit that it provides several parameters which allow the user to tailor the characteristics of the hierarchy that is created to a given application. For our web search processing system, we used these parameters to keep the size of the hierarchy and number of pages in each cluster reasonable.

In this section we will describe the important implementation details of our search system.

6.2.1 *Asynchronous search*

The system that we have created for processing the search results returned by a search engine performs what we call asynchronous search. Unlike most conventional search engines which return a ranked list of documents which match the query within a few seconds, our system works by handling the search and processing off-line. The user submits his query and then is immediately free to go and perform other tasks. Once the search results have been processed the user is notified by e-mail and can view them at his or her leisure. Even though conventional search engines return results quickly, the user is often required to spend time browsing through the results, perhaps having to re-query in order to properly focus the search (*e.g.* from "Amazon" to "Amazon rain forest"). The main benefit to performing an asynchronous search over the conventional method is that, because users do not have to keep an active connection once a request is submitted, the system can perform some time consuming processing to improve the results since they are not required right away. The user is not kept waiting for a response and he can perform whatever other tasks he wishes while the request is being processed. Thus asynchronous search makes the best use of the user's time: he or she is not kept waiting while the results are processed and he or she is able to work with the results more efficiently when they are available. In addition, the e-mail with a link to the search results can be saved by the user and revisited at a later time; the results are not lost once the user exits the browser or switches to a different computer.

6.2.2   *Implementation, input preparation and pre-processing*

The basic operation of our system is as follows. First, the user submits a query request to the system via a web form. The request is eventually picked up by our system which in turn queries a standard web search engine (by default we used Google [Goo]) for web pages matching the user's query. Using the description and title information returned by the search engine or the full text of the web page itself obtained by downloading each URL, we create a list of terms associated with each page. The list of terms associated with each page is used to create the membership table (Step 1 in the CHCA algorithm), which is reduced (Step 2) and passed on to a program that performs the rest of the CHCA algorithm: it creates a cluster hierarchy (Step 3) and assigns each page to a cluster (Step 4). Finally the clusters with small numbers of pages are removed (Step 5). The user is e-mailed with a URL where he can review the results of the algorithm.

By parsing the full text or the description and title of each URL we generate a list of terms which appear on each web page. This is equivalent to creating a row vector in the membership table for each accessible URL. However, the number of columns in the membership table is equal to the number of unique terms encountered over all of the pages. This can be a huge number (thousands), so to both ease memory requirements and speed processing we reduce the number of terms (columns) to a fixed threshold, called MTT (Maximum Term Threshold). The terms that are selected are those that appeared on the largest number of pages. After examining experimental results, we chose a 30 term threshold. This essentially makes the time complexity of CHCA for this implementation $O(n^2)$ since m is now a constant (recall that n is the number of web pages and m is the number of terms). We note here that in our original system we downloaded and parsed the entire HTML of each page. Using only the description and title "snippets" provided by the search engine, the system produces results much more quickly.

6.2.3   *Selection of parameters for web search*

Previously we described the three user defined parameters used in CHCA, MCT, MDT, and MPT, which are used to change the characteristics of the created hierarchy. However we have not yet given what values we have used for them in our web application. We performed many experiments with these parameters (as well as MTT) in order to determine values which produce reasonable results over a variety of searches. From our experimental results we chose to limit the number of clusters (MCT) at 100. This may seem too high, but it turns out the number of clusters created is small (about 10–20), due to reasons we will explain in a moment. From experimental results, we chose a distance threshold (MDT) of 2 and chose an MPT of 5 pages per cluster.

By setting the MCT to 100, we are essentially allowing up to 100 clusters to be created. The distance threshold, MDT, further limits the number of potential clusters. A larger minimum page per cluster threshold, MPT, causes the hierarchy to be pruned of more clusters, eventually resulting in usually about 10 to 20 reasonably sized clusters for our chosen MCT. A plot of the average number of clusters created (taken over the variation of the other parameters for a fixed set of values) as a function of MCT for three separate queries (specified in the legend) that illustrates the relationship is given in Fig. 6.3. A similar plot for MPT is given in Fig. 6.4. Note that for these graphs the MCT assumes a maximum value of 40.

It is worth noting that the parameters, once set to values which produced acceptable hierarchies, do not need to be changed for each query. In our experiments, the choice of search engine(s) has a greater interaction with the parameters than the topic of the query. This is due to the fact that different search engines return varying amounts of results (pages) as well as varying sizes and types of snippets from which to extract the term list of each result.

6.3   Examples of Results

In this section we present examples of cluster hierarchies produced by our method and compare them with the output of other systems which cluster

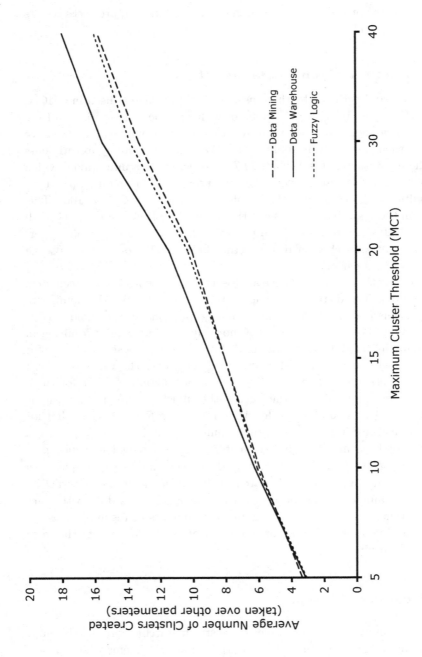

Fig. 6.3   Average number of clusters created as a function of Maximum Cluster Threshold (*MCT*) for three queries.

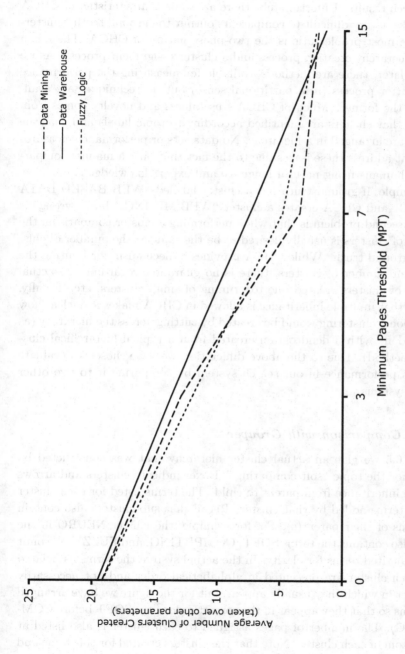

Fig. 6.4 Average number of clusters created as a function of Minimum Pages Threshold (*MPT*) for three queries.

web search results. Unfortunately, there are some characteristics of CHCA that make it very difficult to compare its output to "ground truth" clustering. The most problematic is the two-phase nature of CHCA. There is a cluster hierarchy creation process and a cluster assignment process. As we will see later, there are methods available for measuring the performance of the latter process (in a partitional sense) but no techniques are available for the former. Much of CHCA's usefulness and novelty comes from the fact that clusters are identified according to topic labels and that the clusters are arranged in a hierarchy. No data sets or performance measures exist that address these issues due to the fact that only a manual comparison by humans using natural language and expert knowledge can suffice. For example, if ground truth has a cluster labeled "WEB BASED DATA MINING" and CHCA creates a cluster "WEB MINING," how "wrong" is this? A second problem is that when performing a cluster comparison, the number of clusters is usually desired to be the same as the number of clusters in ground truth. While CHCA provides a mechanism for limiting the maximum number of clusters, there is no guarantee regarding the actual number of clusters created due to pruning of small clusters, etc. Finally, the fact that multiple inheritance is allowed in CHCA makes it unclear how a partitional clustering would be created by cutting across the hierarchy (as can be done with a dendrogram created from a typical hierarchical clustering method). Due to the above difficulties, we have chosen to evaluate CHCA's performance in our search system by comparing it to two other similar systems.

6.3.1   *Comparison with Grouper*

In Fig. 6.5 we give an actual cluster hierarchy that was constructed by CHCA for the topic "soft computing." Boxes indicate clusters and arrows indicate inheritance from parent to child. The terms listed for each cluster are the terms added by that cluster. Recall that sub-clusters also contain the terms of their parent(s). So, for example, the cluster NEURO in the figure also contains the terms SOFT, COMPUTING, and FUZZY. We omit these inherited terms for clarity. In the actual system the terms associated with each cluster are presented in alphabetical order and not necessarily the order in which they usually appear, but for the figure we have arranged the terms so that they appear in the correct order (*e.g.* SOFT before COMPUTING). The number of pages assigned to each cluster is also listed at the bottom of each cluster. Note that the clusters created for this topic and the hierarchy itself are quite reasonable. We should mention that the WSC term used in one of the clusters is the World Conference on Soft Computing and Engineering Design and Manufacturing, abbreviated to WSC.

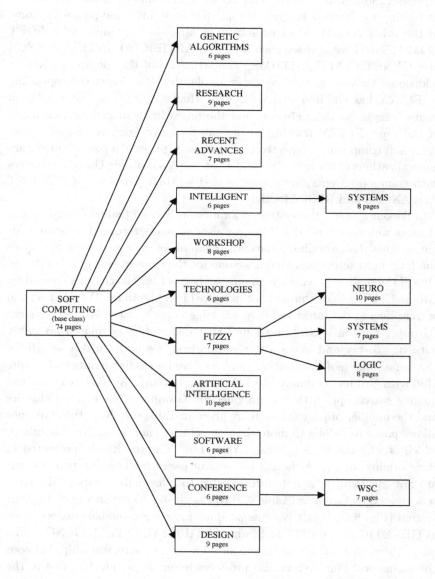

Fig. 6.5   Cluster hierarchy created by CHCA for the query "soft computing."

This cluster hierarchy is a knowledge representation about a domain (*i.e.* the topic specified by the query, soft computing) induced from data. So in essence we have performed a web mining task in creating this knowledge representation. But what exactly do we gain from the cluster hierarchy? One thing we discover is, given a topic (query string) as input, what some of the other related topics or sub-topics are. For example, with SOFT COMPUTING we also see such topics as ARTIFICIAL INTELLIGENCE and GENETIC ALGORITHMS. The structure of the hierarchy gives us additional knowledge. We see, for example, that the cluster corresponding to FUZZY has children such as LOGIC (fuzzy logic) and NEURO (as in neuro-fuzzy). So these clusters and the pages in them are specializations of the topic FUZZY relating to the sub-topics of fuzzy logic and neuro-fuzzy soft computing, respectively. Conversely, pages of a parent cluster are generalizations of those in the child clusters. Also, sibling clusters (clusters with common parents) are topics related by their parents (*e.g.* RECENT ADVANCES and RESEARCH).

Like our system, the system of Zamir and Etzioni (called Grouper) also clusters web search results. Grouper uses snippets returned by search engines rather than examining the entire contents of the web documents, so we similarly used snippets with our system for the experiments in this section. One of the main differences with our method is that the clusters created by Grouper's STC algorithm are not arranged in a hierarchy. We tried several searches using the latest publicly available version of the Grouper system (Grouper Custom) [Gro] and found that our system compared favorably with it. To try and make a fair comparison, we performed a search for the same topic (soft computing) and retrieved a similar number of results (186 with Grouper compared to 194 for our system). We also used the best quality search option that is provided by Grouper. The created clusters and the number of pages in each are given in Table 6.2. Note that Grouper allows pages to belong to more than one cluster (non-exclusive clustering), which is why the total is greater than 186. The results are presented in their original order. Although the sets of pages used by the two systems are not identical, it is not unreasonable to informally compare the clusters created by Grouper (Table 6.2) to the cluster hierarchy created by our system (Fig. 6.5). Both systems produce mostly reasonable clusters, such as GENETIC ALGORITHM(S) and ARTIFICIAL INTELLIGENCE. The major difference is that our system also illustrates the relationships between these clusters. Our system also produces fewer, larger clusters due to the parameters we selected. Grouper seemingly produces too many clusters

Table 6.2   Results of the Grouper Custom system for the query "soft computing."

Cluster Title	Number of Pages in Cluster
soft computing strategies in life sciences	15
fuzzy logic	40
mammut soft computing ag banking software	12
genetic algorithm	19
artificial intelligence	20
probabilistic reasoning	14
premier on-line event on soft computing and it	5
uncertainty and partial truth	6
partial truth to achieve tractability	4
fuzzy set	12
original paper	9
data mining	8
takeshi furuhashi	6
lotfi zadeh	9
rudolf kruse	6
neuronale netze	5
drug discovery	6
computational intelligence	8
evolutionary computation	6
fuzzy control	10
pattern recognition	5
current research	7
rapport with reality	4
recent advances	5
technische universit	4
tolerance for imprecision	5
nature biotechnology	4
consortium of methodologies	4
chaos theory	5
initiative in soft computing	8
machine intelligence	6
on-line tutorial	4
drug design	5
machine learning	5
all others	83

overall (35 created by Grouper vs. 17 for our system), and some of those clusters appear irrelevant (such as DRUG DESIGN or RAPPORT WITH REALITY). The results of a search for the topic "data compression" are given for our system and Grouper in Fig. 6.6 and Table 6.3, respectively. Like the results for the other topic, our system creates fewer (35 vs. 10 clusters), larger, and generally more relevant clusters than Grouper.

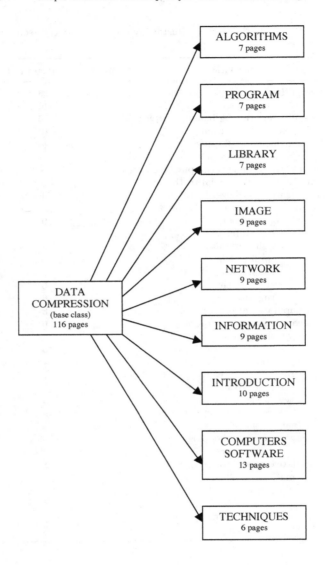

Fig. 6.6   Cluster hierarchy created by CHCA for the query "data compression."

6.3.2   *Comparison with Vivísimo*

We also compared our system with the commercial Vivísimo system [Viv], which performs a hierarchical clustering of web search results. We submitted the same 10 query strings to each system (shown in Table 6.4) and

Table 6.3   Results of the Grouper Custom system for the query "data compression."

cluster title	number of pages in cluster
data compression asp component control library bv	5
mitsuharu arimura bookmark on source data coding	4
arithmetic coding	12
mark nelson	8
mitsuhara arimura	7
huffman coding	10
video teleconference	8
audio teleconference	8
compression techniques	17
submit a url	5
dobb journal	5
compression algorithm	20
source code	7
calgary corpus	4
mobile computing	4
compression ratio	9
webopedia definition and link	4
teleconference planner	4
teleconference phones	4
signal processing	4
teleconference calling	4
lossy compression	9
teleconference service	4
fixed length	4
introduction to data	11
fewer bit	4
teleconference equipment	4
teleconference center	4
teleconference services	4
adaptive huffman	4
image compression	11
data compression library	8
original string	4
lossless data	9
all others	103

compared the resulting cluster hierarchies. The query strings reflect a wide range of topics, from air quality modeling to wedding photography (they were selected from search strings submitted by users of our system). The amount of pages clustered were roughly comparable in each case; for these experiments we used AltaVista with our system, which returned up to 200 pages. Vivísimo also returned a maximum of 200 pages from AltaVista (using the customized search option). Both systems removed duplicate results and worked with snippets (title and description) provided by the search engines in lieu of the full text of the pages. We evaluated the systems by four measurements: 1. total number of clusters created, 2. maximum hierarchy depth, 3. number of base clusters, and 4. average number of children of base clusters. The results are presented in Table 6.5. In the table, the value in the left column (C) represents our system using CHCA, and the value in the right column (V) represents Vivísimo. Vivísimo allows the user to expand the initial hierarchy by clicking on a "More" link. In our evaluation, we consider only the clusters that are initially displayed by the system. Further, Vivísimo includes unspecified clusters entitled "Other Topics"; these clusters were ignored.

Table 6.4   List of query strings used for comparison.

query	string
#1	nuclear medicine
#2	linux
#3	wedding photography
#4	nursery system
#5	pentium processor
#6	human genome project
#7	scuba diving equipment
#8	stamp collection
#9	voice recognition
#10	air quality modeling

We can make the following observations from the data and our personal experience from using the system:

(1) Vivísimo creates more clusters than our system. This can be observed directly from the total number of clusters for each query, as well as from the mean. The more clusters in the hierarchy, the more difficult it is to browse.

(2) Vivísimo always created a single base cluster, which corresponds to the topic specified by the search string. In contrast, our method creates base clusters as appropriate to each search (*i.e.* the search topic is not necessarily the root). Consider query #7, which is "scuba diving equipment." Our system created 3 base clusters for this query: "scuba," "diving," and "equipment" and then created the necessary combinations (*e.g.* "scuba diving") though multiple inheritance. This makes

Table 6.5 Summary of comparison for 10 Searches (C: CHCA, V: Vivísimo).

query	number of clusters		maximum depth		number of base clusters		avg. children per base cluster	
	C	V	C	V	C	V	C	V
#1	18	30	2	3	1	1	16	10
#2	15	18	2	2	1	1	12	10
#3	17	35	2	4	1	1	15	10
#4	17	35	2	2	10	1	0.8	10
#5	15	29	2	3	2	1	3.5	10
#6	14	51	1	3	1	1	13	10
#7	15	22	3	2	3	1	0.66	10
#8	9	25	2	2	1	1	3	10
#9	17	28	2	3	1	1	14	10
#10	12	48	3	3	5	1	0.6	10
Mean	14.9	32.1	2.1	2.7	2.6	1.0	7.86	10.0

sense since the search returned, for example, pages that contained the term "diving" but not the terms "scuba" and "diving" together. For query #4, "nursery system," our system created ten base clusters. This seems reasonable given the rather vague nature of the query; search engines returned pages on everything from health care to plants for this query. Thus, our system does not force the search topic to appear at the root (although it can appear at the root when appropriate, *e.g.* query #2 "linux"), which allows for the investigation of more general topics as well as those that are more specific.

(3) Vivísimo created a fairly constant number of children for base clusters. Recall that we did not examine all the results for Vivísimo, only the initially displayed default results. This appears to limit the number of second level clusters to a constant number.

(4) Comparing the average maximum depths from each system, we see that our method creates a shallower hierarchy than Vivísimo. Thus less "digging" to reach clusters at lower levels is required for our system.

(5) By subtracting the number of base clusters and number of children of base clusters (computed by multiplying the number of base cluster by the average number of children of base clusters) from the total number of clusters, we can derive the number of clusters residing at the lower hierarchy levels. By comparing this number with the total number of clusters and the hierarchy depth, we see that our system often placed most of the clusters at the top two levels (base clusters and their chil-

dren). On the other hand, Vivísimo had many clusters residing at the lower levels, leading to hierarchies that often produced many branches and that were very wide at the lower levels. Such hierarchies are difficult to examine since they either require much "digging" and backtracking (in the depth-first sense) or they require displaying increasingly many nodes at each level (in the breadth-first sense).

(6) Vivísimo's hierarchies were much slower to browse than those of our system. This is probably due to the fact that Vivísimo includes the pages themselves in the hierarchy display, leading to longer loading and rendering times. Our system includes only clusters in the hierarchy; pages are displayed separately.

6.4　Graph Hierarchy Construction Algorithm (GHCA)

In this section, we describe a graph-based version of CHCA, GHCA. GHCA performs clustering using graph representations of web documents rather than the binary term–vector representations we previously used for CHCA. Both the input (the web documents) and the output (the clusters) are represented by graphs. In Sec. 6.4.1 we give an explanation of the user provided algorithm parameters. In Sec. 6.4.2 we describe the pre-processing used to transform the web documents into their graph representations. We present the Graph Hierarchy Construction Algorithm (GHCA) in detail in Sec. 6.4.3.

6.4.1　*Parameters*

GHCA uses five user-provided parameters to control the properties of the resulting cluster hierarchy. Most of these are identical to the CHCA parameters, however the updated version of our system that utilizes GHCA allows the user many new options relating to these parameters. The algorithm parameters are given below, along with their default values (which were determined experimentally across a variety of different searches):

(1) MTT (Maximum Terms Threshold). This parameter restricts the maximum number of vertices in the resulting graph representations of documents. We have two options. We can use the MTT most frequently occurring terms on each page (where frequency means the number of occurrences on a given page). Or we can create a common set of the MTT most frequently occurring terms across all pages (where frequency

(PP.1) Given the set of relevant web pages provided by search engines, download the full text of each page.

(PP.2) Parse the text for each web document and create *page graphs* using the standard representation.

(PP.3) Optionally create separate small *keyword graphs* for each page based only on the *title* web document section (this is the default option).

(PP.4) Optionally remove stop words (*e.g.* "is", "the", *etc.*) from the page graphs and the keyword graphs by deleting the nodes corresponding to the stop words and their incident edges (default option).

(PP.5) Optionally perform stemming by conflating grammatical variants of terms to the most commonly occurring form (default option).

(PP.6) Perform dimensionality reduction using one of the following methods:

(a) Reduce the set of possible terms to the *MTT* terms which appear on the most pages; delete nodes not in this set and their incident edges from all graphs (default method).
(b) Reduce each graph to the *MTT* most frequently occurring terms on that page; delete the infrequently occurring nodes and their incident edges.

(PP.7) Optionally remove edges from the *page graphs* which occur infrequently (*i.e.*, less than 3 times); the default is *not* to remove edges. Note that edges will probably occur infrequently in keyword graphs, so we do not apply this option when using keyword graphs.

(PP.8) Add either the *keyword graphs* (the default) or the *page graphs* to the set of *candidate graphs*.

(PP.9) Optionally generate the maximum common subgraphs of each possible pair of *candidate graphs*, and add them to the set of candidate graphs (default option).

(PP.10) Optionally, for each candidate graph, if the graph contains at least one edge (meaning the graph contains a phrase), delete nodes with no incident edges (*i.e.* extraneous isolated nodes) from that graph, since phrases usually convey more useful information than single-word terms. If there are no phrases, the graph is left as-is (default option).

(PP.11) Remove all duplicate graphs from the set of candidate graphs, leaving only a set of unique graphs. This means that two distinct documents represented by identical graphs are assumed to be related to the same topic.

Fig. 6.7   Pre-processing phase of GHCA.

means the number of pages where a term occurs at least once). The default option is to use the 30 most frequently occurring terms across all pages.

(2) *MPT* (Minimum Pages Threshold). This parameter is used in the pruning section of GHCA by removing clusters that have fewer than MPT native pages assigned to them. The default value is 3.

(3) *MDT* (Maximum Distance Threshold). This parameter is used for restricting the growth of the hierarchy. We do not add clusters to the

hierarchy whose difference in size from their parent(s) is greater than *MDT*. As we mentioned in Chapter 3, the size of a graph is defined as the sum of the number of edges and vertices in the graph. The default value of *MDT* is 2, which is large enough to allow the addition of one new term to an existing phrase (*i.e.* one node and one edge).

(4) *MCT* (Maximum Cluster Threshold). This parameter is used to limit the overall size of the hierarchy. We stop the hierarchy construction phase of the algorithm once it has created *MCT* clusters or we have no candidate graphs remaining. The default value is 50.

(5) *BCST* (Base Cluster Size Threshold). This parameter is used to limit the size of base (top level) clusters. We do not create a new base cluster if its size exceeds *BCST*. The default value of *BCST* is 3. The default value is large enough to admit a two term phrase (*i.e.* two nodes connected by an edge) as a base cluster.

6.4.2   *Graph creation and pre-processing*

The general procedure for creating graphs from web documents and pre-processing is described in Fig. 6.7. The procedure of creating graphs from web documents is similar to what we described in Chapter 3, however some steps are now optional (such as stemming) and we create optionally a separate set of graphs based only the title section information (see Sec. 3.2).

(IHC.1) Find the candidate graph with minimum size, where the *size* of a graph G, $|G|$, is defined as the sum of the number of edges and vertices in the graph, $|V|+|E|$, and select it to be the *cluster candidate*. In case of a tie, select one of the graphs at random.

(IHC.2) Determine the possible parents of the cluster candidate in the hierarchy, such that any parents of the cluster candidate are subgraphs of the cluster candidate and the distance, defined as the difference in size between the two graphs, is minimum.

(IHC.3) If the cluster candidate is a base cluster (it has no parents in step (IHC.2)) and the size of the graph is less than or equal to *BCST*, add the cluster candidate as a base cluster in the hierarchy.

(IHC.4) If the cluster candidate is not a base cluster and the difference in size between the cluster candidate and its parent(s) is less than or equal to *MDT*, add the cluster candidate to the hierarchy.

(IHC.5) Remove the cluster candidate from the set of candidate graphs.

(IHC.6) While the number of clusters in the hierarchy is less than *MCT* and there are still candidate graphs remaining, go to step (IHC.1); otherwise, proceed to the initial document assignment phase.

Fig. 6.8   Initial hierarchy construction phase of GHCA.

6.4.3 *Graph Hierarchy Construction Algorithm (GHCA)*

Given the set of candidate graphs from the previous section, we can perform the Graph Hierarchy Construction Algorithm. The basic steps are initial hierarchy construction (Fig. 6.8), document assignment (Fig. 6.9), and bottom-up cluster pruning (Fig. 6.10.

For every page represented in the set of *page graphs*, determine what clusters in the hierarchy have the smallest distance according to the MCS distance measure.

(DA.1) If the minimum distance is 1, skip this page (go back to step DA.1).

(DA.2) Assign the page to the cluster(s) which have minimum distance as a *native page*.

(DA.3) Also assign the page to super-clusters above the clusters selected in step (DA.2) in the hierarchy as an *inherited page*; continue to propagate the inherited page up the hierarchy from child to parent until a base cluster is reached.

Fig. 6.9   Document assignment phase of GHCA.

The initial hierarchy construction procedure is given in Fig. 6.8. The purpose of this phase of GHCA is it create the initial cluster hierarchy. As mentioned in Chapter 3, the definition of size given in step IHC.1 is necessary because it may be the case that we have, for example, a cluster represented by a graph with 2 vertices and no edges (*e.g.* DATA, MINING) and a cluster represented by a graph with 2 vertices and one edge (DATA→MINING). The first cluster represents pages where the terms "data" and "mining" occur with no particular relationship on the same web document; the second represents pages where the phrase "data mining" occurs (*i.e.*, there is a more specific relationship, the terms appear adjacent to each other in the specified order). If we consider only the number of nodes in computing the size of the graph, these clusters are considered to be equally similar when calculating the distance. This is undesirable because the choice of assignment becomes arbitrary when clearly each graph represents a different concept.

After initial hierarchy construction, the document assignment phase of GHCA (Fig. 6.9) is performed. The purpose of this phase is to assign web documents to the clusters created in the initial hierarchy construction phase. The previous version of our system (described above in Sec. 6.1.3) assigned each web page to only one cluster (exclusive assignment), using tie breaking methods when the distance measures for two or more clusters were equal. We felt this was unnecessarily restrictive, so we have allowed non-exclusive assignment of pages. In addition, base clusters in the induced hierarchy of graphs will have more pages (native + inherited) assigned to them than their descendant clusters; the clusters in the bottom level will represent the most specific topics described by the fewest number of pages.

(CP.1) Starting with the lowest level in the hierarchy, delete all clusters at that level from the hierarchy that have less than *MPT native pages* assigned to them.

(CP.2) Given the new hierarchy, re-assign all the pages from the deleted clusters as described above in steps (DA.1) to (DA.3).

(CP.3) Fix orphaned clusters by updating the parent information as in step (IHC.2) of the initial hierarchy construction.

(CP.4) Repeat steps (CP.1) to (CP.3) going up one level in the hierarchy each iteration until the top level is reached.

Fig. 6.10　　Cluster pruning phase of GHCA.

After initial document assignment, the last phase of GHCA is bottom-up cluster pruning (Fig. 6.10). This removes clusters with less than *MPT* web documents assigned to them, starting with the lowest level clusters.

(R.1) For each cluster, first display the longest simple paths (acyclic paths not contained in any other acyclic paths) in the graph as ordered phrases; next show any isolated nodes as single terms.

(R.2) If the cluster is not a base cluster, show only those phrases or terms which are specific to the graph (i.e., those not displayed for a parent cluster).

Fig. 6.11　　Results display methodology for GHCA.

We use a different method of displaying the terms associated with each cluster than we used for vector-based CHCA. Since the graphs used in GHCA preserve the term ordering information, we can display phrases (groups of related terms) to the user instead of an alphabetical list of single terms for the cluster labels. In order to display the phrases and terms represented by each cluster graph to the user, we use the approach described in Fig. 6.11. For brevity in the output we omit the edge labeling information about the document sections where the terms or phrases were found.

Note that the first three phases above, initial hierarchy construction, initial document assignment, and bottom-up cluster pruning, are directly analogous to Steps 3, 4, and 5, respectively, in CHCA. The following straightforward extensions are performed to go from binary vector-based CHCA to graph-based GHCA:

(1) Instead of the size being determined by the Hamming Weight (the number of 1 bits), the size is determined by the number of nodes and edges in a graph.
(2) Instead of using a bitwise AND operation to determine the subset relationship, we determine if one graph is a subgraph of another directly through the subgraph relationship.
(3) The distance measure used to assign pages to clusters is now Eq. 2.3 rather than Eq. 6.1.

Although there are other changes between CHCA and GHCA as presented here, those are new options or refinements to the search system (such as allowing non-exclusive assignments) rather than changes to the fundamental CHCA algorithm itself. With only the three changes listed above we were able extend the algorithm to work with more complex graphs rather than the simpler bit vectors we used previously.

6.4.4 GHCA examples

In Fig. 6.12 we show the results of performing four different searches for our system with GHCA using the default parameter values and options; the searches are for "data mining" (top left), "soft computing" (top right), "graph theory" (bottom left), and "scuba diving equipment" (bottom right). The total number of pages assigned to each cluster is shown in parentheses. Sub-clusters are indicated by indentation. The phrases and terms associated with each cluster are determined using steps (R.1) and (R.2) in Fig. 6.11 above. For example, the first cluster in the "data mining" hierarchy is displayed as the phrase "data management", meaning the graph contained two nodes ("data" and "management") and an edge from "data" to "management." Distinct phrases or terms are separated by commas. Note that this is an improvement over the case of CHCA, which contained no term ordering or phrase information. Under CHCA, which ordered terms for each cluster alphabetically, we would have clusters identified as "computing soft" or "diving equipment scuba." With GHCA the correct order can be preserved: "soft computing" and "scuba diving equipment." GHCA also allows differentiation of clusters based on the phrase information; *e.g.* "DATA, MINING" is separate cluster from "DATA MINING."

6.5 Comments

In this chapter we presented a system designed to better organize the results returned by conventional web search engines. Novel hierarchical clustering algorithms called CHCA (Cluster Hierarchy Construction Algorithm) and GHCA (Graph Hierarchy Construction Algorithm) were employed to hierarchically cluster web pages by topic using the concept of inheritance. The cluster hierarchy generated by the algorithm can be viewed as a knowledge representation about the domain that has been induced from the web content data. In other words, CHCA and GHCA are web mining algorithms. By creating a cluster hierarchy from the results we are able to cluster web pages as well as determine relationships between the topics related to the search. GHCA modeled web pages as graphs, and worked directly on these representations when clustering. The additional information included ordered phrases; CHCA's vector representation had only alphabetically ordered lists of atomic terms. This allows for better differentiation among the clusters (*i.e.* whether the terms appear together as a phrase, indicating a specific relationship) and for more coherent output of cluster names (the term ordering information is preserved for cluster labels).

The results (the cluster hierarchies) from actual searches show how our system differs from other web search clustering systems. Here is a summary of the main contributions of this chapter:

(1) As shown by the examples of the system output and comparisons with similar systems, our system produces a reasonable and useful clustering of the web pages. Further, the behavior of our system is in-line with clusterings of web pages produced manually by humans when comparing full text processing to snippets.

(2) CHCA and GHCA include several parameters which allow us to direct the characteristics of the cluster hierarchy. This is important since other hierarchical clustering methods, such as the popular agglomerative hierarchical clustering algorithm, can produce very large trees which may be difficult to view and browse. With proper parameters we can achieve a hierarchy of a manageable width and depth. There are versions of the agglomerative hierarchical method that include stopping criteria, but their parameters are topic sensitive [ZE98]. In contrast, our methods' parameters are more sensitive to the search engines used and not to the topics being searched for. We found that when using different search engines we needed to modify the parameters slightly

to account for the number of pages returned and the size and content of the snippets returned by the engine. However, once we arrived at a reasonable set of parameter values for a particular search engine, the results tended to be fairly uniform across searches.

(3) We produce not just a series of nested partitionings, as in conventional hierarchical clustering methods, but a clustering with relationships that include generalization (child to parent), specialization (parent to child) and similarity (between siblings). As a result, we can make statements such as when a parent/child relationship exists, the topic of the child cluster is a specialization of the parent cluster and conversely the topic of the parent cluster is a generalization of the child cluster. Sibling clusters that share common parents are related by the topic of their common parent, *i.e.* they are different specializations of the same cluster. Hierarchies created with conventional hierarchical clustering methods such as the agglomerative and divisive approaches only give us an indication of which clusters include the objects of other clusters (the parent/child relationship) and the similarity between clusters (the sibling relationship). Further, with CHCA and GHCA we are also provided with knowledge of which terms and phrases are used to differentiate and specialize clusters. This gives us an indication of which terms or phrases are most general and how they are used to cause specialization. Such a cluster hierarchy is related to knowledge representation models like frames and semantic networks and by inducing the knowledge from the web content data in effect a web content mining task has been performed.

(4) We do not use any kind of term frequency per document measure except for pre-processing and dimensionality reduction. Thus those pages with intentionally skewed term frequencies intended to improve their ranking are treated the same as well behaved documents.

(5) CHCA and GHCA are applicable to regular text documents in addition to hypertext (linked) documents. Some web mining approaches only consider links (web structure) and thus are not applicable to text documents.

(6) Our system allows asynchronous search. This permits the user to perform other tasks while his/her request is processed and makes possible the examination of the original full content of web pages rather than the snippets stored by search engines, which may be "stale" (out of date).

```
DATA MANAGEMENT (5)

MINING INFORMATION (8)

DATA ANALYSIS (117)
    DATA MINING (117)
        DATA MINING TOOLS (114)

DECISION, PRODUCTS (4)

DATA MINING (164)
    MINING DATA (14)
    DATA MINING SOFTWARE (65)
    DATA ANALYSIS (117)
        DATA MINING TOOLS (114)
    DATA MINING GROUP (41)
    DATA MINING DATABASE (65)

DATABASE, MARKETING, MINING (31)
```

```
SOFTWARE (58)
    DESIGN SOFTWARE (6)
    COMPUTER (51)
    SOFTWARE ENGINEERING (9)
    CONTROL, PROGRAMMING (19)

COMPUTING, SYSTEMS (34)

SYSTEMS DESIGN (8)

COMPUTING, SOFT (135)
    SOFT COMPUTING (133)
        SOFT COMPUTING TECHNOLOGY (94)
        SOFT COMPUTING RESEARCH (99)

COMPUTER SCIENCE (12)

COMPUTER, COMPUTING (52)
    SOFTWARE (50)
```

```
GRAPH COLORING (36)
    GRAPH COLORING PROBLEMS (36)

GRAPH ALGORITHMS (63)
    GRAPH THEORY (63)
        THEORY GRAPH ALGORITHMS (62)

THEORY RESEARCH (7)

GRAPH, THEORY (121)
    GRAPH THEORY (121)
        GRAPH THEORY PAPERS (55)
        GRAPH MATH (57)
        SET THEORY (65)

COMPUTER SCIENCE (11)

PROBLEMS, TREES (4)

COMBINATORICS, GRAPH, MATHEMATICS (95)
    INTEREST, RESEARCH (89)

COLORING, MATHEMATICS, PROBLEMS (11)

COMBINATORICS, GRAPH, SCIENCE (23)

COLORING GRAPH (3)
```

```
SCUBA, SERVICE (14)
    SCUBA DIVING SERVICE (10)

OCEAN SCUBA DIVING (7)

SEA SCUBA DIVING (6)

SCUBA DIVING TRIPS (6)

SCUBA DIVING GEAR (19)

DIVING, SCUBA, UNDERWATER (59)
    SCUBA DIVING, UNDERWATER PHOTO (56)

SCUBA DIVING, SCUBA EQUIPMENT (35)
    SCUBA DIVING EQUIPMENT (32)

SCUBA DIVE, SCUBA DIVING (140)
    SCUBA DIVERS (138)

SCUBA DIVING, WATER DIVING (10)

SCUBA DIVING EQUIPMENT (35)
    SCUBA EQUIPMENT (32)
```

Fig. 6.12   Examples of cluster hierarchies generated by GHCA.

Chapter 7

Conclusions and Future Work

In this book we have introduced several new techniques for performing web content mining tasks when utilizing more descriptive graphs in lieu of the usual case of vector representations. Our first contribution is presenting a number of ways by which web document content can be modeled as graphs. These graph representations retain information that is usually lost when using a vector model, such as term order and document section information. We demonstrated how with careful selection of a graph representation, namely a representation with unique node labels, we can perform the graph similarity task in $O(n^2)$ time (n being the number of nodes). In general, graph similarity using maximum common subgraph is an NP-complete problem, so this is an important result that allows us to forgo sub-optimal approximation approaches and find the exact solution in polynomial time.

Another contribution of this work is far more wide reaching: we extended classical, well-known machine learning techniques, such as the k-means clustering algorithm and k-nearest neighbors classification algorithm, to allow them to work directly with graphs as data items, instead of more limited vectors. This is a major contribution because: 1. it allows for complex, structured data, such as web documents, to be represented by a more robust model that has the potential to retain information that is usually discarded when using a vector representation and 2. we can use many existing, proven machine learning algorithms with these graph representations without having to create new, specialized methods. This opens up the possibility of using a variety of different techniques with graph-based data, where previously sets of atomic (often purely numeric) data were required due to theoretical limitations. Because the extended graph-theoretical versions of these well-known algorithms do not limit the form of the graphs, they are applicable to any graph-based representation of data. Thus we can change graph representations or even application domains without reformulating the underlying algorithms.

In this book we modeled web documents as graphs and performed experiments comparing the performance of clustering and classification when using the traditional vector representation and our novel graph-based representations. We introduced six different graph representations and five graph-theoretical distance measures. Experiments were performed on three web document data sets and performance was measured using clustering performance measures as compared to ground truth, cluster validity indices (such as the Dunn index), or accuracy measured by leave-one-out (for classification procedures). Experimental results consistently show an improvement in performance over the comparable vector-based methods when using graph-based approaches. In addition, some of our experiments also showed an improvement in execution time over the vector model.

Lastly, we demonstrated a practical system that performed content-based clustering of web search results in order to allow for easier browsing by users. We showed how the system was upgraded in a straightforward manner from using vector representations to using graphs and the benefits this had for the system. Namely, term order information was retained for the cluster labels and the presence of specific phrases could be detected and used to better organize the cluster hierarchy. We also gave some implementation details of this system, examples of its output, and compared it with some similar systems.

A number of exciting avenues of future work related to graph-theoretic machine learning exist. First, other machine learning algorithms can be adapted to work with graph-based data. Second, new graph representations which may further improve performance can be envisioned. In Chapter 3 we described several different methods of representing web documents using graphs. It is possible to create other, more elaborate representations that include even more information, such as information about HTML tags or document elements such as sentences, paragraphs, sections, tables, images, lists and so forth. Future experiments may compare the performance of such representations to the results presented here. Third, as we saw earlier, multidimensional scaling combined with graphs promises to be an extremely interesting area of research. Scaling can be applied to graph-based data when using different graph representations and distance measures in order to visualize the impact each approach has. Other types of complex, structured data, such as software code, can also be visualized with this method. In addition to visualization, the Euclidean vector representation of the original data opens up the possibility of using a wide array of additional techniques on graph-based data, such as neural networks. Future experiments could compare, for example, graph-based k-means clustering performance to the performance of vector-based k-means when using the scaled graph-based data. The optimal number of dimensions to use during scaling is also an issue that needs to be addressed experimentally, as there is a trade-off between the number of dimensions and the amount of information lost during the scaling.

The work described in Sec. 5.2 is, to the knowledge of the authors, the first on classifier ensembles in the domain of structural pattern recognition. Our future work will be directed toward examining the effect of other parameters which were not considered in the experiments presented here, such as the maximum number of nodes after dimensionality reduction (m) and the number of nodes used for random node selection. We also plan to vary the number of classifiers in the ensemble over a wider ranger of values. As we saw in our experiments, examining the accuracy of the ensemble as if it were an oracle showed a significant potential improvement in performance. This is a strong motivation to look at further refining the classifier combination method. There are many other open issues to explore as well. For example, instead of random node selection, we could select nodes based on some criteria, such as their degree (*i.e.*, the number of incident edges) or a particular structural pattern they form with other nodes in the graph (chains, cliques, *etc.*). We have previously experimented with various other graph representations of web documents (Sec. 3.2), such as those that capture frequency information about the nodes and edges; using these representations in the context of ensemble classifiers will be a subject of future experiments. Ensemble performance could perhaps be further improved by analyzing the documents on which the baseline graph classifier outperformed the ensemble. We can also create different graph-based classifiers for an ensemble by changing the graph-theoretic distance measures used or through more well-known techniques such as bagging.

Finally, the methods developed here are applicable to many domains other than web document content. File directories, organizational charts, images, and networks are just some examples of domains that naturally employ graph models of data. Now that we have introduced methods that allow standard machine learning algorithms to deal with graph-based representations, these types of data can be handled directly, without having to discard the structural information in favor of a simpler vector model or create new theoretical models to deal with the particular domain.

Appendix A

Graph Examples

In this appendix we give detailed examples of creating graphs from web documents. We show several web documents, including their HTML source and view when rendered in a web browser. We also show the resulting graphs that can be created from the web page content. The documents, which are taken from the University of South Florida web site, are:

(1) Document 1: the section of the undergraduate catalog pertaining to the College of Engineering (http://www.ugs.usf.edu/catalogs/0304/enggen.htm)

(2) Document 2: a page discussing dining and meal plans at the university (http://www.usfdiningservices.com/mealplans.php)

(3) Document 3: a page describing safety issues for students studying abroad (http://web.usf.edu/iac/studyabroad/safety.htm)

Document 1, as it appears when rendered in a web browser, is given in Figs. A.1–A.8. The original HTML source code is presented in Figs. A.9–A.15. We have created a graph from this document, using the standard representation (Sec. 3.2). We did not do any dimensionality reduction by removing nodes. This graph was then exported to DOT format and rendered using GraphViz.[1] The resulting graph is too large and complex to display easily, but we show the largest connected component in Fig. A.16. Nodes with large degrees include: ENGINEER, COLLEGE, STUDENT, PROGRAM, SYSTEM, DESIGN, and COMPUTER. Because the individual nodes can not be seen clearly, we have provided close-ups of sections of Fig. A.16 in Figs. A.17–A.32. To accomplish this, we have divided Fig. A.16 into sixteen equal sections using a grid. We refer to each section as (r,c), where r gives the row of the section, and c gives the column. For example,

---

[1]http://graphviz.org

section (2,3) is the section in the third column (from the left) and second row (from the top). Thus section (1,1) is the top left corner, (1,4) is the top right, (4,1) is the bottom left, and (4,4) is the bottom right.

Similarly, we give the rendered view of document 2 in Figs. A.33 and A.34. The HTML source code of this document is presented in Figs. A.35–A.43. The graph of this document, with isolated nodes (*i.e.* those with no edges) omitted for clarity, is given in Fig. A.44. Nodes with high degree in this graph include DINING, MEMBERSHIP, SEMESTER, and OFFER.

The rendering of document 3 can be found in Figs. A.45–A.49, while the source code is located in Figs. A.50–A.56. The graph for this page, again with isolated nodes omitted for brevity, is given in Figs. A.57–A.59. An enlargement of Fig. A.57 is given in Figs. A.60 and A.61. Some nodes with a high degree in this graph include: EMBASSY, ABROAD, STATE, and USF.

USF 2003-2004 Undergraduate Catalog - Pages 147 - 148

College of Engineering

The mission of the USF College of Engineering is to continuously aspire to excellence in teaching, research and public service. The College values academic excellence, professionalism, ethics and cultural diversity among its students, staff and faculty. The College is committed to addressing the needs of its constituencies and gives careful consideration to the urban and suburban populations in our service area.

At the undergraduate level the College is committed to provide students with a strong, broad-based, fundamental engineering education as preparation for careers in industry in a global environment, and government, or as preparation for advanced studies in professional schools of engineering, science, law, business and medicine.

At the graduate level students work in close collaboration with faculty, pursuing advanced topics within their disciplines, which will result in advancements in their fields and society at large.

Utilizing the expertise of its individual and collective faculty, the College is dedicated to the development of new fundamental knowledge and processes or procedures, which will benefit all humanity. The College promotes multi-disciplinary approaches, commitment to life-long learning and awareness of societal issues, which are requisite for meeting technological challenges.

The College provides technical assistance and technology transfer to the region, state and nation. In all facets of teaching, research and service, the College emphasizes close liaison with industry and government to provide students and faculty with the skills and perspectives needed to ensure effective technological leadership.

The College of Engineering offers undergraduate and graduate programs to prepare students for a broad spectrum of professional careers in engineering. Laboratory experience as well as real-world participation in technological problem-solving is a key aspect of a professional engineer's college education. The College of Engineering, in implementing this need, augments its own modern laboratory and research facilities in close collaboration with the professional societies and the many industries in the metropolitan Tampa Bay area. The College of Engineering offers undergraduate degrees in Chemical Engineering, Civil Engineering, Computer Engineering, Computer Science, Information Systems, Electrical Engineering, Industrial Engineering, and Mechanical Engineering.

The engineering programs of the College have been developed with an emphasis on three broad aspects of engineering activity: design, research, and the operation of complex technological systems. Students who are interested in advanced design or research should pursue the 5-Year Program leading to a Master of Science degree in a designated Engineering discipline. The Engineering Accreditation Commission (EAC) of the Accreditation Board for Engineering and Technology, Inc. (ABET) has inspected and accredited the Engineering programs of the College (Chemical Engineering, Civil Engineering, Computer Engineering, Electrical Engineering, Industrial Engineering and Mechanical Engineering). The Bachelor of Science program in Computer Science is accredited by the Computing Accreditation Commission (CAC) of ABET.

The Departments and Programs section that follows contains descriptions of the engineering degrees offered by the College. The "Four Year Programs" section includes courses students need to take, beginning with

Fig. A.1 Document 1 as rendered in a web browser (page 1).

their first semester at USF, to earn the Bachelor of Science in Engineering degree.

Students interested in particular programs offered by the College of Engineering should direct their inquiries to the College of Engineering Office of Student Services (see Advising section below). Information is also available on the College's website: http://www.eng.usf.edu/.

Professional Engineering

The College of Engineering recognizes that modern engineering solutions draw on knowledge of several branches of engineering. It also recognizes that future technological and societal developments will lead to shifting of the relative emphasis on various branches of engineering, triggered by new needs or a reassessment of national goals. For this reason the College's programs include a strong engineering foundation portion, designed to equip the prospective engineer with a broad base of fundamental technical knowledge. To this foundation is added the student's specialization of sufficient depth to prepare him/her to successfully embark on a professional career.

The Bachelor of Science degrees offered in the various engineering disciplines provide the student a broad education with sufficient technical background to contribute effectively in many phases of engineering not requiring the depth of knowledge needed for advanced design or research. The baccalaureate degree is considered the minimum educational credential for participating in the engineering profession and is the first professional degree. Students interested in design and research are strongly encouraged to pursue advanced work beyond the baccalaureate either at this or other institutions. It is becoming increasingly evident that large segments of today's engineering professionals are involved in some form of post baccalaureate study. Engineers are earning advanced degrees to obtain the information and training necessary to meet effectively tomorrow's technological challenges. All are faced with the continuing problem of refurbishing and updating their information skills and most are obtaining advanced information by means of formal graduate study, seminars, special institutes and other such systems designed for this purpose. *Life-long learning is a fact in engineering practice, and graduates must be aware and committed to it.*

The Bachelor of Science degree program in a designated engineering discipline and the Master of Science degree in the same discipline may be pursued simultaneously in a program called the Five-Year Program.

Professional Registration

Students who have attained senior status, and are in good academic standing in an ABET accredited Engineering Program, are eligible to register for examinations leading to licensure as Professional Engineers. The first examination, called the Fundamentals of Engineering (FE) Exam, is offered by the Florida Board of Professional Engineers and is usually taken the semester prior to graduation. In addition to the knowledge acquired through the engineering curriculum, many students take advantage of review courses offered by the Engineering Student College Council and the College of Engineering's distance education program, FEEDS, to prepare for the Fundamentals of Engineering Examination. Registering for the FE exam during the senior year is strongly encouraged for students graduating with an engineering degree.

Preparation for Engineering

Students planning to attend USF's College of Engineering should familiarize themselves thoroughly with the College's admissions standards and requirements for their prospective program, which are more stringent than the University's minimum entrance requirements.

Fig. A.2   Document 1 as rendered in a web browser (page 2).

The high school student anticipating a career in engineering should elect the strongest academic program that is available while in high school, including four years each of English, mathematics and science (preferably including Chemistry, Physics, and Biology), as well as full programs in the social sciences and humanities.

Prospective students considering engineering at the University of South Florida who lack certain preparation in high school must elect to follow a program to overcome their deficiencies. Alternatives for these students, classified as "Pre-Engineering majors" might include preparatory coursework at the University of South Florida. As another alternative, students may wish to avail themselves of the State's system of junior/community colleges which offer a wide range of preliminary coursework; many of these schools also offer full programs in pre-engineering (first two years' coursework).

Junior/community college students planning to transfer to the University of South Florida's engineering program from a State of Florida operated college or university should follow a pre-engineering program leading to an A.A. degree. All transfer students should complete as much of the mathematics and science coursework as is available to them. *In general engineering courses taken for military training, at the lower level, or as part of an A.S. or technology degree are not transferable to the engineering programs.* Transfer students should be aware that the College expects them to meet its admission requirements listed in this section under college regulations for graduation just as it expects its own students to meet these requirements. Junior/community college students intending to pursue an engineering program at USF should contact the advisor at their institution and request a course equivalency list.

The College of Engineering can assist students who are planning to obtain an Engineering degree from the University of South Florida and who have started their studies elsewhere in formulating a sound total program. Interested students should contact the College's Office of Student Services (813/974-2684) furnishing sufficient details to permit meaningful response.

Student Computer Policy

Although it is not mandatory, the College strongly recommends acquisition of either a desktop or a laptop personal computer. Recommended computer configuration for a student to be able to run engineering applications is indicated on the College web page http://www.eng.usf.edu. For further details, contact the Associate Dean of Engineering or the Director of Engineering Computing in the College. Also see the section on "College Computing Facilities."

USF 2003-2004 Undergraduate Catalog - Pages 150 - 151

Departments and Programs

The supervision of the academic programs for the College is the function of the administrative departments together with several coordinators. Each department is responsible for specific professional programs, faculty, laboratories, and student advising.

Chemical Engineering

Undergraduate Degree Offered:

- Bachelor of Science in Chemical Engineering (B.S.C.H.)

Fig. A.3   Document 1 as rendered in a web browser (page 3).

Graduate Degrees Offered:

- Master of Science in Chemical Engineering (M.S.C.H.)
- Master in Chemical Engineering (M.C.H.E.)
- Master of Engineering (M.E.)
- Master of Science in Engineering (M.S.E.)
- Doctor of Philosophy in Chemical Engineering (Ph.D.)
- Doctor of Philosophy in Engineering Science (Ph.D.)

This department offers coursework and study in all areas fundamental to Chemical Engineering. Topics included are thermodynamics, fluid flow, heat transfer, mass transfer, separation processes, reactors, instrumentation and process control, economics, optimization, computational methods, computer aided design techniques, and process/plant design. These courses, together with mathematics, physics, chemistry, other interdisciplinary engineering fundamentals, English, and liberal arts courses, provide the basis for long-range professional progress. Because of the many professional areas available for employment to the chemical engineer, the students are also required to take a number of electives from areas such as biotechnology, materials, and environmental engineering. These electives are designed to broaden the experience, and, therefore, the employment possibilities of our graduates. The Chemical Engineering Department also offers a sequence of courses in Chemical Engineering Science, biotechnology and biomedical engineering.

A sequence of courses in the engineering aspects of biotechnology is currently available within the Chemical Engineering program. Topics include applied microbiology, fermentation, enzyme technology, cell separation technology, biomedical engineering, biomaterials, biotechnology, and biomechanics.

Civil and Environmental Engineering

Undergraduate Degree Offered:

- Bachelor of Science in Civil Engineering (B.S.C.E.)

Graduate Degrees Offered:

- Master of Science in Civil Engineering (M.S.C.E.)
- Master or Science in Engineering (M.S.E.)
- Master of Science in Environmental Engineering (M.S.E.V.)
- Master of Civil Engineering (M.C.E.)
- Master of Engineering (M.E.)
- Master of Environmental Engineering (M.E.V.E.)
- Doctor of Philosophy in Civil Engineering (Ph.D.)
- Doctor of Philosophy in Engineering Science (Ph.D.)

This department offers course work and study pertinent to Civil Engineering, Engineering Mechanics, Material Science, and Environmental Engineering. Areas of concentration are structural engineering, engineering mechanics, geotechnical engineering, transportation engineering, water resources engineering, materials and corrosion engineering, and environmental engineering.

Students completing the program may enter the profession as engineers in civil, structural, geotechnical, transportation, water resources, environmental, hydraulics, or materials disciplines. All of these disciplines share the need for knowledge in the areas of engineering mechanics, civil engineering, material science, and environmental engineering. Through choice of the proper area of concentration, a student has the

Fig. A.4   Document 1 as rendered in a web browser (page 4).

opportunity to channel academic studies specifically towards his/her career choice.

Graduates of the program may commence their engineering careers in either industry, engineering consulting firms, or public service at the federal, state, or local level. Initial assignments may include planning, design and implementation of water resources systems; planning and design of transportation and housing systems; regional planning, design, and management for abatement of air, water and solid waste pollution problems; design of bridges and single and multistory structures; and supervision of construction projects.

Computer Science and Engineering

Undergraduate Degrees Offered:

- Bachelor of Science in Computer Engineering (B.S.Cp.E.)
- Bachelor of Science in Computer Science (B.S.C.S)
- Bachelor of Science in Information Systems (B.S.I.S)

Graduate Degrees Offered:

- Master of Science in Computer Science (M.S.C.S)
- Master of Science in Computer Engineering (M.S.Cp.E.)
- Doctor of Philosophy in Computer Science and Engineering (Ph.D.)
- Doctor of Philosophy in Engineering Science (Ph.D.)

This department offers coursework and study in all areas fundamental to Computer Science, Computer Engineering, and Information Systems. Topics dealt with are computer architecture and hardware design, software engineering, computer system organization, operating systems, algorithms and data structures, computer graphics, user interface, software testing, computer networks, database systems, robotics, theory of computation and artificial intelligence.

Our research areas of faculty concentration are 1) computer architecture and VLSI design/testing, 2) artificial intelligence and robotics, 3) graphics/image processing/computer vision, and 4) networks, 5) software testing.

Computing facilities available to students in the Department include several microprocessor and design laboratories for hardware-oriented studies, personal computer laboratories for general use in programming assignments, and networked SUN workstations for use by majors. The Department maintains a number of research laboratories equipped with special purpose hardware. In addition, the Department has access to a large IBM mainframe facility run by the University Computing Center.

Electrical Engineering

Undergraduate Degree Offered:

- Bachelor of Science in Electrical Engineering (B.S.E.E.)

Graduate Degrees Offered:

- Master of Science in Electrical Engineering (M.S.E.E.)
- Master of Engineering (M.E.)
- Master of Science in Engineering (M.S.E.)

Fig. A.5   Document 1 as rendered in a web browser (page 5).

- Master of Science in Engineering Science (M.S.E.S)
- Doctor of Philosophy in Electrical Engineering (Ph.D).
- Doctor of Philosophy in Engineering Science (Ph.D.)

This department offers study in all areas fundamental to Electrical Engineering and the electrical sciences: circuit analysis and design, electronics, communications, electromagnetics, controls, solid state, system analysis, digital circuit design, microelectromechanical systems (MEMS) and the like. Basic concepts are augmented with well-equipped laboratories in circuits, electronics, digital systems, microwave techniques, wireless circuits & systems, and controls and communications. In addition, a general-purpose computer facility, a microprocessor and digital signal processing laboratory, and a microelectronics fabrication, design/test and metrology laboratory are available to undergraduate and graduate students.

Industrial and Management Systems Engineering

Undergraduate Degree Offered:

- Bachelor of Science in Industrial Engineering (B.S.I.E.)

Graduate Degrees Offered:

- Master of Science in Industrial Engineering (M.S.I.E.)
- Master of Engineering (M.E.)
- Master of Science in Engineering Science (M.S.E.S.)
- Master of Science in Engineering Management (M.S.E.M)
- Master of Industrial Engineering (M.I.E.)
- Doctor of Philosophy in Industrial Engineering (Ph.D.)
- Doctor of Philosophy in Engineering Science (Ph.D.)

This department offers study pertinent to the design, evaluation and operation of a variety of industrial systems, ranging from the analysis of public systems to the operation of manufacturing plants. Topics include production planning and control, production and plant design, applied statistics, operations research, human factors and productivity, manufacturing, and automation. The department has excellent laboratory facilities which support class projects and research in microcomputer applications, computer-aided manufacturing, human performance, automation, and applications of robotics. Evening and off-campus programs are available through the Master of Science in Engineering Management (M.S.E.M.) program. The department also administers the manufacturing option in the M.S.E. program.

Mechanical Engineering

Undergraduate Degree Offered:

- Bachelor of Science in Mechanical Engineering (B.S.M.E.)

Graduate Degrees Offered:

- Master of Mechanical Engineering (M.M.E.)
- Master of Science in Mechanical Engineering (M.S.M.E.)
- Master of Engineering (M.E.)
- Master of Science in Engineering (M.S.E.)
- Doctor of Philosophy in Mechanical Engineering (Ph.D.)
- Doctor of Philosophy in Engineering Science (Ph.D.)

Fig. A.6   Document 1 as rendered in a web browser (page 6).

Coursework includes basic science and mathematics, thermal and fluid sciences, material science, solid mechanics, dynamics, machine design, vibrations, instrumentation and control.

Graduates of this program are employed in research, design, production, marketing, service, installation (contracting), maintenance and operation in such industries as mining, petroleum, paper, food, power, manufacturing, air-conditioning, defense systems, aerospace, data processing, communications, and automotive.

Laboratories are available for basic instrumentation, thermal and fluid sciences, solid mechanics, data acquisition and control, CAD/CAE, vibrations, and aerodynamics.

USF 2003-2004 Undergraduate Catalog - Pages 164 - 165

Computer Service (SC) Courses

These courses marked SC are specifically designed for the non-engineering student.

Recognizing that the general purpose digital computer has made significant contributions to the advancement of all elements of the academic community and that it will have an ever greater impact in the future, the College of Engineering offers several levels of credit coursework, both undergraduate and graduate, to serve students of all colleges in order that they may be prepared to meet the computer challenge.

Computer-oriented courses are offered in two broad categories: (1) those courses which are concerned with the operation, organization and programming of computers and computer systems from the viewpoint of examining the fundamental principles involved in computer usage; and (2) those courses which are concerned with computer applications to a variety of different disciplines, by means of user-oriented-languages such as FORTRAN, COBOL, BASIC, "C," "C++", JAVA, and VISUAL BASIC.

Students in engineering, the physical sciences, and mathematics must consult their advisor for suitable computer courses, since these courses are not acceptable to a number of degree programs.

College Computing Facilities

The College provides access to centralized computing facilities to undergraduate and graduate students. Most engineering departments also provide students with local facilities. The University is an Internet2 site and links are available to directly connect to all major supercomputing centers in the country.

The College provides enterprise level servers for computing, mail, file, web and database services for students and faculty. The College operates teaching and open-access labs for student use. These labs are equipped with large number of modern (Dell) PCs using Windows 2000 operating system and Unix workstations (Sun Ultra 5). All lab computers have all of the necessary software required for coursework as well as other standard productivity software. The College also supports a state-of-the-art multimedia lab with document scanners and CD-ROM burner.

Standard programming languages such as FORTRAN, Basic, Pascal, C, C++ and Java are provided on these machines. General-purpose software such as Office 2000, MS visual studio and specialized engineering software including mathematical packages (MathCad, Matlab, Maple, Macsyma, TK Solver), statistical package (SAS), discipline specific application packages such as Abaqus, Ansys, ARENA, Aspen, Cadence

Fig. A.7   Document 1 as rendered in a web browser (page 7).

and Labview are provided on Unix and Windows 2000 platforms on the network and in the labs. Several database management system software packages such as Oracle 8i, MySQL, MSSQL 8 and MS Access are available for classwork. Multi-media software packages such as MS FrontPage, Adobe Acrobat, Illustrator, Photoshop, Omni Page Pro, Paint Shop Pro, Macromedia Dreamweaver and Flash are available in the multi-media lab. The university has also entered an agreement with Microsoft Corporation for upgrade of standard office application, development tools and desktop operating systems.

The college-wide Ethernet network is connected to the USF campus-wide Gigabit Ethernet backbone. Within the College connections are provided to laboratories via 100 Mbps Ethernet. The university's Internet2 connection links it to more than 150 major universities and research institutions in the nation. Dial-in access is available to students from a large USF modem bank as well as through broadband connection. The distance learning (FEEDS) studios provide computer demonstrations for remote classes through the network. Additionally, most departments operate discipline specific computing lab(s).

Cooperative Education and Internship Programs

A wide variety of industries and government agencies have established cooperative programs for engineering students to provide them the opportunity to become familiar with the practical aspects of industrial operations and engineering careers. Students in the Career Resource Center's Cooperative Education (Co-op) program may alternate periods of paid employment in their major field with like periods of study, or may elect to participate in part-time employment while attending classes every semester. Students following the Co-op program usually encounter no problems in scheduling their program, since required Social Science and Humanities, Mathematics and Science, and Engineering Common courses are offered every semester. Students normally apply for participation in this program during their sophomore year and pursue actual Co-op employment during their sophomore and junior years. The senior year is generally pursued on a full-time study basis, since many specialization courses are not offered every semester. The students receive a Cooperative Education Certificate upon successful completion of a minimum of two work assignments.

Army, Air Force & Navy R.O.T.C. For Engineering Students

The Engineering curriculum, coupled with involvement in the Army, Air Force or Navy R.O.T.C. program, will require a minimum of five (5) years to complete the degree. R.O.T.C. cadets must take additional hours in either military science or aerospace studies. Additionally, summer training programs are scheduled, usually between the junior and senior years.

| Top | Engineering Program Listing | Catalog Table of Contents | Index |

Please send questions or comments to:
Karen M. Hall - webCat@ugs.usf.edu
Effective Date: Semester I, 2003

http://www.ugs.usf.edu/catalogs/0304/enggen.htm

Fig. A.8   Document 1 as rendered in a web browser (page 8).

```
<html>
<head>
    <title>USF 2003-2004 Undergraduate Catalog - College of Engineering General
Information</title>
    <link rel=stylesheet href="http://www.ugs.usf.edu/ugsstyle.css" type="text/css"
media=screen>
</head>

<body class="margin10" bgcolor="#FFFFFF" link="#005A4A" alink="#005A4A" vlink="#005A4A">

<hr>
| <a href="enpl.htm">Engineering Program Listing</a> | <a href="cattoc.htm">Catalog Table of
Contents</a> | <a href="index.htm">Index</a> |
<hr>

<p>USF 2003-2004 Undergraduate Catalog - Pages 147 - 148

<h2>College of Engineering</h2>
<p>The mission of the USF College of Engineering is to continuously aspire to excellence in
teaching, research and public service.  The College values academic excellence,
professionalism, ethics and cultural diversity among its students, staff and faculty.  The
College is committed to addressing the needs of its constituencies and gives careful
consideration to the urban and suburban populations in our service area.
<p>At the undergraduate level the College is committed to provide students with a strong,
broad-based, fundamental engineering education as preparation for careers in industry in a
global environment, and government, or as preparation for advanced studies in professional
schools of engineering, science, law, business and medicine.
<p>At the graduate level students work in close collaboration with faculty, pursuing advanced
topics within their disciplines, which will result in advancements in their fields and society
at large.
<p>Utilizing the expertise of its individual and collective faculty, the College is dedicated
to the development of new fundamental knowledge and processes or procedures, which will benefit
all humanity.  The College promotes multi-disciplinary approaches, commitment to life-long
learning and awareness of societal issues, which are requisite for meeting technological
challenges.
<p>The College provides technical assistance and technology transfer to the region, state and
nation.  In all facets of teaching, research and service, the College emphasizes close liaison
with industry and government to provide students and faculty with the skills and perspectives
needed to ensure effective technological leadership.

<p>The College of Engineering offers undergraduate and graduate programs to prepare students
for a broad spectrum of professional careers in engineering. Laboratory experience as well as
real-world participation in technological problem-solving is a key aspect of a professional
engineerís college education. The College of Engineering, in implementing this need, augments
its own modern laboratory and research facilities in close collaboration with the professional
societies and the many industries in the metropolitan Tampa Bay area. The College of
Engineering offers undergraduate degrees in Chemical Engineering, Civil Engineering, Computer
Engineering, Computer Science, Information Systems, Electrical Engineering, Industrial
Engineering, and Mechanical Engineering.
<p>The engineering programs of the College have been developed with an emphasis on three broad
aspects of engineering activity: design, research, and the operation of complex technological
systems. Students who are interested in advanced design or research should pursue the 5-Year
Program leading to a Master of Science degree in a designated Engineering discipline. The
Engineering Accreditation Commission (EAC) of the Accreditation Board for Engineering and
Technology, Inc. (ABET) has inspected and accredited the Engineering programs of the College
(Chemical Engineering, Civil Engineering, Computer Engineering, Electrical Engineering,
Industrial Engineering and Mechanical Engineering). The Bachelor of Science program in Computer
Science is accredited by the Computing Accreditation Commission (CAC) of ABET.
<p>The Departments and Programs section that follows contains descriptions of the engineering
degrees offered by the College. The íFour Year Programsî section includes courses students need
```

Fig. A.9   Document 1 original HTML source (page 1).

to take, beginning with their first semester at USF, to earn the Bachelor of Science in Engineering degree.
<p>Students interested in particular programs offered by the College of Engineering should direct their inquiries to the College of Engineering Office of Student Services (see <a href="enacainf.htm#advising">Advising</a> section below). Information is also available on the Collegeís website: <a href="http://www.eng.usf.edu/">http://www.eng.usf.edu/</a>.

<h3>Professional Engineering</h3>
<p>The College of Engineering recognizes that modern engineering solutions draw on knowledge of several branches of engineering. It also recognizes that future technological and societal developments will lead to shifting of the relative emphasis on various branches of engineering, triggered by new needs or a reassessment of national goals. For this reason the Collegeís programs include a strong engineering foundation portion, designed to equip the prospective engineer with a broad base of fundamental technical knowledge. To this foundation is added the studentís specialization of sufficient depth to prepare him/her to successfully embark on a professional career.
<p>The Bachelor of Science degrees offered in the various engineering disciplines provide the student a broad education with sufficient technical background to contribute effectively in many phases of engineering not requiring the depth of knowledge needed for advanced design or research. The baccalaureate degree is considered the minimum educational credential for participating in the engineering profession and is the first professional degree. Students interested in design and research are strongly encouraged to pursue advanced work beyond the baccalaureate either at this or other institutions. It is becoming increasingly evident that large segments of todayís engineering professionals are involved in some form of post baccalaureate study. Engineers are earning advanced degrees to obtain the information and training necessary to meet effectively tomorrowís technological challenges. All are faced with the continuing problem of refurbishing and updating their information skills and most are obtaining advanced information by means of formal graduate study, seminars, special institutes and other such systems designed for this purpose. Life-long learning is a fact in engineering practice, and graduates must be aware and committed to it.
<p>The Bachelor of Science degree program in a designated engineering discipline and the Master of Science degree in the same discipline may be pursued simultaneously in a program called the Five-Year Program.

<h3>Professional Registration</h3>
<p>Students who have attained senior status, and are in good academic standing in an ABET accredited Engineering Program, are eligible to register for examinations leading to licensure as Professional Engineers. The first examination, called the Fundamentals of Engineering (FE) Exam, is offered by the Florida Board of Professional Engineers and is usually taken the semester prior to graduation. In addition to the knowledge acquired through the engineering curriculum, many students take advantage of review courses offered by the Engineering Student College Council and the College of Engineeringís distance education program, FEEDS, to prepare for the Fundamentals of Engineering Examination. Registering for the FE exam during the senior year is strongly encouraged for students graduating with an engineering degree.

<a name="prep">
<h3>Preparation for Engineering</h3>
<p>Students planning to attend USFís College of Engineering should familiarize themselves thoroughly with the Collegeís admissions standards and requirements for their prospective program, which are more stringent than the Universityís minimum entrance requirements.
<p>The high school student anticipating a career in engineering should elect the strongest academic program that is available while in high school, including four years each of English, mathematics and science (preferably including Chemistry, Physics, and Biology), as well as full programs in the social sciences and humanities.
<p>Prospective students considering engineering at the University of South Florida who lack certain preparation in high school must elect to follow a program to overcome their deficiencies. Alternatives for these students, classified as íPre-Engineering majorsî might include preparatory coursework at the University of South Florida. As another alternative, students may wish to avail themselves of the Stateís system of junior/community colleges which offer a wide range of preliminary coursework; many of these schools also offer full programs in

Fig. A.10   Document 1 original HTML source (page 2).

pre-engineering (first two yearsí coursework).
<p>Junior/community college students planning to transfer to the University of South Floridaís engineering program from a State of Florida operated college or university should follow a pre-engineering program leading to an A.A. degree. All transfer students should complete as much of the mathematics and science coursework as is available to them. In general engineering courses taken for military training, at the lower level, or as part of an A.S. or technology degree are not transferable to the engineering programs. Transfer students should be aware that the College expects them to meet its admission requirements listed in this section under college regulations for graduation just as it expects its own students to meet these requirements. Junior/community college students intending to pursue an engineering program at USF should contact the advisor at their institution and request a course equivalency list.
<p>The College of Engineering can assist students who are planning to obtain an Engineering degree from the University of South Florida and who have started their studies elsewhere in formulating a sound total program. Interested students should contact the Collegeís Office of Student Services (813/974-2684) furnishing sufficient details to permit meaningful response.

<h3>Student Computer Policy</h3>
<p>Although it is not mandatory, the College strongly recommends acquisition of either a desktop or a laptop personal computer. Recommended computer configuration for a student to be able to run engineering applications is indicated on the College web page <a href="http://www.eng.usf.edu">http://www.eng.usf.edu</a>. For further details, contact the Associate Dean of Engineering or the Director of Engineering Computing in the College. Also see the section on l<a href="#compfac">College Computing Facilities</a>.í

<p>
<hr>
<p>USF 2003-2004 Undergraduate Catalog - Pages 150 - 151
<a name="deptprogs">
<h2>Departments and Programs</h2>
<p>The supervision of the academic programs for the College is the function of the administrative departments together with several coordinators. Each department is responsible for specific professional programs, faculty, laboratories, and student advising.

<h3>Chemical Engineering</h3>
<p>Undergraduate Degree Offered:
<ul>
<li>Bachelor of Science in Chemical Engineering (B.S.C.H.)
</ul>

<p>Graduate Degrees Offered:
<ul>
<li>Master of Science in Chemical Engineering (M.S.C.H.)
<li>Master in Chemical Engineering (M.C.H.E.)
<li>Master of Engineering (M.E.)
<li>Master of Science in Engineering (M.S.E.)
<li>Doctor of Philosophy in Chemical Engineering (Ph.D.)
<li>Doctor of Philosophy in Engineering Science (Ph.D.)
</ul>
<p>This department offers coursework and study in all areas fundamental to Chemical Engineering. Topics included are thermodynamics, fluid flow, heat transfer, mass transfer, separation processes, reactors, instrumentation and process control, economics, optimization, computational methods, computer aided design techniques, and process/plant design. These courses, together with mathematics, physics, chemistry, other interdisciplinary engineering fundamentals, English, and liberal arts courses, provide the basis for long-range professional progress. Because of the many professional areas available for employment to the chemical engineer, the students are also required to take a number of electives from areas such as biotechnology, materials, and environmental engineering. These electives are designed to broaden the experience, and, therefore, the employment possibilities of our graduates. The Chemical Engineering Department also offers a sequence of courses in Chemical Engineering

Fig. A.11   Document 1 original HTML source (page 3).

Science, biotechnology and biomedical engineering.
<p>A sequence of courses in the engineering aspects of biotechnology is currently available within the Chemical Engineering program. Topics include applied microbiology, fermentation, enzyme technology, cell separation technology, biomedical engineering, biomaterials, biotechnology, and biomechanics.

<h3>Civil and Environmental Engineering</h3>
<p>Undergraduate Degree Offered:
<ul>
<li>Bachelor of Science in Civil Engineering (B.S.C.E.)
</ul>

<p>Graduate Degrees Offered:
<ul>
<li>Master of Science in Civil Engineering (M.S.C.E.)
<li>Master or Science in Engineering (M.S.E.)
<li>Master of Science in Environmental Engineering (M.S.E.V.)
<li>Master of Civil Engineering (M.C.E.)
<li>Master of Engineering (M.E.)
<li>Master of Environmental Engineering (M.E.V.E.)
<li>Doctor of Philosophy in Civil Engineering (Ph.D.)
<li>Doctor of Philosophy in Engineering Science (Ph.D.)
</ul>
<p>This department offers course work and study pertinent to Civil Engineering, Engineering Mechanics, Material Science, and Environmental Engineering. Areas of concentration are structural engineering, engineering mechanics, geotechnical engineering, transportation engineering, water resources engineering, materials and corrosion engineering, and environmental engineering.
<p>Students completing the program may enter the profession as engineers in civil, structural, geotechnical, transportation, water resources, environmental, hydraulics, or materials disciplines. All of these disciplines share the need for knowledge in the areas of engineering mechanics, civil engineering, material science, and environmental engineering. Through choice of the proper area of concentration, a student has the opportunity to channel academic studies specifically towards his/her career choice.
<p>Graduates of the program may commence their engineering careers in either industry, engineering consulting firms, or public service at the federal, state, or local level. Initial assignments may include planning, design and implementation of water resources systems; planning and design of transportation and housing systems; regional planning, design, and management for abatement of air, water and solid waste pollution problems; design of bridges and single and multistory structures; and supervision of construction projects.

<h3>Computer Science and Engineering</h3>
<p>Undergraduate Degrees Offered:
<ul>
<li>Bachelor of Science in Computer Engineering (B.S.Cp.E.)
<li>Bachelor of Science in Computer Science (B.S.C.S)
<li>Bachelor of Science in Information Systems (B.S.I.S)
</ul>

<p>Graduate Degrees Offered:
<ul>
<li>Master of Science in Computer Science (M.S.C.S)
<li>Master of Science in Computer Engineering (M.S.Cp.E.)
<li>Doctor of Philosophy in Computer Science and Engineering (Ph.D.)
<li>Doctor of Philosophy in Engineering Science (Ph.D.)
</ul>
<p>This department offers coursework and study in all areas fundamental to Computer Science, Computer Engineering, and Information Systems. Topics dealt with are computer architecture and hardware design, software engineering, computer system organization, operating systems, algorithms and data structures, computer graphics, user interface, software testing, computer

Fig. A.12   Document 1 original HTML source (page 4).

networks, database systems, robotics, theory of computation and artificial intelligence.
<p>Our research areas of faculty concentration are 1) computer architecture and VLSI
design/testing, 2) artificial intelligence and robotics, 3) graphics/image processing/computer
vision, and 4) networks, 5) software testing.
<p>Computing facilities available to students in the Department include several microprocessor
and design laboratories for hardware-oriented studies, personal computer laboratories for
general use in programming assignments, and networked SUN workstations for use by majors. The
Department maintains a number of research laboratories equipped with special purpose hardware.
In addition, the Department has access to a large IBM mainframe facility run by the University
Computing Center.

<h3>Electrical Engineering</h3>
<p>Undergraduate Degree Offered:
<ul>
<li>Bachelor of Science in Electrical Engineering (B.S.E.E.)
</ul>

<p>Graduate Degrees Offered:
<ul>
<li>Master of Science in Electrical Engineering (M.S.E.E.)
<li>Master of Engineering (M.E.)
<li>Master of Science in Engineering (M.S.E.)
<li>Master of Science in Engineering Science (M.S.E.S)
<li>Doctor of Philosophy in Electrical Engineering (Ph.D).
<li>Doctor of Philosophy in Engineering Science (Ph.D.)
</ul>
<p>This department offers study in all areas fundamental to Electrical Engineering and the
electrical sciences: circuit analysis and design, electronics, communications,
electromagnetics, controls, solid state, system analysis, digital circuit design,
microelectromechanical systems (MEMS) and the like. Basic concepts are augmented with
well-equipped laboratories in circuits, electronics, digital systems, microwave techniques,
wireless circuits & systems, and controls and communications. In addition, a general-purpose
computer facility, a microprocessor and digital signal processing laboratory, and a
microelectronics fabrication, design/test and metrology laboratory are available to
undergraduate and graduate students.

<h3>Industrial and Management Systems Engineering</h3>
<p>Undergraduate Degree Offered:
<ul>
<li>Bachelor of Science in Industrial Engineering (B.S.I.E.)
</ul>

<p>Graduate Degrees Offered:
<ul>
<li>Master of Science in Industrial Engineering (M.S.I.E.)
<li>Master of Engineering (M.E.)
<li>Master of Science in Engineering Science (M.S.E.S.)
<li>Master of Science in Engineering Management (M.S.E.M)
<li>Master of Industrial Engineering (M.I.E.)
<li>Doctor of Philosophy in Industrial Engineering (Ph.D.)
<li>Doctor of Philosophy in Engineering Science (Ph.D.)
</ul>
<p>This department offers study pertinent to the design, evaluation and operation of a variety
of industrial systems, ranging from the analysis of public systems to the operation of
manufacturing plants. Topics include production planning and control, production and plant
design, applied statistics, operations research, human factors and productivity, manufacturing,
and automation. The department has excellent laboratory facilities which support class projects
and research in microcomputer applications, computer-aided manufacturing, human performance,
automation, and applications of robotics. Evening and off-campus programs are available through
the Master of Science in Engineering Management (M.S.E.M.) program. The department also

Fig. A.13   Document 1 original HTML source (page 5).

administers the manufacturing option in the M.S.E. program.

```
<h3>Mechanical Engineering</h3>
<p>Undergraduate Degree Offered:
<ul>
<li>Bachelor of Science in Mechanical Engineering (B.S.M.E.)
</ul>

<p>Graduate Degrees Offered:
<ul>
<li>Master of Mechanical Engineering (M.M.E.)
<li>Master of Science in Mechanical Engineering (M.S.M.E.)
<li>Master of Engineering (M.E.)
<li>Master of Science in Engineering (M.S.E.)
<li>Doctor of Philosophy in Mechanical Engineering (Ph.D.)
<li>Doctor of Philosophy in Engineering Science (Ph.D.)
</ul>
<p>Coursework includes basic science and mathematics, thermal and fluid sciences, material
science, solid mechanics, dynamics, machine design, vibrations, instrumentation and control.
<p>Graduates of this program are employed in research, design, production, marketing, service,
installation (contracting), maintenance and operation in such industries as mining, petroleum,
paper, food, power, manufacturing, air-conditioning, defense systems, aerospace, data
processing, communications, and automotive.
<p>Laboratories are available for basic instrumentation, thermal and fluid sciences, solid
mechanics, data acquisition and control, CAD/CAE, vibrations, and aerodynamics.

<p>
<hr>
<p>USF 2003-2004 Undergraduate Catalog - Pages 164 - 165
<a name="compserv">
<h3>Computer Service (SC) Courses</h3>
<p>These courses marked SC are specifically designed for the non-engineering student.
<p>Recognizing that the general purpose digital computer has made significant contributions to
the advancement of all elements of the academic community and that it will have an ever greater
impact in the future, the College of Engineering offers several levels of credit coursework,
both undergraduate and graduate, to serve students of all colleges in order that they may be
prepared to meet the computer challenge.
<p>Computer-oriented courses are offered in two broad categories: (1) those courses which are
concerned with the operation, organization and programming of computers and computer systems
from the viewpoint of examining the fundamental principles involved in computer usage; and (2)
those courses which are concerned with computer applications to a variety of different
disciplines, by means of user-oriented-languages such as FORTRAN, COBOL, BASIC, ìC,î "C++",
JAVA, and VISUAL BASIC.
<p>Students in engineering, the physical sciences, and mathematics must consult their advisor
for suitable computer courses, since these courses are not acceptable to a number of degree
programs.

<a name="compfac">
<h3>College Computing Facilities</h3>
<p>The College provides access to centralized computing facilities to undergraduate and
graduate students. Most engineering departments also provide students with local facilities.
The University is an Internet2 site and links are available to directly connect to all major
supercomputing centers in the country.
<p>The College provides enterprise level servers for computing, mail, file, web and database
services for students and faculty. The College operates teaching and open-access labs for
student use. These labs are equipped with large number of modern (Dell) PCs using Windows 2000
operating system and Unix workstations (Sun Ultra 5). All lab computers have all of the
necessary software required for coursework as well as other standard productivity software. The
College also supports a state-of-the-art multimedia lab with document scanners and CD-ROM
burner.
```

Fig. A.14   Document 1 original HTML source (page 6).

```
<p>Standard programming languages such as FORTRAN, Basic, Pascal, C, C++ and Java are provided
on these machines. General-purpose software such as Office 2000, MS visual studio and
specialized engineering software including mathematical packages (MathCad, Matlab, Maple,
Macsyma, TK Solver), statistical package (SAS), discipline specific application packages such
as Abaqus, Ansys, ARENA, Aspen, Cadence and Labview are provided on Unix and Windows 2000
platforms on the network and in the labs. Several database management system software packages
such as Oracle 8i, MySQL, MSSQL 8 and MS Access are available for classwork. Multi-media
software packages such as MS FrontPage, Adobe Acrobat, Illustrator, Photoshop, Omni Page Pro,
Paint Shop Pro, Macromedia Dreamweaver and Flash are available in the multi-media lab. The
university has also entered an agreement with Microsoft Corporation for upgrade of standard
office application, development tools and desktop operating systems.
<p>The college-wide Ethernet network is connected to the USF campus-wide Gigabit Ethernet
backbone. Within the College connections are provided to laboratories via 100 Mbps Ethernet.
The universityís Internet2 connection links it to more than 150 major universities and research
institutions in the nation. Dial-in access is available to students from a large USF modem bank
as well as through broadband connection. The distance learning (FEEDS) studios provide computer
demonstrations for remote classes through the network. Additionally, most departments operate
discipline specific computing lab(s).

<h3>Cooperative Education and Internship Programs</h3>
<p>A wide variety of industries and government agencies have established cooperative programs
for engineering students to provide them the opportunity to become familiar with the practical
aspects of industrial operations and engineering careers. Students in the Career Resource
Centerís Cooperative Education (Co-op) program may alternate periods of paid employment in
their major field with like periods of study, or may elect to participate in part-time
employment while attending classes every semester.  Students following the Co-op program
usually encounter no problems in scheduling their program, since required Social Science and
Humanities, Mathematics and Science, and Engineering Common courses are offered every semester.
Students normally apply for participation in this program during their sophomore year and
pursue actual Co-op employment during their sophomore and junior years.  The senior year is
generally pursued on a full-time study basis, since many specialization courses are not offered
every semester. The students receive a Cooperative Education Certificate upon successful
completion of a minimum of two work assignments.

<h3>Army, Air Force &amp; Navy R.O.T.C. For Engineering Students</h3>
<p>The Engineering curriculum, coupled with involvement in the Army, Air Force or Navy R.O.T.C.
program, will require a minimum of five (5) years to complete the degree. R.O.T.C. cadets must
take additional hours in either military science or aerospace studies. Additionally, summer
training programs are scheduled, usually between the junior and senior years.


<p>
<hr>
|  <a href="#top">Top</a>  |  <a href="enpl.htm">Engineering Program Listing</a>  |  <a
href="cattoc.htm">Catalog Table of Contents</a>  |  <a href="index.htm">Index</a>  |
<hr>

<p>Please send questions or comments to:
<br>Karen M. Hall - <a href="mailto:webCat@ugs.usf.edu">webCat@ugs.usf.edu</a>
<br>Effective Date: Semester I, 2003
<p><b>http://www.ugs.usf.edu/catalogs/0304/enggen.htm</b>

</body>
</html>
```

Fig. A.15   Document 1 original HTML source (page 7).

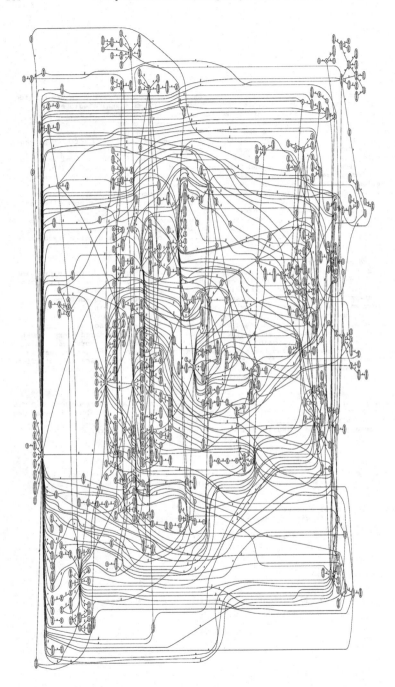

Fig. A.16   Largest connected component of the graph created from the document 1 using the standard representation.

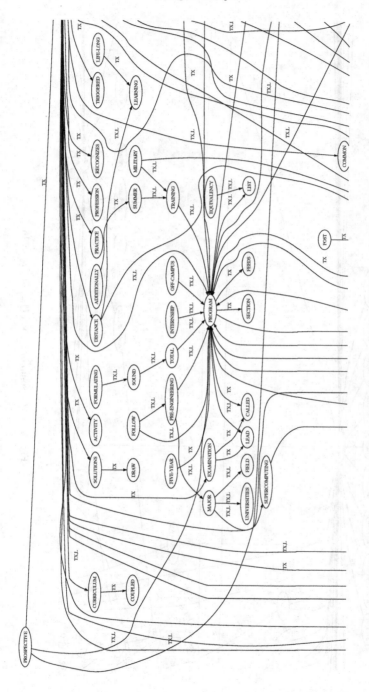

Fig. A.17 Close-up of section (1,1) of Fig. A.16.

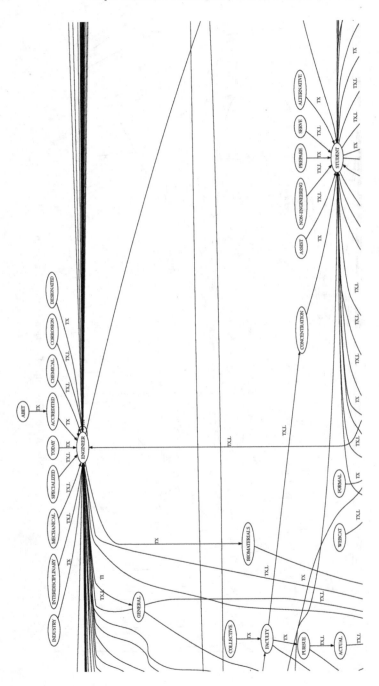

Fig. A.18   Close-up of section (1,2) of Fig. A.16.

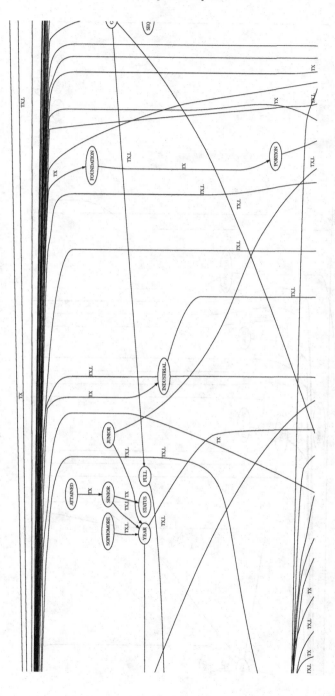

Fig. A.19 Close-up of section (1,3) of Fig. A.16.

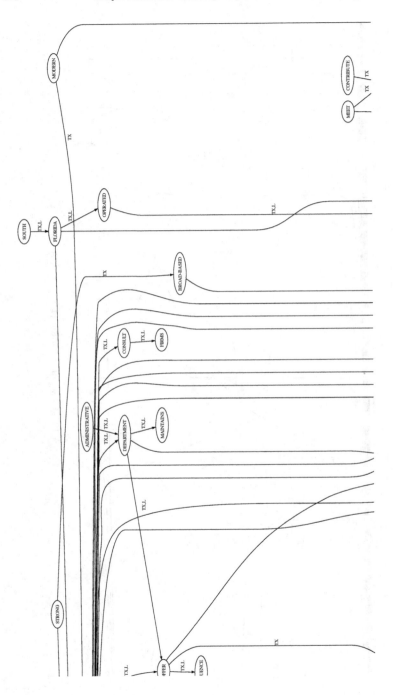

Fig. A.20   Close-up of section (1,4) of Fig. A.16.

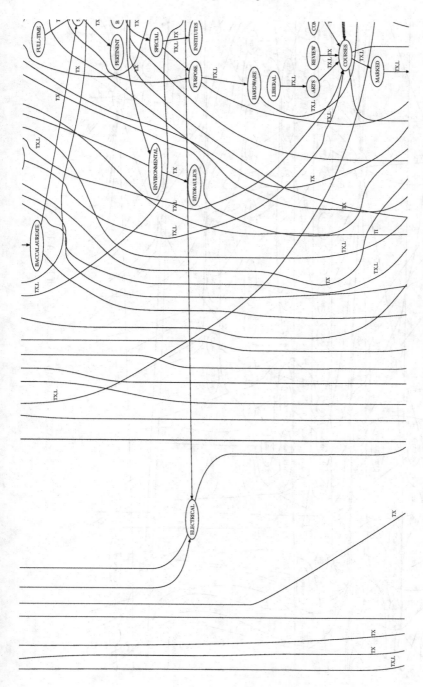

Fig. A.21 Close-up of section (2,1) of Fig. A.16.

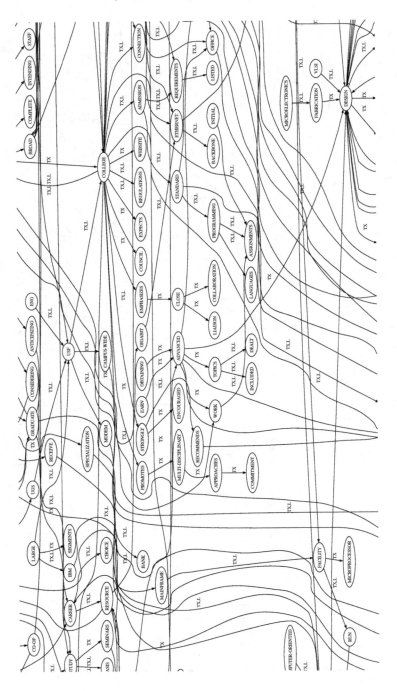

Fig. A.22 Close-up of section (2,2) of Fig. A.16.

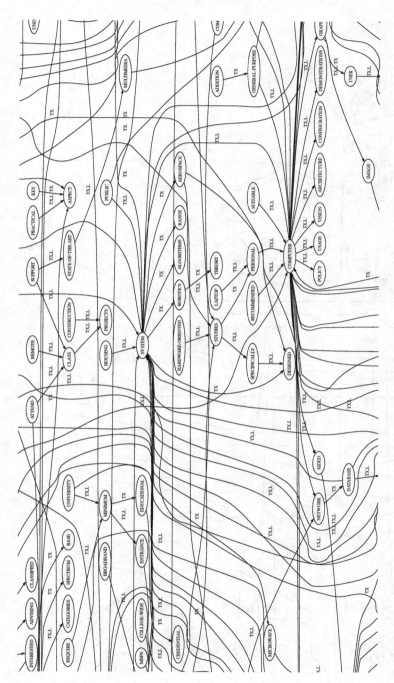

Fig. A.23 Close-up of section (2,3) of Fig. A.16.

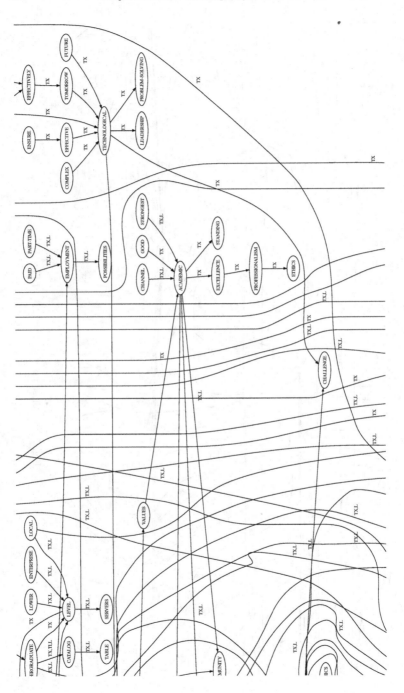

Fig. A.24　Close-up of section (2,4) of Fig. A.16.

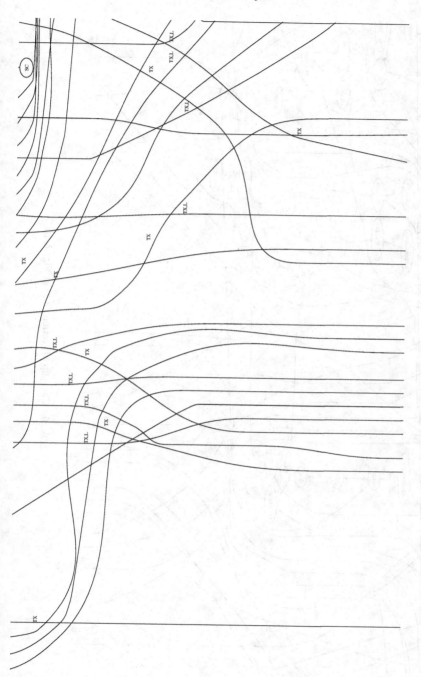

Fig. A.25   Close-up of section (3,1) of Fig. A.16.

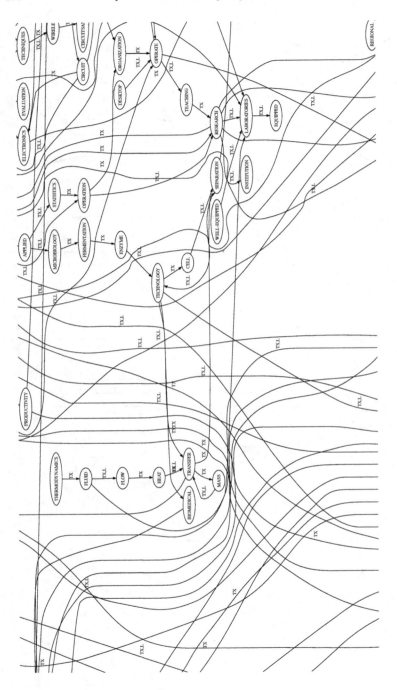

Fig. A.26 Close-up of section (3,2) of Fig. A.16.

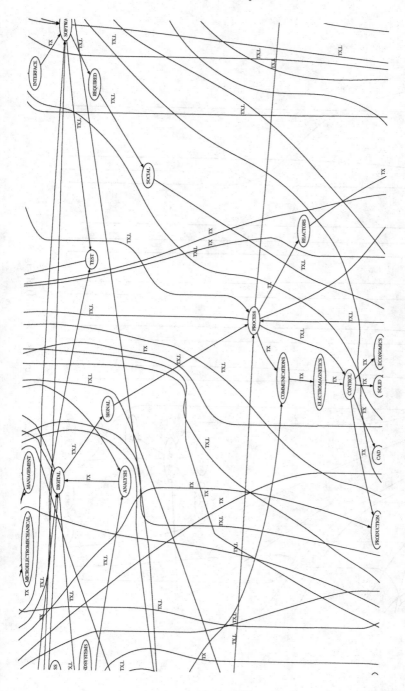

Fig. A.27   Close-up of section (3,3) of Fig. A.16.

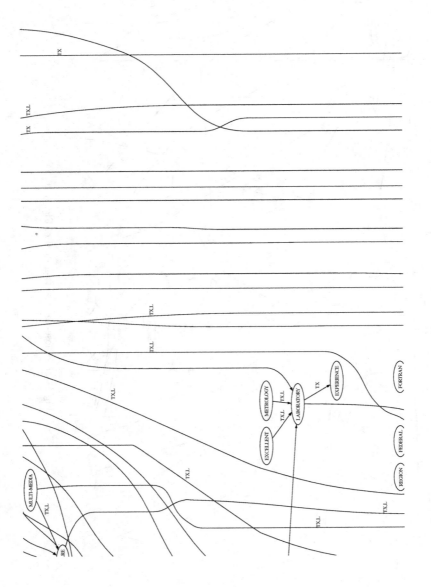

Fig. A.28   Close-up of section (3,4) of Fig. A.16.

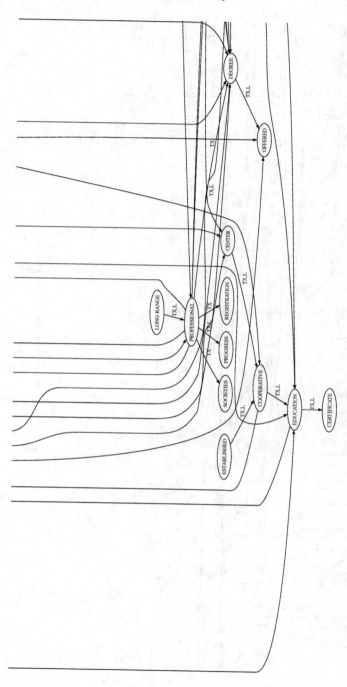

Fig. A.29   Close-up of section (4,1) of Fig. A.16.

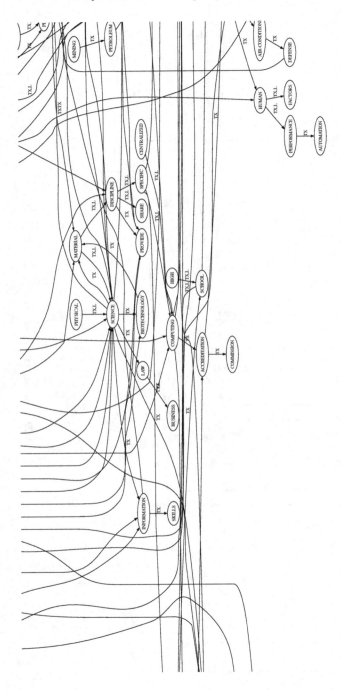

Fig. A.30   Close-up of section (4,2) of Fig. A.16.

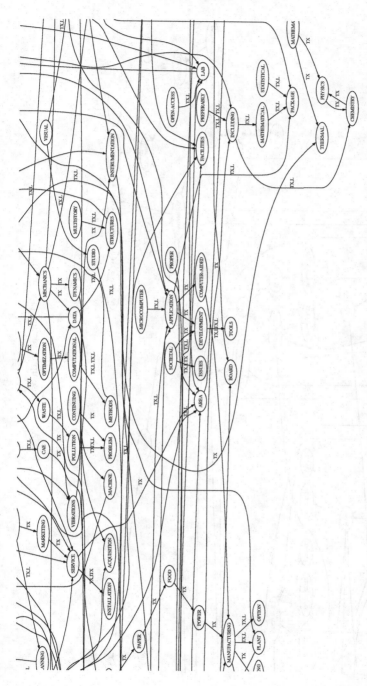

Fig. A.31   Close-up of section (4,3) of Fig. A.16.

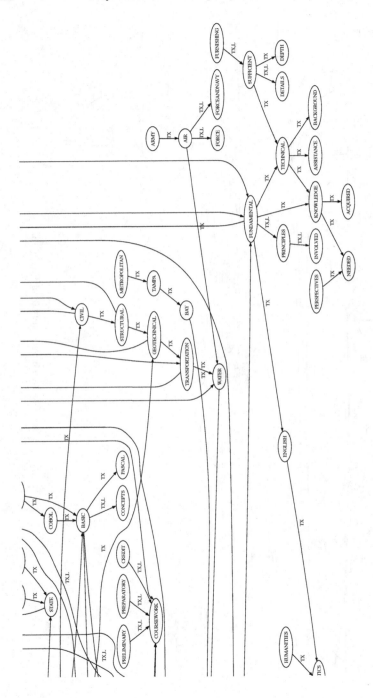

Fig. A.32   Close-up of section (4,4) of Fig. A.16.

home | general info | meal plans | declining balance | locations/menus | catering | employment | feedback

meal plans

Meal Memberships
Summer 2004

Our Summer Meal Memberships offer a weekly plan (Any 15 Plan) or two block plans (BULLBlock 75 or BULLBlock 50). Meal plans are for Summer 2004 Session B only.

For specific details and a contract form that you can print out and bring in, mail, or fax, **click here (requires** acrobat reader**).**

Meal Memberships
Fall 2004/Spring 2005

Meal Memberships provide the most economical way to eat on campus – you can save over 30% off the average cash door price! We know you are busy, that's why we have created several different options to meet your needs.

Weekly Memberships

The most economical memberships are weekly memberships – the Unlimited and the Any 15 Plan – the value cannot be beat! These plans offer unlimited or 15 meals per week that can be used at The Fresh Food Company or Andros Dining Center. Because your meals are rationed for you throughout the semester, you won't have to worry about running out of food. With the Any 15 Plan you can eat for as low as $4.37 a meal! With the weekly membership, you also receive Flex Bucks that can be used at any USF Dining Location. Weekly memberships are available to all students, faculty, and staff members.

Weekly Memberships Details		
Unlimited	$150 Flex and Unlimited entry into FFC and Andros.	$1605.65 ($4.05 per meal)
Any 15 Plan	Most Popular! $300 Flex and 15 meals per week.	$1420.96 ($4.37 per meal)

Note: All Meal Memberships are a two semester commitment. You must sign up for the same dollar value meal membership in the Spring semester as you did in the Fall semester. Prices above are for one semester only, and include tax on the meal membership portion.

Block Memberships

Block memberships provide flexibility to your dining needs by offering a set number of meals per semester – 150, 90, 50. This allows you to ration your meals yourself, eating as often as you like each week. These meals can be used at The Fresh Food Company or Andros Dining Center and with the block membership, you also receive Flex Bucks that can be used at any USF Dining Location.

BULLBlock 150 – Available to all students, faculty, and staff members

BULLBlock 90 – Available to Mandatory students in Greek Village, Holly, Kosove, and Maple Apartments. Also available to Voluntary students, faculty, and staff members.

BULLBlock 50 – Available to faculty, staff, and Voluntary students only.

Semester Block Membership Details	
BULLBlock 150 $150 Flex & 150 meals per semester.	$1265.24 ($6.95 per meal)

Fig. A.33   Document 2 as rendered in a web browser (page 1).

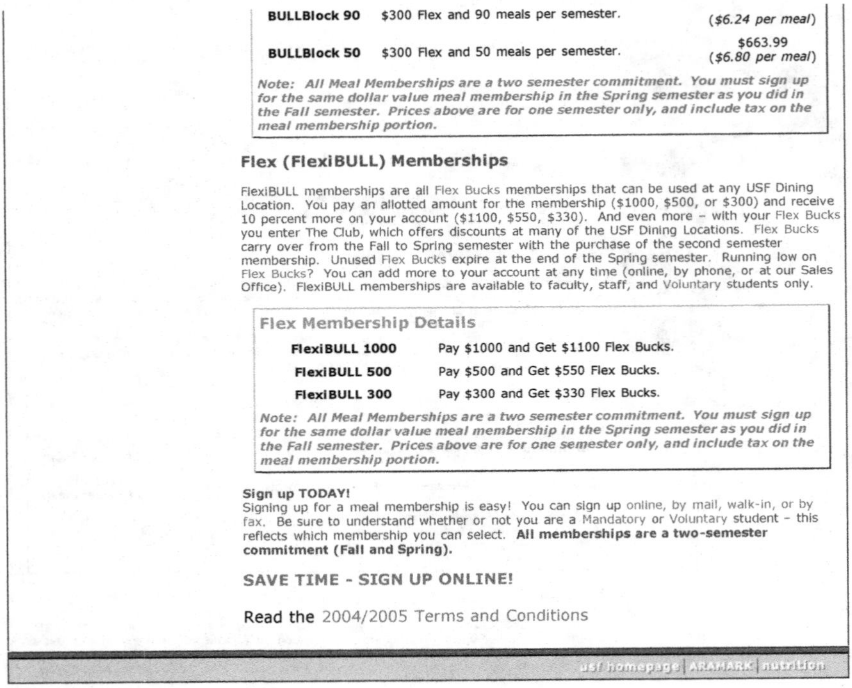

| **BULLBlock 90** | $300 Flex and 90 meals per semester. | *($6.24 per meal)* |
| **BULLBlock 50** | $300 Flex and 50 meals per semester. | $663.99
($6.80 per meal) |

Note: All Meal Memberships are a two semester commitment. You must sign up for the same dollar value meal membership in the Spring semester as you did in the Fall semester. Prices above are for one semester only, and include tax on the meal membership portion.

Flex (FlexiBULL) Memberships

FlexiBULL memberships are all Flex Bucks memberships that can be used at any USF Dining Location. You pay an allotted amount for the membership ($1000, $500, or $300) and receive 10 percent more on your account ($1100, $550, $330). And even more – with your Flex Bucks you enter The Club, which offers discounts at many of the USF Dining Locations. Flex Bucks carry over from the Fall to Spring semester with the purchase of the second semester membership. Unused Flex Bucks expire at the end of the Spring semester. Running low on Flex Bucks? You can add more to your account at any time (online, by phone, or at our Sales Office). FlexiBULL memberships are available to faculty, staff, and Voluntary students only.

Flex Membership Details

FlexiBULL 1000	Pay $1000 and Get $1100 Flex Bucks.
FlexiBULL 500	Pay $500 and Get $550 Flex Bucks.
FlexiBULL 300	Pay $300 and Get $330 Flex Bucks.

Note: All Meal Memberships are a two semester commitment. You must sign up for the same dollar value meal membership in the Spring semester as you did in the Fall semester. Prices above are for one semester only, and include tax on the meal membership portion.

Sign up TODAY!
Signing up for a meal membership is easy! You can sign up online, by mail, walk-in, or by fax. Be sure to understand whether or not you are a Mandatory or Voluntary student – this reflects which membership you can select. **All memberships are a two-semester commitment (Fall and Spring).**

SAVE TIME - SIGN UP ONLINE!

Read the 2004/2005 Terms and Conditions

usf homepage ARAMARK nutrition

Fig. A.34   Document 2 as rendered in a web browser (page 1).

```
<!DOCTYPE html PUBLIC "-//W3C//DTD HTML 4.01 Transitional//EN">

<HTML>
<HEAD>
<TITLE>USF Dining Services</TITLE>
<META HTTP-EQUIV="Content-Type" CONTENT="text/html; charset=iso-8859-1">
        <csscriptdict import>
            <script type="text/javascript" src="CSScriptLib.js"></script>
        </csscriptdict>
        <csactiondict>
            <script type="text/javascript"><!--
var preloadFlag = false;
function preloadImages() {
    if (document.images) {
        over_RolloverImage = newImage(/*URL*/'images/nr_04.gif');
        over_RolloverImage2 = newImage(/*URL*/'images/nr_05.gif');
        over_RolloverImage3 = newImage(/*URL*/'images/nr_06.gif');
        over_RolloverImage4 = newImage(/*URL*/'images/nr_07.gif');
        over_RolloverImage5 = newImage(/*URL*/'images/nr_08.gif');
        over_RolloverImage6 = newImage(/*URL*/'images/nr_09.gif');
        over_RolloverImage7 = newImage(/*URL*/'images/nr_10.gif');
        over_RolloverImage8 = newImage(/*URL*/'images/nr_11.gif');
        over_f1 = newImage(/*URL*/'images/fr_03.gif');
        over_f2 = newImage(/*URL*/'images/fr_04.gif');
        over_f3 = newImage(/*URL*/'images/fr_05.gif');
        over_main = newImage(/*URL*/'images/mr_04.gif');
        over_mp = newImage(/*URL*/'images/save2.gif');
        over_mp = newImage(/*URL*/'images/dbgr.gif');
        preloadFlag = true;
    }

}
function openwindow(url, name, w, h) {
  l = (screen.availWidth-10 - w) / 2;
  t = (screen.availHeight-20 - h) / 2;

  features = "width="+w+",height="+h+",left="+l+",top="+t;
  features += ",screenX="+l+",screenY="+t;
  features += ",scrollbars=1,resizable=0,location=0";
  features += ",menubar=0,toolbar=0,status=0";

  window.open(url, name, features);
}
// --></script>
        </csactiondict>
        <LINK REL=StyleSheet HREF="astyle.css">
    </HEAD>
<BODY onload="preloadImages();" BGCOLOR=#333333 LEFTMARGIN=0 TOPMARGIN=0 MARGINWIDTH=0
MARGINHEIGHT=0 background="images/backgroundpalm7.gif">
<!-- ImageReady Slices (finalnav.psd) -->
<div align="center">
  <center>
<TABLE class="tb" WIDTH=700 BORDER=0 CELLPADDING=0 CELLSPACING=0 style="border-collapse:
collapse" bordercolor="#111111">
    <TR>
        <TD COLSPAN=5>
            <IMG SRC="images/n_01.gif" ALT="" width="344" height="93"></TD>
        <TD COLSPAN=5>
            <img border="0" src="images/n_02.gif" width="356" height="93"></TD>
    </TR>
```

Fig. A.35   Document 2 original HTML source (page 1).

```
<TR>
    <TD>
        <IMG SRC="images/n_03.gif" ALT="" width="9" height="18"></TD>
        <TD><a onmouseover="changeImages(
/*CMP*/'RolloverImage',/*URL*/'images/nr_04.gif');return true" onmouseout="changeImages(
/*CMP*/'RolloverImage',/*URL*/'images/n_04.gif');return true" href="index.php">
        <IMG SRC="images/n_04.gif" name="RolloverImage" ALT="" border="0" width="49"
height="18"></a></TD>
        <TD><a onmouseover="changeImages(
/*CMP*/'RolloverImage2',/*URL*/'images/nr_05.gif');return true" onmouseout="changeImages(
/*CMP*/'RolloverImage2',/*URL*/'images/n_05.gif');return true" href="generalinfo.php">
        <IMG SRC="images/n_05.jpg" name="RolloverImage2" ALT="" border="0" width="89"
height="18"></a></TD>
        <TD><a onmouseover="changeImages(
/*CMP*/'RolloverImage3',/*URL*/'images/nr_06.gif');return true" onmouseout="changeImages(
/*CMP*/'RolloverImage3',/*URL*/'images/n_06.gif');return true" href="mealplans.php">
        <IMG SRC="images/n_06.gif" name="RolloverImage3" ALT="" border="0" width="82"
height="18"></a></TD>
        <TD>
        <a onmouseover="changeImages( /*CMP*/'RolloverImage4',/*URL*/'images/nr_07.gif');return
true" onmouseout="changeImages( /*CMP*/'RolloverImage4',/*URL*/'images/n_07.gif');return true"
href="declining.php">
        <IMG SRC="images/n_07.gif" name="RolloverImage4" ALT="" border="0" width="115"
height="18"></a></TD>
        <TD>
        <a onmouseover="changeImages( /*CMP*/'RolloverImage5',/*URL*/'images/nr_08.gif');return
true" onmouseout="changeImages( /*CMP*/'RolloverImage5',/*URL*/'images/n_08.gif');return true"
href="dining.php">
        <IMG SRC="images/n_08.gif" name="RolloverImage5" ALT="" border="0" width="122"
height="18"></a></TD>
        <TD><a onmouseover="changeImages(
/*CMP*/'RolloverImage6',/*URL*/'images/nr_09.gif');return true" onmouseout="changeImages(
/*CMP*/'RolloverImage6',/*URL*/'images/n_09.gif');return true" href="catering.php">
        <IMG SRC="images/n_09.gif" name="RolloverImage6" ALT="" border="0" width="66"
height="18"></a></TD>
        <TD><a onmouseover="changeImages(
/*CMP*/'RolloverImage7',/*URL*/'images/nr_10.gif');return true" onmouseout="changeImages(
/*CMP*/'RolloverImage7',/*URL*/'images/n_10.gif');return true" href="employment.php">
        <IMG SRC="images/n_10.gif" name="RolloverImage7" ALT="" border="0" width="91"
height="18"></a></TD>
        <TD><a onmouseover="changeImages(
/*CMP*/'RolloverImage8',/*URL*/'images/nr_11.gif');return true" onmouseout="changeImages(
/*CMP*/'RolloverImage8',/*URL*/'images/n_11.gif');return true" href="feedback.php">
        <IMG SRC="images/n_11.gif" name="RolloverImage8" ALT="" border="0" width="69"
height="18"></a></TD>
        <TD>
        <IMG SRC="images/n_12.gif" ALT="" width="8" height="18"></TD>
    </TR>
    <TR>
        <TD COLSPAN=10>
        <img border="0" src="images/n_13.gif" width="700" height="9"></TD>
    </TR>
</TABLE>
    </center>
</div>
<!-- End ImageReady Slices -->

<!-- ImageReady Slices (concord2.psd) -->
<div align="center">
    <center>
```

Fig. A.36   Document 2 original HTML source (page 2).

```
                <table class="t" border="0" cellpadding="0" style="border-collapse: collapse"
bordercolor="#111111" width="700" id="AutoNumber1" bgcolor="#FFFFFF" cellspacing="0">
                <tr>
                    <td>
                    <table border="0" cellpadding="0" cellspacing="0" style="border-collapse:
collapse" bordercolor="#111111" width="100%" id="AutoNumber4">
                        <tr>
                        <td width="100%" colspan="2" background="images/hbg.gif">
                        <img border="0" src="images/mpheader.gif" width="161" height="25"></td>
                        </tr>
                        <tr><td width="700" height="1" bgcolor="#000000">
                    <img src="images/spacer.gif" width="700" height="1"></td></tr></table>
                    <table border="0" cellpadding="0" style="border-collapse: collapse"
bordercolor="#111111" width="700" id="AutoNumber1" bgcolor="#FFFFFF" cellspacing="0">

                    <tr>
                    <td width="100%">
                    <table border="0" cellpadding="0" cellspacing="0" style="border-collapse:
collapse" bordercolor="#111111" width="700" id="AutoNumber8" height="1">
                        <tr>
                        <td width="192" bgcolor="#F4F4F4" valign="top" height="63">
                        <img border="0" src="images/mppic2new.jpg" width="192"
height="306"><br>

                        <a onmouseover="changeImages(
/*CMP*/'mp',/*URL*/'images/save2.gif');return true" onmouseout="changeImages(
/*CMP*/'mp',/*URL*/'images/save4.gif');return true" href="mealplans2.php">
                        <img name="mp" border="0" src="images/save4.gif" width="192"
height="60"></a></td>
                        <td width="508" valign="top" height="1"><div align="center">
                        <table border="0" cellpadding="4" cellspacing="1"
style="border-collapse: collapse" bordercolor="#111111" width="100%" id="AutoNumber9"
height="100%">

                            <tr>
                            <td width="100%">
                            <b>
                            <font size="2" color="#333333">Meal
                            Memberships</font><br>
                            <font size="1" color="#333333">Summer 2004</font></b><p>
                            <font size="1" color="#333333">Our Summer Meal
                            Memberships offer a weekly plan (Any 15 Plan) or
                            two block plans (BULLBlock 75 or BULLBlock 50). 
                            Meal plans are for Summer 2004 Session B only.</font></p>
                            <p><font size="1" color="#333333">For specific
                            details and a contract form that you can print
                            out and bring in, mail, or fax, <b>
                            <a href="PDFs/2004%20Summer%20Contract.pdf">click
                            here</a></b> </font><font size="1">(requires
                            <a href="http://www.adobe.com/products/acrobat/readstep2.html"
target="_blank">

                            acrobat reader</a>).</font></p>
                            <hr>
                            <p>
                            <b>
                            <font size="2" color="#333333">Meal
                            Memberships</font><br>
                            <font size="1" color="#333333">Fall 2004/Spring
                            2005</font></b><font size="1" color="#333333"><br>
                            <br>
```

Fig. A.37   Document 2 original HTML source (page 3).

```
                              Meal Memberships provide the most economical way
                              to eat on campus ñ you can save over 30% off the
                              average cash door price!  We know you are busy,
                              thatís why we have created several different
                              options to meet your needs.<br>
                              <br>
                              </font>
                              <b>
                              <font size="2" color="#333333">Weekly
Memberships</font></b><font size="1" color="#333333"><br>
                              <br>
                              The most economical memberships are weekly
                              memberships ñ the Unlimited and the Any 15 Plan
                              ñ the value cannot be beat! These plans offer
                              unlimited or 15 meals per week that can be used
                              at The Fresh Food Company or Andros Dining
                              Center.  Because your meals are rationed for you
                              throughout the semester, you wonít have to worry
                              about running out of food.  With the Any 15 Plan
                              you can eat for as low as $4.37 a meal!  With the
                              weekly membership, you also receive <a
href="JavaScript:openwindow('termsFlexBucks.htm','terms',510,300)">Flex Bucks</a>
                              that can be used at any USF Dining Location.  Weekly member
available to all
                              students, faculty, and staff members.<br>
 </font></p>
                              <div align="center">
                                <table class="ta" border="0" cellpadding="4" cellspacing="1"
style="border-collapse: collapse" bordercolor="#111111" width="480" id="table4">
                                  <tr>
                                    <td width="100%" colspan="3" bgcolor="#336633">
                                    <font color="#FFFFFF"><b>Weekly
                                    Memberships Details</b></font></td>
                                  </tr>
                                  <tr>
                                    <td width="16%" bgcolor="#EAEAD5" align="center">
                                    <b><font size="1">Unlimited</font></b></td>
                                    <td width="57%" bgcolor="#EAEAD5" align="center">
                                    <p align="left"><font size="1">$150 Flex
                                    and Unlimited entry into FFC and Andros.
                                    </font></td>
                                    <td width="22%" bgcolor="#EAEAD5" align="center">
                                    <font size="1">$1605.65<br>
                                    (<i>$4.05 per meal</i>)</font></td>
                                  </tr>
                                  <tr>
                                    <td width="16%" bgcolor="#EAEAD5">
                                    <p align="center"><b><font size="1">Any 15
                                    Plan</font></b></td>
                                    <td width="57%" bgcolor="#EAEAD5">
                                    <font size="1">Most Popular! $300 Flex and
                                    15 meals per week.</font></td>
                                    <td width="22%" bgcolor="#EAEAD5">
                                    <p align="center"><font size="1">$1420.96<br>
                                    (<i>$4.37 per meal</i>)</font></td>
                                  </tr>
                                  <tr>
                                    <td width="95%" bgcolor="#FFFF99" colspan="3">
                                    <i><font size="1"
color="#008000"><b><u>Note</u>:</b> 
```

Fig. A.38　Document 2 original HTML source (page 4).

```
                    <b>All
                    Meal Memberships are a two semester
                    commitment.  You must sign up for
                    the same dollar value meal membership in
                    the Spring semester as you did in the
                    Fall semester.  Prices above are
                    for one semester only, and include tax
                    on the meal membership portion.</b></font></i></td>
                  </tr>
                </table>
              </div>
              <p><font size="2" color="#333333">
              <b>Block Memberships<br>
              </b></font><font size="1" color="#333333"><br>
              Block memberships provide flexibility to your
              dining needs by offering a set number of meals
              per semester ñ 150, 90, 50.  This allows you to
              ration your meals yourself, eating as often as
              you like each week.  These meals can be used at
              The Fresh Food Company or Andros Dining Center
              and with the block membership, you also receive
              <a
href="JavaScript:openwindow('termsFlexBucks.htm','terms',510,300)">Flex Bucks</a> that can be
used at any USF Dining
              Location. <br>
              <br>
              BULLBlock 150 ñ Available to all students,
              faculty, and staff members<br>
              <br>
              BULLBlock 90 ñ Available to <a
href="JavaScript:openwindow('termsMandatoryStudent.htm','terms',510,200)">Mandatory</a>
students
              in Greek Village, Holly, Kosove, and Maple
              Apartments.  Also available to
              <a
href="JavaScript:openwindow('termsVoluntaryStudent.htm','terms',510,350)">
              Voluntary</a>
              students, faculty, and staff members.<br>
              <br>
              BULLBlock 50 ñ Available to faculty, staff, and
              <a
href="JavaScript:openwindow('termsVoluntaryStudent.htm','terms',510,350)">
              Voluntary</a> students only.</font></p>
              <div align="center">
                <table class="ta" border="0" cellpadding="4" cellspacing="1"
style="border-collapse: collapse" bordercolor="#111111" width="480" id="table5">
                  <tr>
                    <td width="100%" colspan="3" bgcolor="#336633">
                    <font color="#FFFFFF"><b>Semester Block
                    Membership Details</b></font></td>
                  </tr>
                  <tr>
                    <td width="21%" bgcolor="#EAEAD5" align="center">
                    <b><font size="1">BULLBlock 150</font></b></td>
                    <td width="53%" bgcolor="#EAEAD5" align="center">
                    <p align="left"><font size="1">$150 Flex
                    &amp; 150 meals per semester. </font></td>
                    <td width="21%" bgcolor="#EAEAD5" align="center">
                    <font size="1">$1265.24<br>
                    (<i>$6.95 per meal</i>)</font></td>
```

Fig. A.39 Document 2 original HTML source (page 5).

```
</tr>
<tr>
  <td width="21%" bgcolor="#EAEAD5" align="center">
  <p align="center"><b><font size="1">
  BULLBlock 90</font></b></td>
  <td width="53%" bgcolor="#EAEAD5">
  <font size="1">$300 Flex and 90 meals per
  semester.</font></td>
  <td width="21%" bgcolor="#EAEAD5">
  <p align="center"><font size="1">$900.91<br>
  (<i>$6.24 per meal</i>)</font></td>
</tr>
<tr>
  <td width="21%" bgcolor="#EAEAD5" align="center">
  <b><font size="1">BULLBlock 50</font></b></td>
  <td width="53%" bgcolor="#EAEAD5">
  <font size="1">$300 Flex and 50 meals per
  semester.</font></td>
  <td width="21%" bgcolor="#EAEAD5">
  <p align="center"><font size="1">$663.99<br>
  (<i>$6.80 per meal</i>)</font></td>
</tr>
<tr>
  <td width="95%" bgcolor="#FFFF99" align="center"
colspan="3">
  <p align="left">
  <i><font size="1"
color="#008000"><b><u>Note</u></b>:</b> 
    <b>All
    Meal Memberships are a two semester
    commitment.  You must sign up for
    the same dollar value meal membership in
    the Spring semester as you did in the
    Fall semester.  Prices above are
    for one semester only, and include tax
    on the meal membership portion.</b></font></i></td>
</tr>
</table>
</div>
<p><font size="2" color="#333333">
<b>Flex (FlexiBULL) Memberships</b></font><font size="1"
color="#333333"><br>

  <br>
  FlexiBULL memberships are all <a
href="JavaScript:openwindow('termsFlexBucks.htm','terms',510,300)">Flex Bucks</a>
  memberships that can be used at any USF Dining
  Location.  You pay an allotted amount for the
  membership ($1000, $500, or $300) and receive 10
  percent more on your account ($1100, $550,
  $330).  And even more ñ with your <a
href="JavaScript:openwindow('termsFlexBucks.htm','terms',510,300)">Flex Bucks</a> you
  enter The Club, which offers discounts at many
  of the USF Dining Locations.  <a
href="JavaScript:openwindow('termsFlexBucks.htm','terms',510,300)">Flex Bucks</a> carry
  over from the Fall to Spring semester with the
  purchase of the second semester membership. 
  Unused <a
href="JavaScript:openwindow('termsFlexBucks.htm','terms',510,300)">Flex Bucks</a> expire at the
end of the
  Spring semester.  Running low on <a
```

Fig. A.40   Document 2 original HTML source (page 6).

```
href="JavaScript:openwindow('termsFlexBucks.htm','terms',510,300)">Flex Bucks</a>?  You
                            can add more to your account at any time
                            (online, by phone, or at our Sales Office). 
                            FlexiBULL memberships are available to faculty,
                            staff, and
                            <a
href="JavaScript:openwindow('termsVoluntaryStudent.htm','terms',510,350)">
                            Voluntary</a> students only.</font></p>
                            <div align="center">
                              <table class="ta" border="0" cellpadding="4" cellspacing="1"
style="border-collapse: collapse" bordercolor="#111111" width="480" id="table6">
                                <tr>
                                  <td width="100%" colspan="2" bgcolor="#336633">
                                  <font color="#FFFFFF"><b>Flex Membership
                                  Details</b></font></td>
                                </tr>
                                <tr>
                                  <td width="30%" bgcolor="#EAEAD5" align="center">
                                   <b><font size="1">FlexiBULL 1000</font></b></td>
                                  <td width="66%" bgcolor="#EAEAD5" align="center">
                                   <p align="left"><font size="1">Pay $1000
                                  and Get $1100 Flex Bucks.</font></td>
                                </tr>
                                <tr>
                                  <td width="30%" bgcolor="#EAEAD5" align="center">
                                   <p align="center"><b><font size="1">
                                  FlexiBULL 500</font></b></td>
                                  <td width="66%" bgcolor="#EAEAD5">
                                  <font size="1">Pay $500 and Get $550 Flex
                                  Bucks.</font></td>
                                </tr>
                                <tr>
                                  <td width="30%" bgcolor="#EAEAD5" align="center">
                                  <b><font size="1">FlexiBULL 300</font></b></td>
                                  <td width="66%" bgcolor="#EAEAD5">
                                  <font size="1">Pay $300 and Get $330 Flex
                                  Bucks.</font></td>
                                </tr>
                                <tr>
                                  <td width="96%" bgcolor="#FFFF99" align="center"
colspan="2">

                                  <p align="left">
                                  <i><font size="1"
color="#008000"><b><u>Note</u>:</b> 
                                  <b>All
                                  Meal Memberships are a two semester
                                  commitment.  You must sign up for
                                  the same dollar value meal membership in
                                  the Spring semester as you did in the
                                  Fall semester.  Prices above are
                                  for one semester only, and include tax
                                  on the meal membership portion.</b></font></i></td>
                                </tr>
                              </table>
                              </div>
                            <p><font size="1" color="#333333"><b>Sign up TODAY!</b><br>
                            Signing up for a meal membership is easy!  You
                            can sign up <a href="mealplans2.php">online,
                            by mail, walk-in, or by fax</a>.  Be sure to understand whe
                            or not you are a <a
```

Fig. A.41   Document 2 original HTML source (page 7).

```
href="JavaScript:openwindow('termsMandatoryStudent.htm','terms',510,200)">Mandatory</a> or <a
href="JavaScript:openwindow('termsVoluntaryStudent.htm','terms',510,350)">Voluntary</a>
                          student ñ this reflects which membership you can
                          select.  <b>All memberships are a two-semester
                          commitment (Fall and Spring). </b> <br>
                          <br>
                          </font>
                          <font size="2" color="#333333">
                          <b><a href="mealplans2.php">SAVE TIME - SIGN UP
                          ONLINE!</a></b></font><font size="1" color="#333333"><br>
                          </font><br>
                          Read the <a href="mealplans2.php">2004/2005 Terms and
                          Conditions</a><br>
                           </td>
                        </tr>
                      </table></center>
                    </div></td>
                  </tr>
                </table>
              </td>
            </tr>
          </table>
        </td>
      </tr>
    </table>

  </center>
</div>
<!-- End ImageReady Slices -->
<div align="center">
  <center>
  <table border="0" cellpadding="0" cellspacing="0" style="border-collapse: collapse"
bordercolor="#111111" width="700" id="AutoNumber7" bgcolor="#000000">
    <tr>
      <td width="100%">
        <img border="0" src="images/spacer.gif" width="1" height="1"></td>
    </tr>
  </table>
  </center>
</div>

<!-- ImageReady Slices (Untitled-2) -->
<div align="center">
  <center>
<TABLE class="tab" WIDTH=700 BORDER=0 CELLPADDING=0 CELLSPACING=0>
    <TR>
        <TD COLSPAN=4>
            <IMG SRC="images/f_01.gif" ALT="" width="700" height="4"></TD>
    </TR>
    <TR>
        <TD>
            <IMG SRC="images/f_02.gif" ALT="" width="449" height="21"></TD>
        <TD>
        <a onmouseover="changeImages( /*CMP*/'f1',/*URL*/'images/fr_03.gif');return true"
onmouseout="changeImages( /*CMP*/'f1',/*URL*/'images/f_03.gif');return true" target="_blank"
href="http://www.usf.edu/">
            <IMG SRC="images/f_03.gif" name="f1" ALT="" border="0" width="114"
height="21"></a></TD>
        <TD><a onmouseover="changeImages( /*CMP*/'f2',/*URL*/'images/fr_04.gif');return true"
```

Fig. A.42   Document 2 original HTML source (page 8).

```
onmouseout="changeImages( /*CMP*/'f2',/*URL*/'images/f_04.gif');return true"
href="http://www.aramark.com" target="_blank">
        <IMG SRC="images/f_04.gif" name="f2" ALT="" border="0" width="61" height="21"></a></TD>
        <TD>
        <a onmouseover="changeImages( /*CMP*/'f3',/*URL*/'images/fr_05.gif');return true"
onmouseout="changeImages( /*CMP*/'f3',/*URL*/'images/f_05.gif');return true" target="_self"
href="nutrition.php">
        <IMG SRC="images/f_05.gif" name="f3" ALT="" border="0" width="76" height="21"></a></TD>
    </TR>
</TABLE>
   </center>
</div>
<!-- End ImageReady Slices -->
</BODY>
</HTML>
```

Fig. A.43   Document 2 original HTML source (page 9).

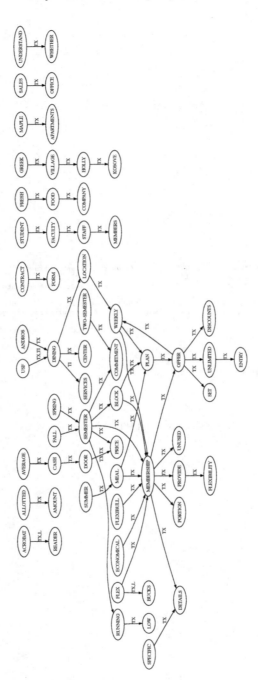

Fig. A.44   Graph created from the document 2 using the standard representation with isolated nodes omitted.

INTERNATIONAL AFFAIRS
Bridging the World

Home

Programs

Safety Abroad

Financial Information

Study Abroad Basics

FAQs

Applications/Forms

Announcements/Events

For USF Faculty

About Us

International Affairs

USF Home

Cooper Hall, Room 468
University of South Florida
4202 E. Fowler Ave., CPR107
Tampa, FL 33620-5550 USA
Tel: (813) 974-4314
Fax: (813) 974-4613
studyabroad@iac.usf.edu

Study Abroad Office

Dear USF Study Abroad Student,

As you already know, your safety abroad is of great concern to us. In this ever-changing world, situations within the global community cause us all to remain diligent and alert. It is with this in mind that the Office of Study Abroad is sending out the following information concerning your safety while you are overseas.

First, you should register with the U.S. Consulate or Embassy in your country. If you have not done this, please do it immediately. It is important that the Consulate/Embassy staff know where you are living abroad and how to contact you; you should also have the phone number of the Consulate/Embassy in case you need to contact them.

Secondly, we urge you to maintain a "low profile" while you are abroad. This means blending in to the local culture as much as possible. Do not travel in large packs, speaking English loudly, and wearing clothes with your school logo. Travel around the city and country in small groups, quietly, and dress like someone who lives in this country.

If a world emergency arises while you are abroad, do not panic. It is likely that a war in Iraq, for example, will have no effect on your daily life. But do remain in close contact with the International Student Office at your university where you are studying. They, in turn, are in constant contact with us, and we are with them. You should also keep in contact with your family while you are away, because they will worry more about you. Phone them or send them e-mail frequently to reassure them.

If you are traveling on the weekend, it is important that someone know where you are. Leave contact information, or an itinerary with a roommate, a flat-mate, or a friend. And return when you say you are planning to, or telephone to tell your friends that you are staying later. It is important that someone know where you are when you are away from campus. Take with you when you travel the telephone number of the international office at your host university, and, if they have one, their emergency phone number, and use these if you need to.

If an emergency situation arises when you are away from school, and you cannot contact your host university, call the Office of Study Abroad at USF immediately. Our contact numbers are below.

We also urge you to avoid any crowd activity while you are away. Do not join demonstrations for or against anything! Keep away from such demonstrations, as crowd behavior can be unpredictable. Do not enter into arguments or heated

Fig. A.45   Document 3 as rendered in a web browser (page 1).

discussions in pubs or clubs where there may be anti-American, or anti-American-policy opinions expressed. Again... keep a low profile.

We are including the web site links listed below for additional information concerning safety abroad, and we ask you to visit these sites. You will find the information very helpful and of use during your time abroad, regardless of any changes in the world. It is practical information which applies to all Americans abroad, and some material that is specifically geared towards you, those participating on academic programs abroad. You'll find information on how to "blend in" as much as possible while abroad.

Feel free to contact this office if you have any questions or concerns regarding any information presented in this message. You will find USF Emergency Contact information, as well as the location and contact details of the closest US Embassy/Consulate to your varied locations abroad, at the end of this message. Please keep these contacts with you at all times in case of emergency. We remain committed to helping you if the need arises.

At the same time, we want you to continue to enjoy your semester abroad. We do not want to alarm you unnecessarily, and we believe you are in no danger, so long as you follow the instructions above and use good common sense about where to go and how to behave. We wish you a good semester and look forward to hearing from you.

Sincerely,

Office of Study Abroad
University of South Florida

From the US State Department:

"A Safe Trip Abroad": http://travel.state.gov/asafetripabroad.html **(Excellent Resource)**

"Tips for Students": http://travel.state.gov/studentinfo.html

"Crises Awareness and Preparedness": http://travel.state.gov/crisismg.html

Emergency Contact Information:

Office of Study Abroad & Exchanges
International Affairs Center
Office Address: 468 Cooper Hall
Mailing Address: 4202 East Fowler Avenue, CPR107
University of South Florida
Tampa, Florida 33620-5550

Front Desk Office Phone: (813) 974-4314
(this phone is answered from 8:00 a.m. until 5:00 p.m., Monday - Friday.)

Fax Number: (813) 974-4613

Phone Numbers / E-mail Addresses for Emergency Contact

Ms. Susan Ansara, Director, Office of Study Abroad & Exchanges
Office Phone: (813) 974-4126
E-mail: ansara@iac.usf.edu

USF Campus Police
Phone: **(813) 974-2628**
* This phone is staffed **24 hours per day** and will contact the Dean of International

Fig. A.46   Document 3 as rendered in a web browser (page 2).

Affairs and the Director of Study Abroad & Exchanges in case of a student emergencies while abroad. The campus telecommunications equipment does not accept collect calls.

Contact Information for US Overseas Embassy/Consular Offices

You can also find information on US Overseas Embassy/Consular Offices at: http://usembassy.state.gov/

AUSTRALIA

Consulate General of the United States- Sydney
MLC Centre, Level 59
19-29 Martin Place
Sydney, NSW 2000
Phone: (61-2) 9373-9200
Fax: (61-2) 9373-9184
E-mail: amvisa@state.gov
Web: http://usembassy-australia.state.gov/sydney

Consulate General of the United States- Melbourne
553 St. Kilda Road
Melbourne, VIC 3004
Phone: (61-3) 9526-5900
Fax: (61-3) 9525-0769
E-mail: MelbourneACS@state.gov
Web: http://usembassy-australia.state.gov/melbourne

Consulate General of the United States- Perth
16 St. George's Terrace, 13th Floor
Perth, WA 6000
Phone: (61-8) 9202-1224
Phone (After Hour Emergencies): (08) 9476-0081
Fax: (08) 9231-9444
E-mail: usgperth@starwwon.com.au
Web: http://usembassy-australia.state.gov/perth/

COSTA RICA

United States Embassy, San Jose, Costa Rica
Calle 120 Avenida 0
Pavas, San Jose, Costa Rica
Phone: (506) 220-3939
After Hour Emergencies: (506) 220-3127
Fax: (506) 220-2305
E-mail: consular@usembassy.or.cr
Web: http://usembassy.or.cr/index.html

FRANCE

US Embassy Paris, Consular Section
2, rue Saint-Florentin
75382 Paris Cedex 8
Phone: 01-4312-2222
Fax: 01-4261-6140
Web: http://www.amb-usa.fr/consul/oas_home.htm

GERMANY

Fig. A.47   Document 3 as rendered in a web browser (page 3).

Embassy of the United States Berlin
Clayallee 170
14195 Berlin
Federal Republic of Germany
Phone: (030) 832-9233
Fax: (030) 8305-1215
E-mail: ConsBerlin@state.gov
Web: http://www.usembassy.de/e0.htm

US Consulate General Munich
Königinstraße 5
80539 Munchen
Federal Republic of Germany
Phone: (089) 2880-0
Fax: (089) 280-9998
Web: http://www.usembassy.de/e0.htm

JAPAN

American Citizen Services
American Consulate General Osaka-Kobe
11-5 Nishitenma 2-chome
Kita-ku, Osaka 530-8543
Phone: (06) 6315-5912
Fax: (06) 6315-5914
E-mail: acsok@gol.com
Web: http://www.senri-i.or.jp/amcon/usa_01.html

MEXICO

Citizen Consular Services
Embassy of the United States of America
Paseo de la Reforma 305
Colonia Cuauhtemoc
06500 Mexicao, D.F.
Phone (in Mexico): (01-55) 5080-2000
Phone (from US): 011-52-55-5080-2000
Fax: (01-55) 5525-5040
Web: http://www.usembassy-mexico.gov/emenu.html

SPAIN

American Embassy- Madrid
American Consular Services
Calle Serrano 75
28006 Madrid
Phone: 91-587-2240
Phone (after hour emergencies): 91-587-2200 (ask to speak to the duty officer)
Web: http://www.embusa.es/indexbis.html

UNITED KINGDOM

American Embassy, London
24 Grosvenor Square
London, W1A 1AE
United Kingdom
Phone: (44) (0) 20 7499-9000
Web: http://www.usembassy.org.uk

US Consulate General, Edinburgh, Scotland
Consulate General

Fig. A.48   Document 3 as rendered in a web browser (page 4).

3 Regent Terrace
Scotland, EHY 5BW
Phone: (44) (0) 131 556-8315
Fax: (44) (0) 131 557-6023
Web: http://www.usembassy.org.uk

Updated 10/17/2003. © 2003 *USF International Affairs Center.*
Please send comments, questions, or suggestions to the *Webmaster.*

Fig. A.49 Document 3 as rendered in a web browser (page 5).

```
<html>
 <head>
 <title>Safety | USF Study Abroad &amp; Exchanges Home | International Affairs Center -
University of South Florida</title>

<meta name="usf" content="iac@iac.usf.edu">
<meta name="keywords" content="overseas, study abroad, international, france, germany, iceland,
tahiti, ireland, russia, brazil,
 mexico, england, cambridge, costa rica, spain, italy, europe">
<meta name="description" content="USF's Study Abroad programs are
designed to appeal to all types of students.
Through classes and field trips, students earn USF credit abroad.
Teachers may update their linguistic skills or earn credits toward
recertification.  Programs are directed by USF faculty members with
expertise in the field of study being offered and an in-depth knowledge
of the country in which the program takes place.">
 </head>
<body background="globe_background.gif" alink="gold" vlink="green" link="darkgreen">
<span style="font-family: arial"> <a name="Top"></a></span>
<TABLE align="center" width="717">
  <TR>
    <TH> <span style="font-family: arial"> <img src="iaclogo1.jpg" border=0
usemap="#Map"></span>
  </TR>
  <TR>
    <TH BGCOLOR="GOLD"></TH>
  </TR>
</TABLE>

<table cellpadding=7 cellspacing="2" width="718" align="center" height="231">
  <tr>
    <td height="2" width="26%">
      <div align="left"><font size="2" face="Arial, Helvetica, sans-serif"><b><span
style="font-family: arial"><a href="index.html">Home</a></span></b></font></div>
    </td>
    <th height="2" width="74%" bgcolor="#FFFFCC"><b><font size="4" face="Arial, Helvetica,
sans-serif" color="#336600">Study
      Abroad Office</font></b></th>
  </tr>
  <tr>
    <td width="26%" height="0">
      <div align="left"><font size="2" face="Arial, Helvetica, sans-serif"><b><span
style="font-family: arial"><span style="font-family: arial"><a
href="programs.htm">Programs</a></span></span></b></font></div>
    </td>
    <td height="157" rowspan="13" width="74%">
      <p><font face="Arial, Helvetica, sans-serif" size="2">Dear USF Study Abroad
        Student,</font></p>
      <p><font face="Arial, Helvetica, sans-serif" size="2">As you already know,
        your safety abroad is of great concern to us. In this ever-changing world,
        situations within the global community cause us all to remain diligent
        and alert. It is with this in mind that the Office of Study Abroad is
        sending out the following information concerning your safety while you
        are overseas. <br>
        <br>
        First, you should register with the U.S. Consulate or Embassy in your
        country. If you have not done this, please do it immediately. It is important
        that the Consulate/Embassy staff know where you are living abroad and
        how to contact you; you should also have the phone number of the Consulate/Embassy
        in case you need to contact them. </font></p>
```

Fig. A.50   Document 3 original HTML source (page 1).

```
<p><font face="Arial, Helvetica, sans-serif" size="2">Secondly, we urge
you to maintain a &quot;low profile&quot; while you are abroad. This means
blending in to the local culture as much as possible. Do not travel in
large packs, speaking English loudly, and wearing clothes with your school
logo. Travel around the city and country in small groups, quietly, and
dress like someone who lives in this country. </font></p>
<p><font face="Arial, Helvetica, sans-serif" size="2">If a world emergency
arises while you are abroad, do not panic. It is likely that a war in
Iraq, for example, will have no effect on your daily life. But do remain
in close contact with the International Student Office at your university
where you are studying. They, in turn, are in constant contact with us,
and we are with them. You should also keep in contact with your family
while you are away, because they will worry more about you. Phone them
or send them e-mail frequently to reassure them.</font></p>
<p><font face="Arial, Helvetica, sans-serif" size="2">If you are traveling
on the weekend, it is important that someone know where you are. Leave
contact information, or an itinerary with a roommate, a flat-mate, or
a friend. And return when you say you are planning to, or telephone to
tell your friends that you are staying later. It is important that someone
know where you are when you are away from campus. Take with you when you
travel the telephone number of the international office at your host university,
and, if they have one, their emergency phone number, and use these if
you need to.</font></p>
<p><font face="Arial, Helvetica, sans-serif" size="2">If an emergency situation
arises when you are away from school, and you cannot contact your host
university, call the Office of Study Abroad at USF immediately. Our contact
numbers are below. </font></p>
<p><font face="Arial, Helvetica, sans-serif" size="2">We also urge you to
avoid any crowd activity while you are away. Do not join demonstrations
for or against anything! Keep away from such demonstrations, as crowd
behavior can be unpredictable. Do not enter into arguments or heated discussions
in pubs or clubs where there may be anti-American, or anti-American-policy
opinions expressed. Again... keep a low profile.</font></p>
<p><font face="Arial, Helvetica, sans-serif" size="2">We are including the
web site links listed below for additional information concerning safety
abroad, and we ask you to visit these sites. You will find the information
very helpful and of use during your time abroad, regardless of any changes
in the world. It is practical information which applies to all Americans
abroad, and some material that is specifically geared towards you, those
participating on academic programs abroad. You'll find information on
how to &quot;blend in&quot; as much as possible while abroad.</font></p>
<p><font face="Arial, Helvetica, sans-serif" size="2">Feel free to contact
this office if you have any questions or concerns regarding any information
presented in this message. You will find USF Emergency Contact information,
as well as the location and contact details of the closest US Embassy/Consulate
to your varied locations abroad, at the end of this message. Please keep
these contacts with you at all times in case of emergency. We remain committed
to helping you if the need arises.</font></p>
<p><font face="Arial, Helvetica, sans-serif" size="2">At the same time,
we want you to continue to enjoy your semester abroad. We do not want
to alarm you unnecessarily, and we believe you are in no danger, so long
as you follow the instructions above and use good common sense about where
to go and how to behave. We wish you a good semester and look forward
to hearing from you.</font></p>
<p><font face="Arial, Helvetica, sans-serif" size="2">Sincerely,</font></p>
<p><font face="Arial, Helvetica, sans-serif" size="2">Office of Study Abroad<br>
University of South Florida<br>

--------------------------------------------------------------------------------</font></p>
<p><font face="Arial, Helvetica, sans-serif" size="2"><b>From the US State
```

Fig. A.51 Document 3 original HTML source (page 2).

```
    Department:</b></font></p>
  <p><font face="Arial, Helvetica, sans-serif" size="2">&quot;A Safe Trip
    Abroad&quot;:  <a href="http://travel.state.gov/asafetripabroad.html"
target="_blank">http://travel.state.gov/asafetripabroad.html</a>
    (Excellent Resource)</font></p>
  <p><font face="Arial, Helvetica, sans-serif" size="2">&quot;Tips for Students&quot;:
    <a href="http://travel.state.gov/studentinfo.html"
target="_blank">http://travel.state.gov/studentinfo.html</a></font></p>
  <p><font face="Arial, Helvetica, sans-serif" size="2">&quot;Crises Awareness
    and Preparedness&quot;:  <a href="http://travel.state.gov/crisismg.html"
target="_blank">http://travel.state.gov/crisismg.html</a></font></p>
  <p><font face="Arial, Helvetica, sans-serif" size="2"><br>
    <b>Emergency Contact Information:</b></font></p>
  <p><font face="Arial, Helvetica, sans-serif" size="2">Office of Study Abroad
    &amp; Exchanges<br>
    International Affairs Center<br>
    Office Address: 468 Cooper Hall<br>
    Mailing Address: 4202 East Fowler Avenue, CPR107<br>
    University of South Florida<br>
    Tampa, Florida 33620-5550</font></p>
  <p><font face="Arial, Helvetica, sans-serif" size="2">Front Desk Office
    Phone: (813) 974-4314<br>
    (this phone is answered from 8:00 a.m. until 5:00 p.m., Monday - Friday.)</font></p>
  <p><font face="Arial, Helvetica, sans-serif" size="2">Fax Number: (813)
    974-4613</font></p>
  <p><font face="Arial, Helvetica, sans-serif" size="2"><b>Phone Numbers /
    E-mail Addresses for Emergency Contact</b></font></p>
  <p><font face="Arial, Helvetica, sans-serif" size="2">Ms. Susan Ansara,
    Director, Office of Study Abroad &amp; Exchanges<br>
    Office Phone: (813) 974-4126<br>
    E-mail: <a href="mailto:ansara@iac.usf.edu">ansara@iac.usf.edu</a></font></p>
  <p><font face="Arial, Helvetica, sans-serif" size="2">USF Campus Police<br>
    Phone: <b>(813) 974-2628</b><br>
    * This phone is staffed<b> 24 hours per day</b> and will contact the Dean
    of International Affairs and the Director of Study Abroad &amp; Exchanges
    in case of a student emergencies while abroad. The campus telecommunications
    equipment does not accept collect calls.</font></p>
  <p><font face="Arial, Helvetica, sans-serif" size="2"><br>
    <b>Contact Information for US Overseas Embassy/Consular Offices</b></font></p>
  <p><font face="Arial, Helvetica, sans-serif" size="2">You can also find
    information on US Overseas Embassy/Consular Offices at: <a
href="http://usembassy.state.gov/">http://usembassy.state.gov/</a></font></p>
  <p><font face="Arial, Helvetica, sans-serif" size="2"><b>AUSTRALIA</b></font></p>
  <p><font face="Arial, Helvetica, sans-serif" size="2">Consulate General
    of the United States- Sydney<br>
    MLC Centre, Level 59<br>
    19-29 Martin Place<br>
    Sydney, NSW 2000<br>
    Phone: (61-2) 9373-9200<br>
    Fax: (61-2) 9373-9184<br>
    E-mail: <a href="mailto:amvisa@state.gov">amvisa@state.gov</a><br>
    Web: <a href="http://usembassy-australia.state.gov/sydney"
target="_blank">http://usembassy-australia.state.gov/sydney</a></font></p>
  <p><font face="Arial, Helvetica, sans-serif" size="2">Consulate General
    of the United States- Melbourne<br>
    553 St. Kilda Road<br>
    Melbourne, VIC 3004<br>
    Phone: (61-3) 9526-5900<br>
    Fax: (61-3) 9525-0769<br>
    E-mail: <a href="mailto:MelbourneACS@state.gov">MelbourneACS@state.gov</a><br>
```

Fig. A.52   Document 3 original HTML source (page 3).

```
        Web: <a href="http://usembassy-australia.state.gov/melbourne"
target="_blank">http://usembassy-australia.state.gov/melbourne</a></font></p>
        <p><font face="Arial, Helvetica, sans-serif" size="2">Consulate General
        of the United States- Perth<br>
        16 St. George's Terrace, 13th Floor<br>
        Perth, WA 6000<br>
        Phone: (61-8) 9202-1224<br>
        Phone (After Hour Emergencies): (08) 9476-0081<br>
        Fax: (08) 9231-9444<br>
        E-mail: <a href="mailto:usgperth@starwwon.com.au">usgperth@starwwon.com.au</a><br>
        Web: <a href="http://usembassy-australia.state.gov/perth/"
target="_blank">http://usembassy-australia.state.gov/perth/</a></font></p>
        <p><font face="Arial, Helvetica, sans-serif" size="2"><b>COSTA RICA</b></font></p>
        <p><font face="Arial, Helvetica, sans-serif" size="2">United States Embassy,
        San Jose, Costa Rica<br>
        Calle 120 Avenida 0<br>
        Pavas, San Jose, Costa Rica<br>
        Phone: (506) 220-3939<br>
        After Hour Emergencies: (506) 220-3127<br>
        Fax: (506) 220-2305<br>
        E-mail: <a href="mailto:consular@usembassy.or.cr">consular@usembassy.or.cr</a><br>
        Web: <a href="http://usembassy.or.cr/index.html"
target="_blank">http://usembassy.or.cr/index.html</a></font></p>
        <p><font face="Arial, Helvetica, sans-serif" size="2"><b>FRANCE</b></font></p>
        <p><font face="Arial, Helvetica, sans-serif" size="2">US Embassy Paris,
        Consular Section<br>
        2, rue Saint-Florentin<br>
        75382 Paris Cedex 8<br>
        Phone: 01-4312-2222<br>
        Fax: 01-4261-6140<br>
        Web: <a href="http://www.amb-usa.fr/consul/oas_home.htm"
target="_blank">http://www.amb-usa.fr/consul/oas_home.htm</a></font></p>
        <p><font face="Arial, Helvetica, sans-serif" size="2"><b>GERMANY</b></font></p>
        <p><font face="Arial, Helvetica, sans-serif" size="2">Embassy of the United
        States Berlin<br>
        Clayallee 170<br>
        14195 Berlin<br>
        Federal Republic of Germany<br>
        Phone: (030) 832-9233<br>
        Fax: (030) 8305-1215<br>
        E-mail: <a href="mailto:ConsBerlin@state.gov">ConsBerlin@state.gov</a><br>
        Web: <a href="http://www.usembassy.de/e0.htm"
target="_blank">http://www.usembassy.de/e0.htm</a></font></p>
        <p><font face="Arial, Helvetica, sans-serif" size="2">US Consulate General
        Munich<br>
        K&ouml;niginstra&szlig;e 5<br>
        80539 Munchen<br>
        Federal Republic of Germany<br>
        Phone: (089) 2880-0<br>
        Fax: (089) 280-9998<br>
        Web: <a href="http://www.usembassy.de/e0.htm"
target="_blank">http://www.usembassy.de/e0.htm</a></font></p>
        <p><font face="Arial, Helvetica, sans-serif" size="2"><b>JAPAN</b></font></p>
        <p><font face="Arial, Helvetica, sans-serif" size="2">American Citizen Services<br>
        American Consulate General Osaka-Kobe<br>
        11-5 Nishitenma 2-chome<br>
        Kita-ku, Osaka 530-8543<br>
        Phone: (06) 6315-5912<br>
        Fax: (06) 6315-5914<br>
        E-mail: <a href="mailto:acsok@gol.com">acsok@gol.com</a><br>
```

Fig. A.53   Document 3 original HTML source (page 4).

```
          Web: <a href="http://www.senri-i.or.jp/amcon/usa_01.html"
target="_blank">http://www.senri-i.or.jp/amcon/usa_01.html</a></font></p>
        <p><font face="Arial, Helvetica, sans-serif" size="2"><b>MEXICO</b></font></p>
        <p><font face="Arial, Helvetica, sans-serif" size="2">Citizen Consular Services<br>
        Embassy of the United States of America<br>
        Paseo de la Reforma 305<br>
        Colonia Cuauhtemoc<br>
        06500 Mexicao, D.F.<br>
        Phone (in Mexico): (01-55) 5080-2000<br>
        Phone (from US): 011-52-55-5080-2000<br>
        Fax: (01-55) 5525-5040<br>
        Web: <a href="http://www.usembassy-mexico.gov/emenu.html"
target="_blank">http://www.usembassy-mexico.gov/emenu.html</a></font></p>
        <p><font face="Arial, Helvetica, sans-serif" size="2"><b>SPAIN</b></font></p>
        <p><font face="Arial, Helvetica, sans-serif" size="2">American Embassy-
        Madrid<br>
        American Consular Services<br>
        Calle Serrano 75<br>
        28006 Madrid<br>
        Phone: 91-587-2240<br>
        Phone (after hour emergencies): 91-587-2200 (ask to speak to the duty
        officer)<br>
        Web: <a href="http://www.embusa.es/indexbis.html"
target="_blank">http://www.embusa.es/indexbis.html</a></font></p>
        <p><font face="Arial, Helvetica, sans-serif" size="2"><b>UNITED KINGDOM</b></font></p>
        <p><font face="Arial, Helvetica, sans-serif" size="2">American Embassy,
        London<br>
        24 Grosvenor Square<br>
        London, W1A 1AE<br>
        United Kingdom<br>
        Phone: (44) (0) 20 7499-9000<br>
        Web: <a href="http://www.usembassy.org.uk"
target="_blank">http://www.usembassy.org.uk</a></font></p>
        <p><font face="Arial, Helvetica, sans-serif" size="2">US Consulate General,
        Edinburgh, Scotland<br>
        Consulate General<br>
        3 Regent Terrace<br>
        Scotland, EHY 5BW<br>
        Phone: (44) (0) 131 556-8315<br>
        Fax: (44) (0) 131 557-6023<br>
        Web: <a href="http://www.usembassy.org.uk"
target="_blank">http://www.usembassy.org.uk</a></font></p>
    </tr>
    <tr>
      <td width="26%" height="0"><font size="2" face="Arial, Helvetica, sans-serif"><b>Safety
        Abroad </b></font></td>
    </tr>
    <tr>
      <td width="26%" height="2"><b><font face="Arial, Helvetica, sans-serif" size="2"><span
style="font-family: arial"><a href="financial.htm">Financial
        Information</a></span></font></b></td>
    </tr>
    <tr>
      <td width="26%" height="2">
        <div align="left"><font size="2" face="Arial, Helvetica, sans-serif"><b><span
style="font-family: arial"><a href="basics.htm">Study
        Abroad Basics</a> </span></b></font></div>
      </td>
    </tr>
    <tr>
```

Fig. A.54   Document 3 original HTML source (page 5).

```
   <td width="26%" height="4">
      <div align="left"><font size="2" face="Arial, Helvetica, sans-serif"><b><a
href="faq.htm">FAQs</a></b></font></div>
   </td>
  </tr>
  <tr>
   <td width="26%" height="2">
      <div align="left"><font size="2" face="Arial, Helvetica, sans-serif"><b><a
href="SA-FORMS.htm">Applications/Forms</a></b></font></div>
   </td>
  </tr>
  <tr>
   <td width="26%">
      <div align="left"><font size="2" face="Arial, Helvetica, sans-serif"><b><a
href="announcements.htm">Announcements/Events</a></b></font></div>
   </td>
  </tr>
  <tr>
   <td width="26%" height="8"><font face="Arial, Helvetica, sans-serif" size="2"><b><a
href="faculty-info.htm">For
      USF Faculty</a></b></font> </td>
  </tr>
  <tr>
   <td width="26%" height="8">
      <p><font size="2" face="Arial, Helvetica, sans-serif"><b><span style="font-family:
arial"><a href="about.htm">About
      Us</a></span></b></font></p>
   </td>
  </tr>
  <tr>
   <td width="26%" height="28"><b><font size="2"><span style="font-family: arial"><a
href="http://web.usf.edu/iac/">International
      Affairs </a></span></font></b></td>
  </tr>
  <tr>
   <td width="26%" height="2">
      <p><font size="2"><span style="font-family: arial"><b><a href="http://www.usf.edu">USF
      Home</a> </b></span></font></p>
   </td>
  </tr>
  <tr>
   <td width="26%" height="159"><span style="font-family: arial"><font face="Arial, Helvetica,
sans-serif" size="1">Cooper
      Hall, Room 468</font></span><font face="Arial, Helvetica, sans-serif" size="1"><br>
      University of South Florida <br>
      4202 E. Fowler Ave., CPR107<br>
      Tampa, FL 33620-5550 USA</font><font size="1"><br>
      <span style="font-family: arial"><font face="Arial, Helvetica, sans-serif"><span
style="font-family: arial">Tel:
      (813) 974-4314<br>
      Fax: (813) 974-4613<br>
      <a href="mailto:studyabroad@iac.usf.edu">
studyabroad@iac.usf.edu</a></span></font></span></font>
   </td>
  </tr>
  <tr>
   <td width="26%" height="3202"> </td>
  </tr>
</table>
<span style="font-family: arial"></span>
```

Fig. A.55   Document 3 original HTML source (page 6).

```
<div align="center">
  <table width="77%" border="0" cellspacing="5" cellpadding="5" align="center" height="8">
    <tr>
      <td width="22%" height="2"> </td>
      <td width="56%" height="2">
        <div align="center">
          <map name="Map">
            <area shape="rect" coords="2,2,482,106" href="http://web.usf.edu/iac/"
alt="International Affairs Home | University of South Florida" title="International Affairs
Home | University of South Florida">
            <area shape="circle" coords="527,61,32" href="http://www.usf.edu/" alt="University
of South Florida Home" title="University of South Florida Home">
          </map>
          <p align="center"><span style="font-family: arial"><b><em><font size="-3">
            Updated 10/17/2003. &copy 2003<a href="http://web.usf.edu/iac/"> USF
            International Affairs Center</a>.<br>
            Please send comments, questions, or suggestions to the <a
href="mailto:studyabroad@iac.usf.edu">Webmaster</a>.</font></em></b></span>
          </p>
        </div>
      </td>
      <td width="22%" height="2"> </td>
    </tr>
  </table>
</div>
</body>
</html>
```

Fig. A.56   Document 3 original HTML source (page 7).

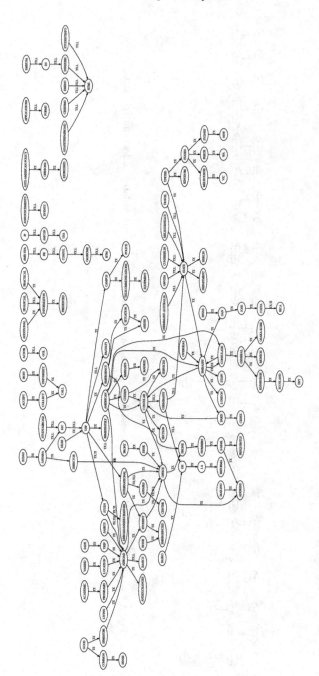

Fig. A.57   Graph created from the document 3 using the standard representation with isolated nodes omitted (part 1).

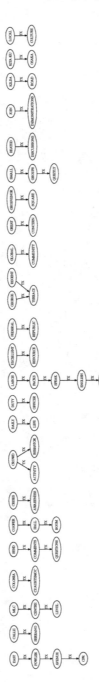

Fig. A.58   Graph created from the document 3 using the standard representation with isolated nodes omitted (part 2).

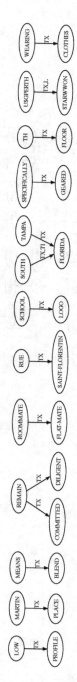

Fig. A.59 Graph created from the document 3 using the standard representation with isolated nodes omitted (part 3).

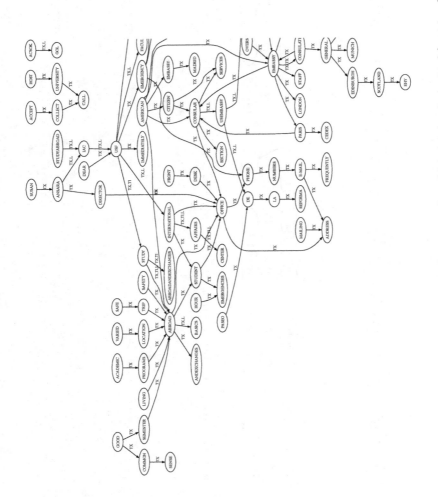

Fig. A.60   Graph created from the document 3 using the standard representation with isolated nodes omitted (part 1, enlargement, left side).

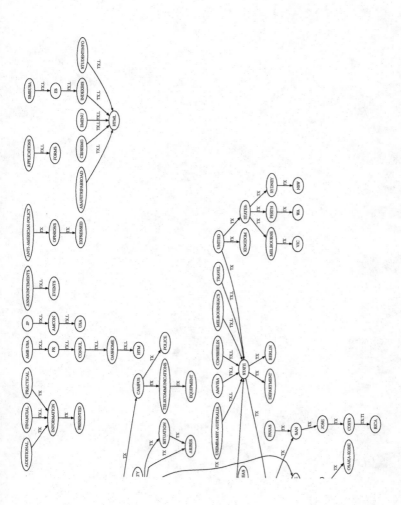

Fig. A.61 Graph created from the document 3 using the standard representation with isolated nodes omitted (part 1, enlargement, right side).

Appendix B

List of Stop Words

Table B.1 List of stop words.

A	ABOUT	ABOVE
ACCORDING	ACCORDINGLY	ACROSS
ACTUALLY	AFTER	AFTERWARDS
AGAIN	AINT	ALL
ALLOW	ALLOWS	ALMOST
ALONE	ALONG	ALREADY
ALSO	ALTHOUGH	ALWAYS
AMONG	AMONGST	AN
AND	ANOTHER	ANY
ANYBODY	ANYHOW	ANYONE
ANYTHING	ANYWAY	ANYWAYS
ANYWHERE	APART	APPEAR
APPRECIATE	APPROPRIATE	APPROXIMATELY
ARE	ARENT	AROUND
AS	ASIDE	ASK
ASKING	ASSOCIATED	AT
AVAILABLE	AVE	AWAY
AWFULLY	BACK	BE
BECAME	BECAUSE	BECOME
BECOMES	BECOMING	BEEN
BEFORE	BEFOREHAND	BEHIND
BEING	BELIEVE	BELOW
BESIDE	BESIDES	BEST
BETTER	BETWEEN	BEYOND
BLVD	BOTH	BRIEF
BROWSER	BUT	BY
CAME	CAN	CANNOT
CANT	CAUSE	CAUSES
CERTAIN	CERTAINLY	CHANGES
CLEARLY	CLICK	CMON
CO	COM	COME

215

Table B.2   List of stop words.

COMES	COMMENT	CONCERNING
CONTACT	CONTAIN	CONTAINING
CONTAINS	COPYRIGHT	CORRESPONDING
COULD	COULDNT	COURSE
CURRENTLY	DATE	DEFINITELY
DESCRIBED	DESPITE	DID
DIDNT	DIFFERENT	DO
DOES	DOESNT	DOING
DONE	DONT	DOWN
DOWNLOAD	DOWNWARDS	DR
DUE	DURING	EACH
EDU	EG	EIGHT
EITHER	ELSE	ELSEWHERE
EMAIL	ENOUGH	ENTIRELY
ESPECIALLY	ET	ETC
EVEN	EVER	EVERY
EVERYBODY	EVERYONE	EVERYTHING
EVERYWHERE	EX	EXACTLY
EXAMPLE	EXCEPT	FAR
FAX	FEW	FIFTH
FIND	FIRST	FIVE
FL	FOLLOWED	FOLLOWING
FOLLOWS	FOR	FORMER
FORMERLY	FOUND	FOURTH
FOUR	FRAME	FREE
FROM	FTP	FURTHER
FURTHERMORE	GET	GETS
GETTING	GIVE	GIVEN
GIVES	GIVING	GO
GOES	GOING	GONE
GOT	GOTTEN	GOV

Table B.3   List of stop words.

GREETINGS	HAD	HADNT
HAPPENS	HARDLY	HAS
HASNT	HAVE	HAVENT
HAVING	HE	HES
HELLO	HELP	HOME
HENCE	HER	HERE
HERES	HEREAFTER	HEREBY
HEREIN	HEREUPON	HERS
HERSELF	HI	HIM
HIMSELF	HIS	HITHER
HOPEFULLY	HOW	HOWBEIT
HOWEVER	HTTP	I
ID	IE	IF
IGNORED	ILL	IM
IMMEDIATE	IN	INASMUCH
INC	INCLUDE	INCLUDES
INDEED	INDEX	INDICATE
INDICATED	INDICATES	INNER
INSOFAR	INSTEAD	INTERNET
INTO	INWARD	IS
ISNT	IT	ITD
ITLL	ITS	ITSELF
IVE	JUST	KEEP
KEEPS	KEPT	KNOW
KNOWS	KNOWN	KG
KM	LARGELY	LAST
LATELY	LATER	LATTERLY
LEAST	LESS	LEST
LET	LETS	LIKE
LIKED	LIKELY	LINK
LINKS	LITTLE	LOOK

Table B.4   List of stop words.

LOOKING	LOOKS	LTD
MADE	MAIL	MAINLY
MAKE	MANY	MAY
MAYBE	ME	MEAN
MEANWHILE	MERELY	MIGHT
MIN	ML	MM
MORE	MOREOVER	MOST
MOSTLY	MORE	MOST
MOSTLY	MR	MRS
MS	MUCH	MUST
MY	MYSELF	NAME
NAMELY	NEAR	NEARLY
NECESSARY	NEED	NEEDS
NEITHER	NET	NEVER
NEVERTHELESS	NEW	NEXT
NINE	NO	NOBODY
NON	NONE	NOONE
NOR	NORMALLY	NOT
NOVEL	NOW	NOWHERE
NUMBER	OBTAIN	OBTAINED
OBVIOUSLY	OF	OFF
OFTEN	OH	OK
OKAY	OLD	ON
ONCE	ONE	ONES
ONLY	ONTO	OR
ORG	OTHER	OTHERS
OTHERWISE	OUGHT	OUR
OURS	OURSELVES	OUT
OUTSIDE	OVER	OVERALL
OWN	PAGE	PARTICULAR
PARTICULARLY	PER	PERHAPS

Table B.5   List of stop words.

PLACED	PLEASE	PLUS
POSSIBLE	PRESUMABLY	PREVIOUS
PREVIOUSLY	PROBABLY	PROVIDES
QUE	QUITE	QV
RATHER	RD	RE
REALLY	REASONABLY	REGARDING
REGARDLESS	REGARDS	RELATIVELY
RESERVED	RESPECTIVELY	RESULTED
RESULTING	RIGHT	RIGHTS
SAID	SAME	SAW
SAY	SAYING	SAYS
SEARCH	SECOND	SECONDLY
SEE	SEEING	SEEM
SEEMED	SEEMING	SEEMS
SEEN	SELF	SELVES
SENSIBLE	SENT	SERIOUS
SERIOUSLY	SEVEN	SEVERAL
SHALL	SHE	SHOULD
SHOULDNT	SHOW	SHOWED
SHOWN	SHOWS	SIGNIFICANT
SIGNIFICANTLY	SINCE	SITE
SIX	SO	SOME
SOMEBODY	SOMEHOW	SOMEONE
SOMETHING	SOMEWHAT	SOMEWHERE
SOON	SORRY	SPECIFIED
SPECIFY	SPECIFYING	ST
STILL	SUB	SUCH
SUGGEST	SUP	SURE
TAKE	TAKEN	TELL
TENDS	THAN	THANK
THANKS	THANX	THAT

Table B.6   List of stop words.

THATS	THE	THEIR
THEIRS	THEM	THEMSELVES
THEN	THENCE	THERE
THERES	THEREAFTER	THEREBY
THEREFORE	THEREIN	THERES
THEREUPON	THESE	THEY
THEYD	THEYLL	THEYRE
THEYVE	THINK	THIRD
THIS	THOROUGH	THOROUGHLY
THOSE	THOUGH	THREE
THROUGH	THOROUGHLY	THRU
THUS	TIME	TITLE
TO	TOGETHER	TOP
TOO	TOOK	TOWARD
TOWARDS	TRIED	TRIES
TRULY	TRY	TRYING
TWICE	TWO	UN
UNDER	UNFORTUNATELY	UNLESS
UNLIKELY	UNTIL	UNTITLED
UNTO	UP	UPDATED
UPON	US	USE
USED	USEFUL	USES
USING	USUALLY	UUCP
VALUE	VARIOUS	VERSION
VERY	VIA	VIZ
VOL	VS	WANT
WANTS	WAS	WASNT
WAY	WE	WEB
WED	WELCOME	WELL
WENT	WERE	WERE
WERENT	WEVE	WHAT

Table B.7   List of stop words.

WHATS	WHATEVER	WHEN
WHENCE	WHENEVER	WHERE
WHEREAFTER	WHEREAS	WHEREBY
WHEREIN	WHEREUPON	WHEREVER
WHICH	WHILE	WHITHER
WHO	WHOS	WHOEVER
WHOLE	WHOM	WHOSE
WHY	WIDE	WILL
WILLING	WISH	WITH
WITHIN	WITHOUT	WONT
WONDER	WORLD	WOULD
WOULDNT	WWW	YES
YET	YOU	YOUD
YOULL	YOUR	YOURE
YOUVE	YOUR	YOURS
YOURSELF	YOURSEVES	ZERO

Bibliography

C. Apte, F. Damerau, and S. M. Weiss. Automated learning of decision rules for text categorization. *ACM Transactions on Information Systems*, 12:233–251, 1994.

H. Ahonen, O. Heinonen, M. Klemettinen, and A. I. Verkamo. Applying data mining techniques in text analysis. Technical Report C-1997-23, University of Helsinki, Department of Computer Science, March 1997.

R. Agrawal, R. J. Bayardo Jr., and R. Srikant. Athena: Mining-based interactive management of text databases. In *Proceedings of the 7th Conference on Extending Database Technology*, 2000.

D. Beeferman and A. Berger. Agglomerative clustering of a search engine query log. In *Proceedings of the 6th International Conference on Knowledge Discovery and Data Mining ACM SIGKDD*, 2000.

D. Boley, M. Gini, R. Gross, E. H. Han, K. Hastings, G. Karypis, B. Mobasher, and J. Moore. Partitioning-based clustering for web document categorization. *Decision Support Systems*, 27:329–341, 1999.

D. Boley, M. Gini, R. Gross, E.-H. (Sam) Han, K. Hastings, G. Karypis, V. Kumar, B. Mobasher, and J. Moore. Document categorization and query generation on the World Wide Web using WebACE. *AI Review*, 13, 1999.

H. Bunke, S. Gnter, and X. Jiang. Towards bridging the gap between statistical and structural pattern recognition: Two new concepts in graph matching. In S. Singh, N. Murshed, and W. Kropatsch, editors, *Advances in Pattern Recognition — ICAPR 2001*, volume 2013 of *Lecture Notes in Computer Science*, pages 1–11. Springer-Verlag, 2001.

H. Bunke, X. Jiang, and A. Kandel. On the minimum common supergraph of two graphs. *Computing*, 65:13–25, 2000.

H. Bunke and A. Kandel. Mean and maximum common subgraph of two graphs. *Pattern Recognition Letters*, 21:163–168, 2000.

D. L. Boley. Principal direction divisive partitioning. *Data Mining and Knowledge Discovery*, 2(4):325–344, 1998.

P. De Boeck and S. Rosenberg. Hierarchical classes: Model and data analysis. *Psychometrika*, 53(3):361–381, 1988.

L. Breiman. Bagging predictors. *Machine Learning*, 24(2):123–140, 1996.

H. Bunke and K. Shearer. A graph distance metric based on the maximal common subgraph. *Pattern Recognition Letters*, 19:255–259, 1998.

H. Bunke. On a relation between graph edit distance and maximum common subgraph. *Pattern Recognition Letters*, 18:689–694, 1997.

H. Bunke. Error correcting graph matching: On the influence of the underlying cost function. *IEEE Transactions on Pattern Analysis and Machine Intelligence*, 21(9):917–922, September 1999.

H. Bunke. Recent developments in graph matching. In *Proceedings of the 15th International Conference on Pattern Recognition*, volume 2, pages 117–124, 2000.

R. Baeza-Yates and B. Ribeiro-Neto. *Modern Information Retrieval*. Addison-Wesley, 1999.

T. F. Cox and M. A. A. Cox. *Multidimensional Scaling*. Chapman and Hall, 1994.

D. B. Crouch, C. J. Crouch, and G. Andreas. The use of cluster hierarchies in hypertext information retrieval. In *Proceedings of the ACM Hypertext '89 Conference*, pages 225–237, 1989.

D. Conte, P. Foggia, C. Sansone, and M. Vento. Thirty years of graph matching in pattern recognition. *International Journal of Pattern Recognition and Artificial Intelligence*, 18(3):265–298, 2004.

C.-H. Chang and C.-C. Hsu. Customizable multi-engine search tool with clustering. *Computer Networks and ISDN Systems*, 29:1217–1224, 1997.

G. Chartrand, G. Kubicki, , and M. Schultz. Graph similarity and distance in graphs. *Aequationes Mathematicae*, 55:129–145, 1998.

T. H. Cormen, C. E. Leiserson, and R. L. Rivest. *Introduction to Algorithms*. The MIT Press, 1997.

T. M. Cover and J. A. Thomas. *Elements of Information Theory*. Wiley, 1991.

M. Crochemore and R. Vérin. Direct construction of compact directed acyclic word graphs. In A. Apostolico and J. Hein, editors, *CPM97*, volume 1264 of *Lecture Notes in Computer Science*, pages 116–129. Springer-Verlag, 1997.

S. Chakrabarti, M. H. van den Berg, and B. E. Dom. Distributed hypertext resource discovery through examples. In *Proceedings of the 25th International Conference on Very Large Databases*, pages 375–386, 1999.

A. D. J. Cross, R. C. Wilson, and E. R. Hancock. Inexact graph matching using genetic search. *Pattern Recognition*, 30(6):953–970, 1997.

D. Davies and D. Bouldin. A cluster separation measure. *IEEE Transactions on Pattern Recognition and Machine Intelligence*, 1(2):209–224, 1979.

P. J. Dickinson, H. Bunke, A. Dadej, , and M. Kraetzl. Application of median graphs in detection of anomalous change in communication networks. In *Proceedings of the World Multiconference on Systemics, Cybernetics and Informatics*, volume 5, pages 194–197, 2001.

P. Dickinson, H. Bunke, A. Dadej, and M. Kretzl. On graphs with unique node labels. In *Proceedings of the 4th International Workshop on Graph Based Representations in Pattern Recognition*, volume 2726 of *Lecture Notes in Computer Science*, pages 13–23. Springer-Verlag, 2003.

S. Dumais and H. Chen. Hierarchical classification of web content. In *Proceed-*

ings of SIGIR-00, 23rd ACM International Conference on Research and Development in Information Retrieval, pages 256–263, 2000.

S. Deerwester, S. Dumais, T. Furnas, T. Landaur, and R. Harshman. Indexing by latent semantic analysis. *Journal of the American Society for Information Science*, 41(6):391–407, 1990.

L. Denoyer and P. Gallinari. A belief networks-based generative model for structured documents. An application to the XML categorizaion. In *Proceedings of the International Conference on Machine Learning and Data Mining*, volume 2734 of *Lecture Notes in Artificial Intelligence*, pages 328–342. Springer-Verlag, 2003.

T. G. Dietterich. Ensemble methods in machine learning. In J. Kittler and F. Roli, editors, *First International Workshop on Multiple Classifier Systems*, volume 1857 of *Lecture Notes in Computer Science*. Springer-Verlag, 2000.

J. Dunn. Well separated clusters and optimal fuzzy partitions. *Journal of Cybernetics*, 4:95–104, 1974.

M. A. Eshera and K.-S. Fu. A graph distance measure for image analysis. *IEEE Transactions on Systems, Man, and Cybernetics*, SMC-14(3):398–408, May/June 1984.

M. Eirinaki and M. Vazirgiannis. Web mining for web personalization. *ACM Transactions on Internet Technology*, 3(1):1–27, 2003.

H. Frigui and R. Krishnapuram. A robust algorithm for automatic extraction of an unknown number of clusters from noisy data. *Pattern Recognition Letters*, 17:1223–1232, 1996.

M.-L. Fernández and G. Valiente. A graph distance metric combining maximum common subgraph and minimum common supergraph. *Pattern Recognition Letters*, 22:753–758, 2001.

A. M. Finch, R. C. Wilson, and E. R. Hancock. An energy function and continuous edit process for graph matching. *Neural Computation*, 10:1873–1894, 1998.

S. Günter and H. Bunke. Self-organizing map for clustering in the graph domain. *Pattern Recognition Letters*, 23:405–417, 2002.

D. A. Grossman and O. Frieder. *Information Retrieval: Algorithms and Heuristics*. Klewer Academic Publishers, 1998.

L. Goodman and W. Kruskal. Measures of associations for cross-validations. *Journal of the American Statistical Association*, 49:732–764, 1954.

Google. http://www.google.com.

A. D. Gordon. Hierarchical classification. In P. Arabie, L. J. Hubert, and G. De Soete, editors, *Clustering and Classification*, pages 65–122. World Scientific Publishing Company, 1996.

S. Gold and A. Rangarajan. A graduated assignment algorithm for graph matching. *IEEE Transactions on Pattern Analysis and Machine Intelligence*, 18(4):377–388, April 1996.

Grouper. http://www.cs.washington.edu/research/clustering.

S. C. Grossman. Chemical ordering of molecules: a graphic theoretical approach to structure-property studies. *International Journal of Quantum Chemistry*, 28(1):1–16, 1985.

A. Hardy. On the number of clusters. *Computational Statistics and Data Analysis*, 23:83–96, 1996.

X. He, C. Ding, H. Zha, and H. D. Simon. Automatic topic identification using webpage clustering. In *Proceedings of the IEEE International Conference on Data Mining*, pages 195–202, 2001.

K. Haris, S. N. Efstratiadis, N. Maglaveras, C. Pappas, J. Gourassas, and G. Louridas. Model-based morphological segmentation and labeling of coronary angiograms. *IEEE Transactions on Medical Imaging*, 18(10):1003–1015, October 1999.

B. Huet and E. R. Hancock. Shape recognition from large image libraries by inexact graph matching. *Pattern Recognition Letters*, 20:1259–1269, 1999.

T. K. Ho, J. J. Hull, and S. N. Srihari. On multiple classifier systems for pattern recognition. In *Proceedings of the 11th International Conference on Pattern Recognition*, pages 84–87, September 1992.

P. Hannappel, R. Klapsing, , and G. Neumann. Mseec a multi search engine with multiple clustering. In *Proceedings of the 99 Information Resources Management Association International Conference*, May 1999.

T. K. Ho. The random subspace method for constructing decision forests. *IEEE Transactions on Pattern Analysis and Machine Intelligence*, 20(8):832–844, 1998.

M. Hearst and J. Pedersen. Reexamining the cluster hypothesis: Scatter/gather on retrieval results. In *Proceedings of the 19th Annual International ACM/SIGIR Conference on Research and Development in Information Retrieval*, 1996.

L. Hubert and J. Schultz. Quadratic assignment as a general data-analysis strategy. *British Journal of Mathematical and Statistical Psychology*, 29:190–240, 1976.

A. K. Jain and R. C. Dubes. *Algorithms for Clustering Data*. Prentice-Hall, 1988.

A. K. Jain, M. N. Murty, and P. J. Flynn. Data clustering: a review. *ACM Computing Surveys*, 31(3):264–323, September 1999.

R. Kosala and H. Blockeel. Web mining research: a survey. *SIGKDD Explorations*, 2:1–15, 2000.

J. Kittler, M. Hatef, R. Duin, and J. Matas. On combining classifiers. *IEEE Transactions on Pattern Analysis and Machine Intelligence*, 20(3):226–239, 1998.

T. Kohonen, S. Kaski, K. Lagus, J. Salojrvi, J. Honkela, V. Paatero, and A. Saarela. Self organization of a massive document collection. *IEEE Transactions on Neural Networks*, 11(3):574–585, May 2000.

W. J. Krzanowski and F. H. C. Marriott. *Multivariate Analysis Part 2: Classification, covariance structures and repeated measurements*. Arnold, 1995.

R. Kothari and D. Pitts. On finding the number of clusters. *Pattern Recognition Letters*, 20:405–416, 1999.

L. Kaufman and P. J. Rousseeuw. *Finding Groups in Data: an Introduction to Cluster Analysis*. John Wiley and Sons, 1990.

R. Kumar, P. Raghavan, S. Rajagopalan, and A. Tomkins. Extracting large-scale knowledge bases from the web. In *Proceedings of the 25th International*

Conference on Very Large Databases, pages 639–649, 1999.

G. J. Klir and B. Yuan. *Fuzzy Sets and Fuzzy Logic: Theory and Applications.* Prentice Hall, 1995.

M. Lazarescu, H. Bunke, and S. Venkatesh. Graph matching: fast candidate elimination using machine learning techniques. In *Advances in Pattern Recognition, Joint IAPR International Workshops SSPR and SPR 2000*, volume 1876 of *Lecture Notes in Computer Science*, pages 236–245. Springer-Verlag, 2000.

J. Liang and D. Doermann. Logical labeling of document images using layout graph matching with adaptive learning. In D. Lopresti, J. Hu, and R. Kashi, editors, *Document Analysis Systems V*, volume 2423 of *Lecture Notes in Computer Science*, pages 224–235. Springer-Verlag, 2002.

V. Levenshtein. Binary codes capable of correcting deletions, insertions, and reversals. *Soviet Physics-Doklady*, 10:707–710, 1966.

G. Levi. A note on the derivation of maximal common subgraphs of two directed or undirected graphs. *Calcolo*, 9:341–354, 1972.

L. Lam, Y.-S. Huang, and C. Suen. Combination of multiple classifier decisions for optical character recognition. In H. Bunke and P. Wang, editors, *Handbook of Character Recognition and Document Image Analysis*, pages 79–101. World Scientific Publishing Company, 1997.

J. B. Lovins. Development of a stemming algorithm. *Mechanical Translation and Computational Linguistics*, 11(1-2):22–31, March 1968.

B. Luo, A. Robles-Kelly, A. Torsello, R. C. Wilson, and E. R. Hancock. Clustering shock trees. In *Proceedings of the 3rd IAPR-TC15 Workshop on Graph-based Representations in Pattern Recognition*, pages 217–228, 2001.

G. F. Luger and W. A. Stubblefield. *Artificial Intelligence: Structures and Strategies for Complex Problem Solving.* The Benjamin/Cummings Publishing Company, 1993.

X. Lu. Document retrieval: a structural approach. *Information Processing and Management*, 26(2):209–218, 1990.

A. Likas, N. Vlassis, and J. J. Verbeek. The global k-means algorithm. *Pattern Recognition*, 36:451–461, 2003.

D. Lopresti and G. Wilfong. Applications of graph probing to web document analysis. In *Proceedings of the 1st International Workshop on Web Document Analysis*, pages 51–54, 2001.

D. Lopresti and G. Wilfong. A fast technique for comparing graph representations with applications to performance evaluation. *International Journal on Document Analysis and Recognition*, 6:219–229, 2004.

B. T. Messmer and H. Bunke. A new algorithm for error-tolerant subgraph isomorphism detection. *IEEE Transactions on Pattern Analysis and Machine Intelligence*, 20(5):493–504, May 1998.

S. A. Macskassy, A. Banerjee, B. D. Davison, and H. Hirsh. Human performance on clustering web pages: a preliminary study. In *Proceedings of The 4th International Conference on Knowledge Discovery and Data Mining*, pages 264–268, 1998.

C. T. Meadow, B. R. Boyce, and D. H. Kraft. *Text Information Retrieval Systems.*

Academic Press, 2000.

S. K. Madria, S. S. Bhowmick, W.-K. Ng, and E.-P. Lim. Research issues in web data mining. *Data Warehousing and Knowledge Discovery*, pages 303–312, 1999.

J. J. McGregor. Backtrack search algorithms and the maximal common subgraph problem. *Software Practice and Experience*, 12:23–34, 1982.

M. Merzbacher. Discovering semantic proximity for web pages. In *Proceedings of the 11th International Symposium on Methodologies for Intelligent Systems*, pages 244–252, 1999.

G. A. Miller. Wordnet: a lexical database for english. *Communications of the ACM*, 38(11):39–41, 1995.

B. Mirkin. *Mathematical Classification and Clustering*. Kluwer Academic Publishers Group, 1996.

T. M. Mitchell. *Machine Learning*. McGraw-Hill, 1997.

S. Medasani, R. Krishnapuram, and Y. S. Choi. Graph matching by relaxation of fuzzy assignments. *IEEE Transactions on Fuzzy Systems*, 9(1):173–182, February 2001.

A. McCallum and K. Nigam. A comparison of event models for naïve Bayes text classification. In *AAAI-98 Workshop on Learning for Text Categorization*, 1998.

F. Masseglia, P. Poncelet, and R. Cicchetti. Webtool: an integrated framework for data mining. In *Proceedings of the 10th International Conference and Workshop on Database and Expert Systems Applications*, pages 892–901, 1999.

G. L. Marcialis, F. Roli, and A. Serrau. Fusion of statistical and structural fingerprint classifiers. In Josef Kittler and Mark S. Nixon, editors, *Proceedings of the 4th International Conference on Audio- and Video-Based Biometric Person Authentication*, volume 2688 of *Lecture Notes in Computer Science*, pages 310–317. Springer-Verlag, 2003.

C. Magnusson and H. Vanharanta. Visualizing sequences of text using collocational networks. In *Proceedings of the International Conference on Machine Learning and Data Mining*, number 2734 in Lecture Notes in Artificial Intelligence, pages 276–283. Springer-Verlag, 2003.

R. Myers, R. C. Wilson, , and E. R. Hancock. Bayesian graph edit distance. *IEEE Transactions on Pattern Analysis and Machine Intelligence*, 22(6):628–635, June 2000.

O. Nasraoui, H. Frigui, A. Joshi, and R. Krishnapuram. Mining web access logs using relational competitive fuzzy clustering. In *Proceedings of the 8th International Fuzzy Systems Association World Congress*, pages 869–873, 1999.

E. Nakamura and N. Kehtarnavaz. Determining number of clusters and prototype locations via multi-scale clustering. *Pattern Recognition Letters*, 19:1265–1283, 1998.

U. Y. Nahm and R. J. Mooney. A mutually beneficial integration of data mining and information extraction. In *Proceedings of the 17th National Conference on Artificial Intelligence*, July 2000.

O. Owolabi. An efficient graph approach to matching chemical structures. *Journal of Chemical Information and Computer Sciences*, 28(4):221–226, 1988.

N. R. Pal and J. Biswas. Cluster validation using graph theoretic concepts. *Pattern Recognition*, 30(6):847–857, 1997.

T. Peterson. Coping with infoglut. http://www.computerworld.com/databasetopics/data/story/0,10801,82314,00%.html.

B. Piwowarski and P. Gallinari. A machine learning model for information retrieval with structured documents. In *Proceedings of the International Conference on Machine Learning and Data Mining*, volume 2734 of *Lecture Notes in Artificial Intelligence*, pages 425–438. Springer-Verlag, 2003.

A. T. P. and C. Siva Ram Murthy. Optimal task allocation in distributed systems by graph matching and state space search. *The Journal of Systems and Software*, 46:59–75, 1999.

M. F. Porter. An algorithm for suffix stripping. *Program*, 14(3):130–137, July 1980.

S. K. Pal, V. Talwar, and P. Mitra. Web mining in soft computing framework: Relevance, state of the art and future directions. *IEEE Transactions on Neural Networks*, 13(5):1163–1177, 2000.

W. M. Rand. Objective criteria for the evaluation of clustering methods. *Journal of the American Statistical Association*, 66:846–850, 1971.

M. R. Rezaee, B. P. F. Lelieveldt, and J. H. C. Reiber. A new cluster validity index for the fuzzy c-mean. *Pattern Recognition Letters*, 19:237–246, 1998.

S. Rosenberg, I. Van Mechelen, and P. De Boeck. A hierarchical classes model: Theory and method with applications in psychology and psychopathology. In P. Arabie, L. J. Hubert, and G. De Soete, editors, *Clustering and Classification*, pages 123–155. World Scientific Publishing Company, 1996.

S. Russell and P. Norvig. *Artificial Intelligence: a Modern Approach*. Prentice-Hall, 1995.

G. Salton. *Automatic Text Processing: The Transformation, Analysis, and Retrieval of Information by Computer*. Addison-Wesley, 1989.

A. Sanfeliu and K. S. Fu. A distance measure between attributed relational graphs for pattern recognition. *IEEE Transactions on Systems, Man, and Cybernetics*, 13:353–363, 1983.

A. Strehl, J. Ghosh, and R. Mooney. Impact of similarity measures on web-page clustering. In *AAAI-2000: Workshop of Artificial Intelligence for Web Search*, pages 58–64, 2000.

A. Schenker, M. Last, H. Bunke, and A. Kandel. Classification of web documents using a graph model. In *Proceedings of the 7th International Conference on Document Analysis and Recognition*, pages 240–244, 2003.

A. Schenker, M. Last, H. Bunke, and A. Kandel. Clustering of web documents using a graph model. In A. Antonacopoulos and J. Hu, editors, *Web Document Analysis: Challenges and Opportunities*, pages 3–18. World Scientific Publishing Company, 2003.

A. Schenker, M. Last, H. Bunke, and A. Kandel. A comparison of two novel algorithms for clustering web documents. In *Proceedings of the 2nd International Workshop on Web Document Analysis*, pages 71–74, 2003.

A. Schenker, M. Last, H. Bunke, and A. Kandel. Classification of documents using graph matching. *International Journal of Pattern Recognition and Artificial Intelligence*, 18(3):475–496, 2004.

A. Schenker, M. Last, and A. Kandel. Design and implementation of a web mining system for organizing search engine results. In *Proceedings of CAiSE'01 Workshop Data Integration over the Web*, pages 62–75, June 2001.

A. Schenker, M. Last, and A. Kandel. A term-based algorithm for hierarchical clustering of web documents. In *Proceedings of IFSA / NAFIPS 2001*, pages 3076–3081, July 2001.

A. Schenker, M. Last, and A. Kandel. Design and implementation of a web mining system for organizing search engine results. *International Journal of Intelligent Systems*, to appear.

H. Schütze and C. Silverstein. Projections for efficient document clustering. In *Proceedings of the 20th Annual International ACM SIGIR Conference on Research and Development in Information Retrieval*, pages 74–81, 1997.

A. Sanfeliu, F. Serratosa, and R. Alquézar. Clustering of attributed graphs and unsupervised synthesis of function-described graphs. In *Proceedings of the 15th International Conference on Pattern Recognition*, volume 2, pages 1026–1029, 2000.

J. Stefanowski and D. Weiss. Carrot² and language properties in web search results. In *Proceedings of th First International Atlantic Web Intelligence Conference on Advances in Web Intelligence*, volume 2663 of *Lecture Notes in Artificial Intelligence*, pages 240–249. Springer-Verlag, 2003.

K.-C. Tai. The tree-to-tree correction problem. *Journal of the Association for Computing Machinery*, 26(3):422–433, 1979.

S. Theodoridis and K. Koutroumbas. *Pattern Recognition*. Academic Press, 1999.

C.-M. Tan, Y.-F. Wang, and C.-D. Lee. The use of bigrams to enhance text categorization. *Information Processing and Management*, 38:529–546, 2002.

J. R. Ullman. An algorithm for subgraph isomorphism. *Journal of the Association for Computing Machinery*, 23:31–42, 1976.

Vivísimo. http://vivisimo.com/.

S. M. Weiss, C. Apte, F. J. Damerau, D. E. Johnson, F. J. Oles, T. Goetz, and T. Hampp. Maximizing text-mining performance. *IEEE Intelligent Systems*, 14(4):63–69, July/August 1999.

C.-C. Wong, C.-C. Chen, and M.-C. Su. A novel algorithm for data clustering. *Pattern Recogniton*, 34:425–442, 2001.

R. A. Wagner and M. J. Fischer. The string-to-string correction problem. *Journal of the Association for Computing Machinery*, 21:168–173, 1974.

L. Wiskott, J.-M. Fellous, N. Krüger, and C. von der Malsburg. Face recognition by elastic bunch graph matching. In *Proceedings of the 7th International Conference on Computer Analysis of Images and Patterns*, pages 456–463, 1997.

R. C. Wilson and E. R. Hancock. Structural matching by discrete relaxation. *IEEE Transactions on Pattern Analysis and Machine Intelligence*, 19(6):634–647, 1997.

R. C. Wilson and E. R. Hancock. Graph matching with hierarchical discrete relaxation. *Pattern Recognition Letters*, 20:1041–1052, June 1999.

S. Wei, S. Jun, and Z. Huicheng. A fingerprint recognition system by use of graph matching. In *Proceedings of SPIE*, volume 4554, pages 141–146, 2001.

W. D. Wallis, P. Shoubridge, M. Kraetz, and D. Ray. Graph distances using graph union. *Pattern Recognition Letters*, 22:701–704, 2001.

M. L. Williams, R. C. Wilson, and E. R. Hancock. Multiple graph matching with Bayesian inference. *Pattern Recognition Letters*, 18:1275–1281, 1997.

J. T. L. Wang, K. Zhang, and G.-W. Chirn. Algorithms for approximate graph matching. *Information Sciences*, 82:45–74, 1995.

C. T. Zahn. Graph-theoretical methods for detecting and describing gestalt structures. *IEEE Transactions on Computers*, C-20:68–86, 1971.

N. Zahid, O. Abouelala, M. Limouri, and A. Essaid. Unsupervised fuzzy clustering. *Pattern Recognition Letters*, 20:123–129, 1999.

O. Zamir and O. Etzioni. Web document clustering: a feasibility demonstration. In *Proceedings of the 21st Annual International ACM SIGIR Conference on Research and Development in Information Retrieval*, pages 46–54, 1998.

N. Zahid, M. Limouri, and A. Essaid. A new cluster-validity for fuzzy clustering. *Pattern Recognition*, 332:1089–1097, 1999.

N. Zhong, J. Liu, and Y. Yao. In search of the wisdom web. *Computer*, 35(11):27–31, 2002.

Index